FERDINAND LASSALLE

FERDINAND LASSALLE

BY

GEORGE BRANDES

AUTHOR OF
"WILLIAM SHAKESPEARE," ETC.

"Flectere si nequeo Superos, Acheronta movebo"
(If I cannot bend the will of Heaven, I will cause turmoil in hell)
VERGIL

GREENWOOD PRESS, PUBLISHERS
WESTPORT, CONNECTICUT

Originally published in 1911
by The Macmillan Company

First Greenwood Reprinting 1970

SBN 8371-2800-5

PRINTED IN UNITED STATES OF AMERICA

NOTE

THE master hand of George Meredith has made Lassalle a permanent figure in English literature. Those who know Lassalle only as Alvan, the passionate lover of the " Tragic Comedians," will wish to know him also as the democratic leader, the man of letters and of law, and to observe from a wider outlook the progress of the restless career which ended in profound catastrophe.

v

PREFACE

THE first draft of this essay was published by instalments in 1874 and 1875, in the monthly magazine the *Nineteenth Century*. In his preface to "Captain Mansana," Björnstjerne Björnsen (1879) referred to the character-drawing in the essay. Some ten thousand copies were at once printed in Germany in the form of magazine articles, and several thousand copies in book form were also sold at a later date: the work was well received, and enjoyed a considerable circulation, even in Russia.

Old white-haired democrats of 1848 have thanked me for my portrait of Lassalle with the speaking look and hand-clasp which are the author's best reward. The chief representative of modern political economy at Berlin University—Professor Adolf Wagner—wrote an appreciative review of the book at the time of its publication. With his theories in general I am unable to agree, but in the preface to his edition of Lassalle's letters to Rodbertus he did me the honour of characterizing my work as "brilliant." Well meant as the expression doubtless was, it does not describe the nature of my efforts with reference to this portrait, or to the art of portraiture in general. My ideal is Velasquez, and his ideal was not brilliance, but truth. In this preface, however, Professor Wagner made one assertion concerning Lassalle which I can subscribe with entire conviction. He said that, divergent as were the judgments which had been pronounced upon this man, both the friends and the enemies of the great Socialist agitator would readily agree that his work had made him an historical personality of first-rate importance. It was this conviction which induced me seven years ago to make a first draft of this literary portrait of Lassalle, the first and the only attempt of the kind that had then been made. I have now completed the picture, and have done my best to give it life and reality.

Lassalle's Socialism has reappeared in present-day Germany under the form of State Socialism, and therefore is interesting as one of the burning questions of the day. In neither form, however, does Socialism form the subject of this work.

Its chief subject is the historical development during one generation of the spirit which inspires modern Germany—a subject which certainly can never be a matter of indifference. I have, moreover, sought to excite interest by making one personality the point of connection between a series of ideas. This is a method which I have invariably employed, and which I regard as natural. The description of an individual inevitably presupposes in my case a number of general ideas. As Sören Kierkegaard represents an individual fragment of the history of Danish culture, so does Ferdinand Lassalle personify a period of modern jurisprudence and political economy. The attraction of the subject for me is, on the one hand, the purely individual element, " a thing that never was before and never again can be," to borrow the definition of individualism given by Lenbach, the distinguished portrait-painter of Munich ;

on the other hand, I am attracted by the great and permanent ideas of the age upon its civilization, and by the problems which have confronted antiquity, and will constantly recur. Subjects which provide interesting personalities and ideas of such importance seem to me especially worthy of treatment, and the method of handling them which I have gradually evovled gives due weight both to the individual character and to the general ideas which that character may evoke.

GEORGE BRANDES.

BERLIN, *September,* 1881.

CONTENTS

PART I

PART II

FERDINAND LASSALLE

PART I

LASSALLE BEFORE THE AGITATION

ONE event during the nineteenth century has provoked the greatest surprise and astonishment in Europe. Unsuccessful attempts at its explanation have been, and are still offered by the different European nationalities. This event is the process by which the Germany of Hegel was transformed to the Germany of Bismarck. Some theorists speak as if the old German stock had suddenly died out, and a new race had sprung up without roots ; others, as if the old stock had been destroyed or ennobled by an infusion of Wendish-Slavonic blood. To some, modern Germany is enigmatic as the Iron Mask. The face of the philosopher and the poet was the real countenance, and this has now been hidden by Prussian domination, as the mask concealed the identity of the unhappy prisoner. Others, again, regard the old and pleasant countenance of romance as the mask, hypocritically hiding the real features, which have now become visible. These views are alike injudicious, and are based in either case upon ignorance of the course of development which modern Germany has pursued. If this development is studied in literature, it will be seen how, step by step, the ideas, the methods of action, and the views of life pursued and entertained by the newer generation have developed organically from those of the past age. The gulf which divides the Germany of Hegel from the Germany of Bismarck will gradually be filled before our eyes. The faces upon either side of this gulf will appear as related by similarity of feature ;

while certain interesting and strongly marked countenances which stand out boldly against the background of history will of themselves typify the process of transition and amalgamation which has fused the intellectual individualities of two generations.   Of these special features hardly any is more interesting or more clearly cut than the figure of Ferdinand Lassalle.   He was born on April 11, 1825, and died of a wound received in a duel on August 31, 1864.   He was a distinguished pupil of Hegel, and was spoken of in his time as Bismarck's tutor, and not unreasonably ; for even though he cannot be shown to have influenced Bismarck directly, yet, if we examine the points which decided both the foreign and domestic policy of the great statesman, we shall find that this policy precisely realized the programme propounded by the philosophical agitator.

CHAPTER I

In order to understand Lassalle, we must begin with the study of his fugitive writings. His prose style will stir the least emotional of men ; his unusually wide learning is dominated by eloquence entirely modern, and strictly logical and practical in character ; between the lines the reader can detect a suppressed enthusiasm, which occasionally blazes out in letters of fire. His attacks are delivered with uncommon audacity, which is supported by the iron tenacity with which he conducts his defensive operations ; his language and style are often tasteful and always peculiar to him. Of mere rhetoric there is no trace. The extent of the writer's knowledge and power left no room for rhetorical display. Nor is the weight of his scholarship at any time perceptible. He marches out to battle in full panoply ; but it is rare to see heavy armour so easily worn. Little has been printed that bears upon the life and personality of our author. While travelling in Germany, and afterwards during a residence of several years (1877-1881) in Berlin, it was my fortune to meet a considerable number of men and women, whose judgment I respect, who had known Lassalle personally. After Lassalle's sudden death had silenced the voices of his assailants, we know that public opinion concerning him underwent a change. Public recognition of his capacity and of his importance is by no means uncommon. On the other hand, expressions of private opinion concerning him are for the most part comparatively unfavourable. His private acquaintances displayed but fugitive interest in his writings, and rarely or never shared his views. His weak points were perfectly obvious, and no psychological analysis

3

was required for the discovery of them ; moreover, the private acquaintances of public men and the majority of the educated reading public are inclined to lay undue stress upon unconcealed weaknesses, especially when such failings are entirely disregarded by a band of hero-worshippers. I did not expect to gather many approving judgments from the upper middle classes upon a man who died in feud with the whole middle class in his own country, sustaining the struggle almost single-handed, universally opposed by the Press. At the same time, I must admit that I was surprised to find disapproval so general, and, in my opinion, so unfounded and so keenly antagonistic to the dead man. To this antagonism is probably due the difficulty which now confronts any attempt to form a complete and adequate picture of Lassalle. No systematic, and certainly no complete edition of his writings exists. Most of them can only be procured through a Socialist agent in Leipsic, whose utterly unbusinesslike habits make the result of an application to him entirely problematical ; while such copies as he possesses are printed on the worst of paper, and disfigured by careless misprints, which constantly distort the sense of a phrase.[1] Lassalle's rarer writings are not to be found even in the Royal Library in Berlin. Very few letters and very little biographical material has been printed. But if, as I have said, this want of material is the outcome of an antagonism to Lassalle which has not yet disappeared, at the same time this antagonism has its limits. I have been surprised by the expressions of good feeling, recognition, kindliness, and admiration for the dead man with which I have met—expressions which have been the warmer where intimacy has been close. This fact is a high testimony in favour of Lassalle ; for it is a circumstance which is repeated in the case of every outstanding personality. Some men may dazzle the onlooker by the attraction of their talent or the splendour of their reputation, but closer acquaintanceship will dispel the charm ; the prestige of the Pope is least in Rome. Really great characters secure the most complete devotion from those who know them best. For years I have mentally compared and contrasted these varying judgments and opinions, while

---

[1] Two instances may be given : *Staatsanwalt* is misprinted for *Staatsgewalt*, and *unerlaubten* for *erlaubten*, in the " Trial for High Treason," 1864, 38, 43.

my interest in the study of their subject remained persistent and unimpaired. All these pronouncements, in conjunction with the views and ideas upon Lassalle which I have earlier or later conceived, now form a strange and many-voiced harmony to my mental ear. I know Lassalle as well as anyone can know him who has never seen him or heard him speak. In considering the brighter side of his character, I feel that delight which is necessary for full appreciation of the subject, and I see that the shadows are limited in extent. I cannot do full and exhaustive honour to his manifold energy—this, indeed, would only be possible for one who was no less accomplished a classical scholar, thinker, legal authority, and political economist than Lassalle himself ; but I will attempt to depict the main features of Lassalle's intellectual character.

The doctrines which Lassalle propounded in the last years of his life have aroused an extraordinary number of writers in their defence, and have urged even more to attack. Doubts have been cast upon the truth of his doctrines, and that truth has also been affirmed. A dispute of unusual violence has arisen concerning the advisability of his last practical proposal. I am incompetent to offer any opinion upon this dispute, and I have no inclination to take part in it. One object I desire and will attempt to secure, as no one else has been induced to make an effort in this direction : I wish to explain Ferdinand Lassalle's character, the fundamental principles of his nature, his most profound mental characteristics, and his dominant ideas ; I wish to display the main features of his intellect and the nature of his talent—in short, to draw a picture of him as a man, as a writer, as an orator, and as a great party leader. I am equally anxious to avoid any confusion between this object and the very different task, which to many minds seems remarkably simple, of sitting in judgment upon one of the most difficult and hotly-contested problems with which the present age has to deal.

The life which I am to describe was lived with such passionate vigour and haste that it passed away before the contemporary world had had time to appreciate its importance. Lassalle's scientific works were inaccessible to the ordinary circle of the educated, and his pamphlets were but partially intelligible to the working classes who read them. As a critical thinker, Lassalle remains unvanquished. No institution or person that he attacked was ever able to recover from his onslaught. That a distinguished scholar should have made occasional mistakes is nothing to the purpose. The stream of time sweeps away the errors, and leaves the truth for the inheritance of humanity.

CHAPTER II

THE old Greek thinker Heraclitus, whom Lassalle made the subject of long research, was in the habit of using various symbolical expressions to denote the primary force of existence —Fire, Stream, Justice, War, Invisible Harmony, Bow and Lyre ; these expressions rise involuntarily in the mind if we seek some symbol to represent the dominant principle of Ferdinand Lassalle's life. Somewhere, in one of his letters, which is full of impatient outbursts against the tardiness with which events develop, Lassalle uses the phrase, " my ardent soul." Thousands use the expression as the mere figure of speech which it has become. Lassalle, perhaps, alone could use it without exaggeration, for his innermost being concealed some force akin to fire. His burning love for knowledge and science, his thirst for righteousness and truth, his enthusiasm, his unrestrained self-confidence, his deep self-conceit, his courage, his delight in power—these were characteristics which all found expression in the same fiery and devouring manner. He was a bearer of light and fire to the world ; a bearer of light, bold and defiant as Lucifer himself ; a torch-bearer who delighted to stand in the full glare of the torch with which he brought enlightenment—*grand oseur et grand poseur*. In the world of Heraclitus, the conjunction of bow and lyre denoted the dominant and fundamental force. The lyre is the type of harmony, of full culture. The bow, with its deadly shafts of light, denotes energy and destructive power. Lyre and bow were also conjoined in Lassalle's spirit, as full culture and the restless impulse to activity. Rarely has such a union of theoretical and practical capacity been seen in the history of the world.

7

Any close observer of Lassalle at the outset of his career, if his insight had been both sympathetic and prophetic, might well have applied to him the words which he himself quotes from the neoplatonist thinker, Maximus of Tyre : "I understand Apollo ; an archer is the god, and a musician, and while I love his harmony, I fear his archery."[1]

Lassalle was born in Breslau.   His father was a merchant of no special capacity, but a sound and upright character, by name Heymann Lassal : it was during his stay in Paris in 1846 that his son changed the spelling of his name.   Both parents were of Jewish origin.   Throughout his life, Lassalle was the most loving of sons, and his relations with his family were, as is usual with Jews, very intimate and close.   Lassalle's whole career was followed by his mother with the greatest enthusiasm ; she sympathized with every one of his enterprises and approved their results.

One special hardship he had to endure in childhood.   Whenever he played with other boys—it must be admitted, only as their leader—his parents regarded him as responsible for any damage that was done.   A broken window-pane or a trampled garden was visited upon Ferdinand Lassalle, though innocent. He was bewildered by this circumstance, which he could not understand, though it was due to his natural superiority over all his comrades.   At a certain age, boys become forward and self-assertive, and these characteristics were unusually strongly marked in the case of Lassalle.   What he often in later life referred to as his " impudence " was even then perceptible. Ferdinand Lassalle grew up amid the environment of Jewish society in a provincial town between 1830 and 1840.   It was a society of which the elder members were unable to speak pure German, and living as they did in a period before the emancipation of the Jews, they necessarily clung tenaciously to the fact of their Israelitish descent and to their hereditary manners and customs in general.   In his mature years, Lassalle displayed an extraordinary dislike for the Jews of his time, regarding them as representatives of the materialist and capitalist interests which he strove to crush ; but in boyhood he was keenly conscious of his Jewish descent.   From his

[1] Lassalle, " The Philosophy of Heraclitus the Obscure of Ephesus," i. III.

fifteenth to the end of his sixteenth year he kept a diary, which provides evidence of this feeling, and, indeed, of all the experiences and the general mental life of the early years during which his mature character was in formation. An entry dated February 2, 1840, made when he was only fourteen years of age, states that a friend had expressed surprise at the warmth with which he had defended the Jewish faith. " The ass ! As if one could not eat tripe and yet be a good Jew ! . . . I believe myself to be one of the best Jews in existence, apart from attention to the ceremonial law. Like the Jew in Bulwer's ' Leila,' I would risk my life to free the Jews from the oppression which now burdens them. I would not even shrink from the scaffold, if I could restore them to a position of respect among the nations. Whenever I indulge in childish dreams, I prefer to picture myself sword in hand, at the head of the Jews, leading them to recover their independence."

Towards the end of his life Lassalle was wont to assert : " Two things in the world are my special objects of hatred— journalists and Jews, and I am both." But at the age of fifteen he felt himself a prince in Israel. On May 21, 1840, he writes with reference to the outrages upon the Jews in Damascus, of which he had heard an account that same evening :

" Oh, it is terrible to read and terrible to hear, and one's hair rises and every emotion is turned to fury ! It is dreadful that a people should endure these things, whether they patiently bear their treatment or revenge themselves. True, fearfully true, is the following sentence from the report : ' The Jews in this city endure cruelties which none but these pariahs of the earth would bear, without making dreadful reprisals.' Thus, even the Christians are surprised at our apathy, and wonder that we do not revolt, and that we prefer death by torture to death in battle. Was the oppression which once drove the Swiss to revolt greater than this ? Could any revolution be more righteous than that which the Jews in Damascus would cause, if they were to revolt, to set every corner of the town on fire, blow up the powder magazine, and perish with their tormentors ? Nation of cowards, you deserve no better fate. The trampled worm will turn, yet do you but bow the head more deeply. You cannot die or wreak destruction, you know not the meaning of righteous vengeance ; you cannot bury yourself with your foes and mangle them even in the agony of death. You are born to servitude !" When the silly falsehood that the Jews used the blood of murdered children in their religious ceremonies was again served up, Lassalle wrote, on July 30 : " Again the preposterous story appears, that the Jews make use of the blood of Christians. The same story, in Damascus, in Rhodes, and in Lemberg. The fact that every corner of the world makes the same charge seems to me an indication that the time is ripe for us to help ourselves in reality by the shedding of Christian blood. God helps those who help themselves. The dice are on the board, and only the players are wanted."

Lassalle's relations with his parents during his youth were marked by boyish love and dutifulness : he was devoted to them heart and soul, obedient and anxious to spare them any trouble. His father was a tall, powerful man, with a clever and attractive face, but he was something of a domestic tyrant, violent and choleric in temper ; at the same time, he was a very affectionate father to his son. His mother, who was a little hard of hearing, was a querulous and somewhat trying character. The eldest child, Lassalle's sister Frederike, was a pretty and lively girl ; her first engagement ended unfortunately, and about the year 1840 she was betrothed to her cousin, Ferdinand Friedländer, a very capable man, who was not at that time appreciated by the family. Her brother, notwithstanding his youth, is seen discussing his sister's circumstances with his elders, and calculating with precocious coolness her prospects of marriage, and the extent of the dowry which she would require.

His self-conceit was of early development. It was not, as in the case of other youthful geniuses, the mere shadow cast upon an immature mind by the rising consciousness of great capacities. Even later we are repelled by it, when Lassalle had reached manhood. He enters in his diary every little compliment that was paid him, and we see that his elders not only repeatedly praised his intelligence and sharpness, but even used the term " genius " in reference to him. The self-assertive, or even presumptuous, tendencies of his character may be ascribed to his self-conceit, as also may his animosity towards his teachers, whom he regards as his sworn enemies, and his generally refractory character during boyhood.

He was a hopeless failure as a schoolboy. In spite of his keen intelligence and his unusual abilities, he was congenitally idle, incessantly playing truant and cheating, copying the exercises of his more industrious friends, and absenting himself under false excuses. Even worse misdeeds are recorded. He not only forged notes of excuse from his father to explain his absence from school, but for six months systematically forged first his mother's and then his father's signature to the bad reports which he brought home from school, while he spent his time at billiards and cards. During the same period he cherished the strongest and warmest sense of friendship, and takes himself to task for his wickedness with a fine honesty, as follows : " I do not know why it is, but I play billiards every Saturday, though my father has strictly forbidden this game. I sign my own conduct reports, which is equally wrong, and yet I love my father most intensely, as only a child can love. I would joyfully give my life to be of use to him, and yet . . . But my want of thought is the cause of it all. At bottom I am really good " (January 14, 1840).

The contradiction between his boyish want of thought, to which he alludes, and the extraordinary vehemence of his enthusiasms, is rather apparent than real.

He was of an impetuous and hot-headed disposition. When his father one day gave him a sound thrashing, he resolved in a fit of wounded pride to commit suicide, and was only prevented from executing his intention by the fact that his father followed him, and caught him up at the moment when he was about to throw himself into the Ohle (January 29). When his forgeries in the report-book were discovered, he was only restrained from suicide by the thought of his parents' grief. However, he soon recovered his spirits in thinking how trivial these troubles and this humiliation would seem in future years.

His passionate nature is especially apparent in the intensity of his anger and hatred, and of his thirst for revenge. He swears inextinguishable, burning hatred to anyone who has insulted him or his, and vows to behold the offence before him in letters of fire until he has avenged it.

Even at so early an age he displays a fierce ruthlessness and an inclination to secure his wishes by forcible means ; at the same time, a very prominent feature is the unbounded honesty with which he never spares himself in the examination of his inward self, and of his relations to those about him. His sense of honour in this respect compensates to some extent for the lack of honour which he sometimes shows in his choice of means to secure his ends.

The discovery of the secret by which Lassalle secured good reports in the *gymnasium* at Breslau aroused in him a desire to leave that institution and to be sent to the commercial school in Leipsic. Lassalle's father did not wish him to enter trade. The friends and acquaintances of the family interfered in the discussion, some supporting the father, others the son. The consequence was family disputes and dissensions, which enabled Lassalle to realize for the first time that it is both confusing and foolish to consider or to act upon hints that may be given by people who know little or nothing of the facts of a case. Just at this time he came across the old fable of the peasant and his son, whose readiness to take the advice of the passers-by eventually obliged both of them to walk and to carry their ass ; hence he derived his first principle of practical life, which he often quoted under the formula, " I will not carry the ass."

In desperation at the vexatious annoyances in which he had entangled himself, Lassalle gained his wish, and went to Leipsic in May, 1840. Here, however, his relations with his teachers became even worse than in Breslau. Here, also, he regarded them merely as malevolent enemies. As he became more profoundly conscious that he was no ordinary character, his self-conceit increased. But he suffered from homesickness, and longed for his family, especially for his father, to whom he was always most tenderly devoted, and for his sister, for whom his heartfelt and fine affection only increased with time. In Leipsic he also formed enthusiastic friendships with different companions. Among these was a certain Robert Zander, whose sister Rosalie was Lassalle's first love ; to her the sentimental schoolboy sent many letters and poems, which were unfortunately destroyed after her death in 1876.

Lassalle did not remain at the commercial school after August in 1841. It became clear to him that he had mistaken his vocation and was in no way fitted for a mercantile career. His parents were not surprised to hear the fact, as they had always wished him to be a student. As early as August 3, 1840, in an entry in his diary, he compares himself with Wilhelm Meister, and says that his heart, like the heart of Wilhelm, beats for art, but that the following difference between them exists : Wilhelm's parents urged him to become a merchant, while he himself has voluntarily renounced all æsthetic pursuits ; but he now feels that he cannot renounce a public career, whether it may lie in the path of art or politics. He is more concerned " about freedom than about the prices of goods, utters more violent curses upon the dogs of aristocrats, who deprive man of his highest boon, than upon the rival tradesmen who lower prices. But he will do more than curse."

We now find evidence in the diary which shows how rapidly this boy, who was scarce seventeen years of age, became a young man entirely convinced of the part which he wished to play in life, and with more than a suspicion of the fate which awaited him.

He reads and admires Börne, who became his next ideal. In Börne's " Letters from Paris " he is horrified to find that in Germany " thirty millions of men are plagued by thirty tyrants." He approves Börne's invectives against Europe's despots, but, characteristically enough, his sound political sense cannot accept Börne's childlike hopes for the immediate future. On July 24, 1840, he writes : " But when he says, ' No European ruler is so blind as to suppose that his grandson will ascend his throne,' I must unfortunately doubt his statement. Things will be worse before they are better."

It is very remarkable that, in spite of the strength of his revolutionary tendencies in youth, he can perceive an aristocratic strain in his temperament, and feels that his democratic bias is due rather to circumstances than to natural disposition. On July 19 he writes :

" I went to the theatre ; Löwe gave Fiesco. Upon my word, this Count of Lavagna is a grand character. My sentiments are as revolutionary, as republican, and as democratic as those of anybody, and yet I feel that in Count Lavagna's place I should have acted as he did ; I should not have been content to remain the first citizen of Genoa, but should have stretched forth my hand for the diadem. Hence it seems, if I examine the situation in the light of day, that I am an egoist. If I had been born a prince or a nobleman, I should be an aristocrat heart and soul. But as I am merely of middle-class origin, I shall be a democrat in time."

In the diary we can trace the course of his mental struggles. On August 24 he writes :

" Two opposed principles struggle within me for the mastery. Is expediency or honesty to guide my life ? Shall I spread my cloak to the breeze, flatter the great, intrigue to gain advantage and reputation, or shall I cling to truth and virtue with republican obstinacy, and fix my gaze upon one sole object—to deal a death-blow to aristocracy ? No, I will be no fawning, cowardly courtier, though I may have the capacity to play the part. I will proclaim freedom to the nations, though I should perish in the attempt." And on August 26 : " I am very sorry that I did not continue my studies. It is now clear to me that I shall become a writer. Yes, I will come before the German people and before all nations, and summon them with burning words to fight for freedom. The menacing frown of princes shall not intimidate me : I will not be bribed with orders and titles to betray the cause of freedom, like a second Judas. Never will I rest until they are pale with fear. From Paris, the land of freedom, I will send the word to all the nations of the earth, as Börne did ; the teeth of all princes shall chatter with fear, and they shall see that their time is come."

He spends much time over Heine, with whose work he now becomes acquainted. " I love this Heine ; he is my second self." He does not understand that Heine is an apostate from the cause of freedom, who has torn the Jacobin cap from his head, and replaced it with a gold-laced hat. He cannot believe that Heine is speaking aught but mockery when he says, " I am a royalist and no democrat," nor can he understand how Heine, in view of this statement, can be so affected by the deaths of noble republicans.

The completion of his sixteenth year found Lassalle entirely decided with regard to his principles and his future. He informed his father of his irrevocable determination to study. When his father asked him what branch of learning he wished to pursue, he replied : " The greatest and most comprehensive study in the world, the study which is most entirely bound up with the most sacred interests of humanity—the study of history." His father went on to ask him whether he thought he was a poet.

" No," he replied ; " but I shall devote myself to pamphleteering and agitation. Now is the time when the struggle is in progress for the most sacred objects of humanity. Until the end of the last century the world was bound in the chains of inert superstition. Then the force of intellect aroused a material power which overthrew the existing system amid blood and ruin. The first outburst was terrible, as was inevitable. Since that time the struggle has proceeded without interruption. . . . The struggle for the most noble of purposes will be conducted in the noblest way. Truth must indeed be supported hereafter by physical force, for those in possession of the thrones will have it so. But let our object be to enlighten and instruct the peoples, not to excite them."

For a long time the father was silent ; at length he said : " My son, I am well aware of the truth in your words, but why should you, of all people, become a martyr ? You, our only hope and support ? Freedom must be gained by struggle, but it will be gained even without your help. . . . You alone, what difference can you make ?"

The young Lassalle then wrote in his diary : " Oh yes, he is right. Why should I, of all people, become a martyr ? But if everyone said as much and withdrew with like cowardice, when would a warrior be forthcoming ? Why should I, of all people, become a martyr ? Why ? Because God has put a voice in my heart that calls me to battle ; because God has given me strength and fitted me for battle : I can feel it ! Because I can fight and suffer for a noble cause. Because I will not deceive God in my use of the strength which He has given me for a definite purpose. Because, in one word, I cannot help it !" What Lassalle afterwards spoke of jestingly as his impudence here appears as a consecration to life and struggle.

At this point we encounter the racial characteristic of Lassalle's disposition which was fundamentally distinctive in his temperament : it is apparent in the quality best expressed by the Jewish word " Chutspo," which connotes presence of mind, impudence, temerity, resolution, and effrontery ; it will be readily intelligible to anyone who regards it as an extreme which the growth of culture necessarily and naturally produced by reaction from the timorous and shrinking subservience imposed upon a race that has been harassed and oppressed for more than a thousand years. We have an instance of " Chutspo " when we find Lassalle, during one of his criminal cases, flouting the public prosecutor in the course of his speech for the defence, notwithstanding the threats of the president to deny him a hearing. Even when he has been ordered to keep silent, he obtains the right of speech by initiating a discussion upon the question how far he can legally be deprived of his right to speak. This " Chutspo " sometimes appears in average members of the race in such repulsive forms as " pushfulness " or unjustifiable desire to appear in the forefront. Sometimes it takes the more attractive intellectual form of resolution and determination. In the case of Lassalle, whose mind contained high capacities awaiting development, challenge was the element which appeared as the impulse to personal action, and invariably lent its colouring to his innate energy. His instinct and his capacity for action was not the pure Anglo-Saxon or American spirit of enterprise, which is confined to incessant production and to orderly arrangement. It was an impulse to action which sought opposition, and could live and breathe only in an atmosphere of antagonism. A German writer, who had seen Lassalle only once in a concert-room, said to me : " He looked like defiance incarnate ; but his brow expressed such energy that one could not have felt surprise if he had conquered for himself a throne." Thus the essence of his nature was an energy which sought and conquered obstacles, and utilized every possible element in his character as a means to victory. His coolness, his love of struggle, his ambition, his domineering tendencies, the striking firmness of his attitude at critical moments, became so many means to this end.

During his first imprisonment while under trial, at the age of twenty-three, far from obeying the prison regulations, he issued his own orders to the warders ; and whenever the latter attempted to exert their authority, scenes of great violence were the result. On hearing that his sister had presented a petition on his behalf, he immediately sent a statement to the King to secure himself against any misunderstanding. His youthful character showed points of resemblance to Cæsar, though horrified citizens were afterwards to regard him as a Catiline. He was born for power and marked out for rule, but birth had placed him in the middle class below Princes and nobles, and had made him a member of a down-trodden race ; he therefore became a thinker, a democrat, and an agitator, in order to reach by this path the position for which he was created. We have seen that even in boyhood Lassalle was conscious of his destiny. But even if his ideas upon this matter afterwards became less precise, we must remember that what self-consciousness may regard as an end is often to Nature nothing more than a means, and that Nature urged him to demand power, reputation, and even the applause and prestige which are conceded to the distinguished leader of a people or of a class. We must remember that Nature had also brought him into the world as a member of the extreme Left, and endowed him with the sense that it was his duty to avenge the oppression and the scorn of centuries. Was it not inevitable that he should regard himself from the outset as a revolutionary and a faction leader ? These tendencies were combined with the influence of modern learning, and Lassalle was a born scholar ; but the whole body of modern science naturally promotes the progress of Radicalism, and the more entirely a man is overcome by the spirit of learning, the more profoundly does he feel himself bound to oppose whatever is based only upon the authority of tradition.

Early as Lassalle reached maturity, the child in him was never overgrown or killed. He was not one of those men who have never been children : he was one of those who ever retain something of childhood's nature. Spielhagen's purely poetical description of the hero of " In Reih' und Glied " must not lead us to assume that Lassalle was a pale, quiet, and ever-serious boy, like Leo. As a man, he possessed feeling and sym-

2

pathy. In private life he showed a want of self-control, would give full rein to his animosity and domineering tendencies, and a moment later would concede the point at issue with entire amiability. He could be a child and play childish tricks as well as anyone. His love of outward show and the pleasure he took in display are among his childlike, or even his childish, characteristics. Democrat though he was, he was a dandy, and very fastidious about his dress, though his taste was good. He liked to see his rooms tastefully fitted up, or even decorated. His house was characterized, not only by refinement, but also by a touch of outward show. Early in the decade 1850-1860 Lassalle twice visited the East, and brought back hangings and artistic objects for the adornment of his house. He was a little histrionic, as dominant characters often are : Napoleon and Byron are cases in point. When he entertained his friends, he would have the most elaborate dishes in Berlin, and this at a time when he was appearing as the champion of the working classes. These characteristics are not to be interpreted as the outcome of sheer inconsistency, but as due to the contrast of ideas existing in a deep and complex character, in a Jacobin endowed with a keen sense of beauty, in a soldier of revolution fighting with splendidly decorated weapons, in a man who had never entirely put away childish things. Lassalle's intellectual powers comprised extraordinarily modern and entirely classical elements, and the latter, again, were of a twofold kind. He was an Alcibiades in his love of enjoyment and in his capacity for accommodating himself to any environment, to the society of scholars or of revolutionaries, to a prison or a ballroom. "In his youth he would go to prison with as much indifference as anyone might go to a ball."[1] He was an ancient Roman in his strength of will, his energy, his political insight, and his capacity for conquest and organization.

At the Universities of Breslau and Berlin Lassalle's enthusiasm for classical antiquity led him to the study of philology, and thence to Hegel, whose dialectical method he appropriated with zealous delight. At the same time he was absorbing the revolutionary ideas of Young Germany. After he had left

[1] Trial in Düsseldorf, June 27, 1864, conclusion.

the University, he lived a bachelor life of independence on the Rhine and studied Greek philology and philosophy both at Düsseldorf and during his stay in Paris in 1845. In Paris, Lassalle, who was then twenty years of age, made the acquaintance of Heinrich Heine. The Aristophanes of the age was not easily hoodwinked, and our respect for the young student's powers is considerably increased when we see how Heine was attracted and dazzled by him. Similarly, we can better realize the keenness of the poet's psychological insight when we weigh the terms in which he addresses and mentions one who must have seemed but a child in years and in intelligence when compared with himself. Apparently Lassalle, with his usual energy, interested himself in the question of an inheritance which was then troubling the poet, who was ill and alone : his vigorous championship secured allies for Heine in Germany whose influence was valuable in this matter of importance to the poet's welfare. Heine's letters to Lassalle constantly speak of him as " his dearly-beloved friend," " his dearest brother in arms," and contain such outbursts as the following :

" To-day I will do no more than thank you ; no one has ever done so much for me before. Nor have I ever yet found anyone who combined such warm-heartedness and such clear intelligence in dealing with affairs. You have the right to be impudent : the rest of us merely usurp this divine right, this heavenly privilege. In comparison with you, I am but a modest gnat." And elsewhere : " Farewell, and be assured that my affection for you is inexpressible. How glad I am that I was not mistaken in you ! But I have never trusted anyone so much—I, whom experience, not Nature, has made so mistrustful. Since I have had your letters, my courage has risen and I feel better."[1]

There is something almost pathetic in the sight of the great poet, broken by many sorrows at the age of forty-six, turning for protection to the iron will of the youth, which had been inexorably steeled by the passage of twenty winters, and was ready to confront the many other difficulties and vexations which lay before him. Heine turning to Lassalle for help—

---

[1] Heinrich Heine, " Letters," third part; letters of January and February, 1846.

we think of the antelope asking protection from the young
lion. A reference in a letter to Ferdinand's father shows that
Lassalle introduced himself to Heine as an avowed atheist.
Heine " would like to see his face " when he hears that the poet
on his death-bed had undergone conversion. Other humorous
allusions show what, in any case, was to be expected—that
Lassalle was neither unattracted by women nor unattractive
to them during his stay in Paris. Fortunately, a letter from
Heine to Varnhagen von Ense has preserved a full description
of Ferdinand Lassalle ; the description is not only memorable
as a close portrait drawn by the cleverest pen which Germany
then possessed, but is doubly valuable because it provides us
with a picture of Lassalle as he was before he became a public
character or made his mark in the literary world. We have
here an etching of Lassalle *avant la lettre* :

" My friend, Herr Lassalle, who brings you this letter, is a
young man of the most distinguished intellectual powers. To
the most thorough scholarship, the widest knowledge and the
greatest penetration that I have ever known, he adds the fullest
endowment of imaginative powers, an energy of will and a
dexterity in action which simply astonish me ; and if he retains
his sympathy for myself, I expect that he will promote my
cause most energetically. In any case, this conjunction of
knowledge and power, of talent and character, has been a very
pleasant experience for me. . . . I should say that Herr
Lassalle is a definite and declared modernist. He will have
nothing to do with the renunciation and the modesty with
which we were accustomed, more or less hypocritically, to dream
and prate away our time. The new generation demands full
possession, and insists upon making itself seen and heard. We
elder men were accustomed to bow humbly before the invisible,
aspiring to shadowy kisses and the scent of blue flowers amid
regretful renunciations. At the same time, we were perhaps
happier than those stern gladiators who advance so proudly
to the death-struggle."

What words ! In every line we observe the penetrating eye
of the artist, the hand of the master, and the clever irony of the
satirist, while the concluding sentence contains the prophetic
insight of the seer.

CHAPTER III

On August 11, 1848, there appeared before the Assize Court at Cologne, charged with complicity in the theft of a cash-box, a youth of proud and attractive exterior, who was thus described in the indictment : " Ferdinand Lassalle, twenty-three years of age, of no occupation, born at Breslau, 5 feet 6 inches high, with brown curly hair, an open forehead, brown eyebrows, dark blue eyes, a well-proportioned nose and mouth, a round chin, a narrow face and slender figure." The young man thus described delivered a speech in his defence upon that day of which the worthy tribunal had never heard the like. He was accused of inciting, two years previously, two other young men, Oppenheim and Mendelssohn, to crime. These men belonged to extremely rich and distinguished families, and both, like himself, had vigorously interfered in the Hatzfeldt family quarrels on behalf of the Countess Sophie von Hatzfeldt. Lassalle was charged with inducing them to abstract from the Count's mistress a cash-box, in which a contract was supposed to have been kept securing to this mistress an income of eight thousand thalers a year from the Count. Oppenheim was already a Prussian assessor, no strong recommendation in this case, and his motives for the theft were not likely to be misconstrued, as he was the heir to two or three million thalers ; in December, 1846, he was therefore released, although his hand had abstracted the cash-box. None the less, in January, 1848, a jury condemned Mendelssohn, who was only an accomplice, to five years' imprisonment for theft, and Lassalle's turn had now come. He, however, adopted the attitude rather of accuser than of accused. Far from limiting himself to defence, in the opening sentence of his speech he scornfully brushed aside the charge against him, which stated that he was the "intellectual originator" of the theft. He then identified his own case with that of the Countess, and attacked the exalted enemies of his client with all the passion of a youthful popular orator and the superiority of a born conqueror. He described the torments which the Countess had endured, and then continued :

" The family was silent, but we know that when men hold their peace the stones will cry out. When every human right is outraged, when even the ties of kinship are silent and a helpless being is abandoned by its natural protectors, then the first and the last relation of such a being has the right to rise in the person of another member of the human race. You all know and have all read with indignation the dreadful story of the unfortunate Duchess of Praslin. Which of you would not have thrown himself forward in her defence, when she was struggling for life ? Well, gentlemen, I said to myself, Here is one who is in tenfold worse case than Praslin, for what is the short struggle of an hour compared with the long process of assassination which refined cruelty has set on foot against the whole existence of a human being, against this lamentable figure of a woman whose rights have been daily trampled underfoot for twenty years, whose every claim has been outraged, after every means has been tried to make her the object of scorn and contempt, that she might be ill-treated with impunity."

The young man who was prosecuted in so strange a case, and who thus displayed such chivalrous sympathy, had made the acquaintance at Berlin, when he was twenty years old, of the Countess Hatzfeldt, by birth a Princess ; she was then thirty-nine years of age, but was still handsome and commanding. Deeply moved by her misfortunes, he had assumed the position of her champion. A majestic figure, with nobly-modelled limbs, whose every movement betrayed grace enough to conquer many a man ; finely-formed features ; heavy red-gold hair, with a distinguished bearing and address ; a calm character, and a simple and sensible manner of expression— such were the weapons of the woman who was constantly de-

scribed as a dangerous siren.   But the combative soul of the
passionate youth was stirred, not so much by her beauty as
by the unusual unhappiness which the Countess had had to
endure.   Her husband and cousin, Count Edmund von Hatzfeldt, to whom she had been betrothed at the early age of
fifteen, had hated and ill-treated her from the outset.   He was
the richest member of the powerful Hatzfeldt family, was
worth some five millions of thalers, and possessed all the
privileges of the high Prussian nobility.   Thus, in his behaviour
towards his wife he was far less subject to legal control than
any ordinary man would have been.   What particular wrong
she had done to him is very difficult to discover, but in any
case it cannot have borne any proportion to the meanness of
the Count's revenge, or to the pettifogging and malignant
nature of his persecution.   He confined her in his castles on
the Rhine ; he refused her medical help and advice when she
was ill ; he secretly abducted her children, to whom she clung
with all a mother's tenderness ; he deprived her of the very
means of existence, while he himself not only squandered his
patrimony in debauchery, but kept scribblers in his pay to
calumniate his wife.   The Countess had no parents ; her
brothers and other relations were in high official posts, and
were more anxious to avoid a scandal than to help the sufferer.
However, upon more than one occasion the family—and once
even the King—had interfered, had succeeded in bringing
about a reconciliation between the married couple, and in
wresting a promise from the Count to be more careful in his
behaviour towards his wife.   But his promises were made
merely to be broken.

Only one course of action remained open—an extremely
doubtful one in these circumstances—an appeal to law.

About this time the Mendelssohn who was involved in the
story of the cash-box introduced Lassalle to the Countess.   It
is certain that the handsome bearing of the young man,
his well-made figure, and his unusually beautiful dark blue
eyes, made a very favourable impression upon her.   A friend
of Lassalle has informed me that shortly after his acquaintance
with the Countess he went to the Count and challenged him.
The high-born Junker merely replied from his lofty pedestal

of nobility by laughing in the face of the "silly Jewish boy," and then it was that Lassalle seriously resolved to undertake the cause of the Countess. In one of his letters he expresses himself as follows upon the subject :

" So I said to myself, Never let anyone be able to say that you knew of this and still allowed that woman to be quietly strangled without an effort to help her. If you did this, what right would you have to reproach others for their selfishness and their cowardice ?

" I was a young man, twenty years of age ; I had just left the University, where I had studied philosophy ; I knew nothing of law, but nothing could restrain me.

" I said to the Countess, who was at the end of her resources : ' You know very well that if you begin an action, your relations will abandon you or will turn against you, as you have always been told ; but you also know that you have nothing to expect in that direction except empty words. If, therefore, you are firmly resolved to conquer or to die, I will take up your case ; for though young, I am strong, and will swear to fight for you to the death.'

" She had confidence in her right, in her strength and in mine, and readily accepted my proposal ; and I, a young Jew without influence, advanced to the assault of the most formidable powers."[1]

Lassalle accompanied the Countess to Düsseldorf, and for several years of his life devoted the whole of his abilities to the struggle to secure her property and her social position.

We can understand that at the first moment Lassalle's parents could feel nothing but anxiety and regret when they saw their son turning aside to champion the cause of a person entirely unknown to them. At an early age he had displayed unusual capacity in the department of philology ; such men as Boeckh and Alexander von Humboldt prophesied the most brilliant future for the young scholar—the Wonder Child, as Humboldt called him—and his mother would have been very glad to see her son a professor. However, she was soon reconciled to the course of events, especially when she was informed that every road to the University was closed to

" Une Page d'Amour de Ferdinand Lassalle," 71.

Ferdinand by reason of his Jewish birth. For himself, however, it was undoubtedly a most severe wrench to abandon the studies he had begun. His great work upon Heraclitus, which had been almost finished at the end of 1846, did not appear until 1859, in consequence of this distraction ; to this matter he refers in his speech in his defence :

" My own gaze, gentlemen, had long been directed upon general questions and affairs, and I should have hesitated, perhaps, to devote the whole of my abilities to an individual case of misfortune, to interrupt the whole of my career for some years at least, although it is heartrending for a sympathetic man to see another person whom he regards as good and noble hurled to destruction in the midst of civilization. But in this case I could see that general principles and points were involved : I told myself that the Countess was a victim to her class ; I told myself that no one who was not in the proud position of a Prince or a millionaire would venture, or have ventured, thus to outrage the moral consciousness of society without hesitation. . . . I did not conceal from myself in the smallest degree the difficulties of this enterprise ; I saw very well that it would be a most formidable task to clear up the rights and wrongs of this long-standing and historical misdeed ; that if the matter were brought to the courts, it would demand the whole of my energies, and that the task of carrying through so complicated an affair would necessitate a long interruption to my own career. I knew very well the difficulties of overcoming false appearances ; I realized that rank, wealth, and influence are dangerous opponents, and that they alone can ever find allies in the ranks of the bureaucracy ; I realized, too, that I might be exposing myself to considerable danger. All this I knew, but it did not deter me. I resolved to oppose truth to speciousness, right to rank, intellectual power to the power of money. Obstacles, sacrifices, and dangers in no way deterred me. Even if I had known what unworthy and infamous calumnies were to be heaped upon me, how my purest motives were to be distorted and misinterpreted, and what ready credence would be given to the most miserable lies—well, even then I hope my resolution would have remained unaltered, though at the price of a hard and painful battle."

Circumstances, allusions in the terms of the charge, and the rumours inevitably in circulation, forced Lassalle to refer to the accusation against him—that he was upon terms of affectionate intimacy with his client. Nothing, he said, was more generally believed than this accusation, and to protest against it would be ridiculous. However, he appeals to that which witnesses in reference to this circumstance have expressed as their conviction—to his letters, which are produced, and prove the opposite to be the fact. He then explains why he had been inevitably met with incredulity upon this matter.

" Gentlemen, very distinguished members of this town spoke to me—men who wished me well, who knew my position, and who had received honourable testimony forbidding them to believe that I was actuated by any mean motives of self-interest—and these men themselves expressed their conviction that I absolutely must be upon terms of affectionate intimacy with the Countess ; and when I ventured to ask them what grounds they had for their conclusions, they simply replied that they had none—none, except the fact that such great sacrifices for another's cause are inexplicable upon any other grounds. Gentlemen, I will admit that these men judged as men of experience with knowledge of the world ; but they forgot one thing — they forgot my youth ; they forgot that, though selfishness may be the ruling principle of our century, youth has ever been, and will ever be, the age of disinterestedness, enthusiasm, and ready sacrifice."

In these words there is a certain ring of sincerity and truth. Whatever Lassalle's relations with the Countess were, as a man of honour he was certainly unable publicly to aver that any amorous connection existed between them. But, in my opinion, the mode of his denial plainly shows that, whatever character the relationship between them may shortly afterwards have assumed, it was originally guided, when he plunged into this fierce practical struggle, by no sentimental tendencies, but by his antagonistic temperament, his burning anger, and his purely intellectual inclinations. These motives overcame all misgivings, and he was actuated merely by the desire to make the cause of right prevail against that of might.

Lassalle's relations towards the Countess in the years

immediately following provided his opponents with continual opportunities for attacking his morality and that of his client. The real nature of these relations naturally remained unknown, and it might, indeed, be said that public opinion had not the smallest concern with them. In any case, the intimacy soon assumed the form of a friendship concluded under unusual circumstances between a young man and a middle-aged woman. During Lassalle's later years the attitude of the Countess towards him was in every respect that of a second mother, and in conversation and correspondence she invariably addressed him as " child."

Lassalle's assertion that in this particular affair he could find general rules and principles exemplified may seem to many a mere rhetorical trick. But such suspicions would certainly be unfounded. It is a characteristic of distinguished men to find a universal fate exemplified in the particular instance which they may encounter, and which a thousand others may encounter without regarding it as anything further than an isolated and chance occurrence. Such men immediately divine, by force of momentary inspiration, how large a number of unfortunate people groan beneath calamities similar to the case which they have witnessed. Behind the wrong-doing they see the social cause of it, and direct their attacks upon these causes, where others might think only of the wrong-doer immediately responsible. Lassalle, therefore, means what he says when he expresses the hope that in those days (1848), when the edifice of lies, hypocrisy, and universal oppression collapsed, the daylight of truth would also be bound to break " upon an individual fate and suffering which is as truly a microcosmos as any individual case can ever be, reflecting the universal suffering, the subservience and misery tottering to the grave ; the hope that the light would break upon an honourable endeavour, undeterred by criminal prosecution or any other forms of law from helping outraged right to secure due recognition."[1]

[1] Lassalle, " My Defence against the Accusation of Inciting to the Cash-box Theft," delivered on August 11, 1848, before the Royal Assize Court at Cologne and the jury. " My Criminal Prosecution for Inciting to the Cash-box Theft," or " The Charge of Moral Complicity : A Prosecution with Ulterior Object." Cologne : Wilhelm Greven, 1848. These two pamphlets are not obtainable from booksellers, and are not to be found in the Royal Library at Berlin. I found copies in the Royal Library at Munich.

The speech from which we have quoted some fragments is the first literary work which exists from Lassalle's pen. Its interest consists in the fact that it gives us a glimpse of the mental furniture with which he was provided in the years of his youth. I have already drawn attention to the genuine nature of the feeling which here comes to light. Characteristics of this kind are betrayed by style, and cannot be imitated. A belief in the ultimate triumph of right over might is deeply rooted in his heart, and appears as a warm and youthful enthusiasm. This belief is accompanied by his sense of self-sufficiency. Lassalle believes not so much in the power of intellect as in the power of his own intellect to defy and overcome all difficulties. We here see the motives of chivalrous feeling and love of conflict, while his mode of expression betrays something of the advocate's talent for grasping a situation, turning incidents to account, and laying on the colours with a heavy hand, " the rights of humanity," etc. Yet to say so much is to say almost too much. When such characteristics do appear, they are so delicate and imperceptible that they lend little more than a vague colouring to the speech. But one characteristic does undoubtedly appear, and one that was deeply rooted in Lassalle's nature—his ruthlessness. Ruthlessness is a very modern ideal of conduct. Bismarck somewhere replies in one of his letters to an intellectual friend of long standing, who reproaches him with excessive ruthlessness, in words both sincere and highly instructive : " As a statesman, I am by no means sufficiently ruthless—indeed, rather cowardly." Ruthlessness, which must not be regarded as synonymous with brutality, iconoclasm, or the like, is an ideal which has arisen during the years 1870-1880. It was not the ideal of our forefathers. How often have they quoted Hamlet's words :

" And thus the native hue of resolution
Is sicklied o'er with the pale cast of thought."

Whatever the deficiencies of the present age may be, Hamlet's words are now inapplicable to it. Our resolutions and determinations are carried out. To pursue one's object ruthlessly, careless of opposition from without, and ready to use the means that circumstances provide, is both the merit and defect of modern times. The incident which brought Lassalle into the dock was of the kind in which nothing but an early-developed ruthlessness could have involved him. To stigmatize his attempt to abstract a deed affecting the interests of the Countess as mere theft would be no less ridiculous than stupid ; but a character in any way fastidious about its choice of means would have shrunk from such an action. Even if he was not immediately concerned in the execution of the act, he was indirectly involved by his influence over the participators in it. The domination of his character is indicated by the express statement in the indictment that, though he was the youngest of the defenders of the Countess, his associates obeyed him unquestioningly.

Thus, from the year 1846 onwards Lassalle conducted the case of the Countess. He began by pouring a perfect flood of lawsuits upon the head of the Count. If he had never studied law before, he now began, and worked with unparalleled enthusiasm. Even while he was occupied in the conduct of these successive suits he was advancing his knowledge of jurisprudence. In a few months he could hold his own with any advocate. At the same time he set other forces in motion with a certainty of touch which betrays the future agitator. He appealed to the democratic Press, and a thousand echoes resounded through it at his cry. He ruined the Count's reputation with the public. Whenever the Count considered that he had found a means for the final annihilation of his Countess, his efforts turned against himself under Lassalle's hands.

In January, 1847, the Count was no longer contented with depriving the Countess of all means for the support of herself and her children. She was then living upon money derived from the sale of some jewels belonging to better times. He now attempted to reduce her to subservience by starvation, and for this purpose to destroy her personal credit. He wrote, for instance, to her hotel-keeper in Deutz, and requested him to give the Countess notice, as he would never pay for his wife. The landlord replied with scorn that if he liked to support the wife and children of the Count, who was allowing them to die of hunger, that was no one's concern but his own.

Lassalle, however, turned the Count's clumsiness to his own account. The newspapers soon spread news of the event in Trèves, in Mannheim, and Breslau, and demanded that public beneficence should put the Count to shame, by providing the Countess with the means for taking her case to the lawcourts. It was a war without cessation or truce, a war to the death, in which Lassalle gradually gained fresh allies among the popular party and their Press. One friend alone upon whom he had calculated left him, however, in the lurch. This was Heinrich Heine, who kept silence chiefly because Count Hatzfeldt's mistress, the Baroness Meyendorff, formerly a Russian spy in Paris, was on friendly terms with the Princesse de Lieven, the mistress of Guizot ; and Heine is known to have drawn a yearly pension from Guizot, as did the majority of the *émigrés* settled in France during the July Monarchy.

The task, with all these legal difficulties, became so colossal, and obstacles increased in such number, that Lassalle, though an unparalleled worker, spent nearly nine years of his life in this struggle, instead of one year, as he had thought would be sufficient in 1848. He was no legal authority by profession ; but he gained so thorough a knowledge of law by practice that he was able to produce a theoretical work of permanent value. One who has long been regarded as the first legal authority in Germany, after studying the case, has privately declared that no professional advocate could have conducted it so well. Lassalle brought the case of the Countess before thirty-six courts. Only so strong a will as his could have been capable of the stern tenacity which the case required, and during this period he was at one time in confinement for examination on the charge of complicity in the theft previously mentioned, and at another time was imprisoned on the ground that he had invited people to protect the Constitution by force of arms against the *coup d'état* of 1848. Undismayed, Lassalle continued to conduct the case from his prison cell ; when he was liberated he prosecuted it with yet greater energy, though philosophy, politics, economy, all his studies and all his prospects in life were set aside and postponed until he should be freed from this ungrateful task. Previously to 1848 the verdicts which he gained were, as a rule, favourable. After

1848, when the counter-revolution was triumphant, hardly a week passed in which some one of the large number of cases which Lassalle had set on foot was not lost. Defeats showered upon him, but he recovered new strength and found new devices, though he afterwards himself asserted that he never understood how he had been able to bring the case to a triumphant issue. At length, in August, 1854, his opponent, the Count, was exhausted. The silly Jewish boy had been too much for him. His strength was broken. Lassalle set his foot upon his neck, and dictated terms of peace under conditions most humiliating and dishonourable to the Count. No verdict was announced, but an agreement was secured, and Lassalle gained that for which he had striven, including a princely settlement upon the Countess. While the case was in progress he had shared with her the scanty sum which was annually sent to him by his parents, for during that long period the Countess was penniless. In return he had stipulated, by written contract, for a definite yearly income of four thousand thalers, if success should be attained. Thus from henceforward he was relieved from all anxiety concerning his daily wants, and was able to devote himself to scientific and unremunerative studies, without being forced daily to consider the necessity of earning his bread.

CHAPTER IV

LASSALLE first returned to his work on Heraclitus. As the book now stands, the attentive reader can easily discover the traces of two hands. The mature thinker has collected, arranged, and published what the researches of the youth had discovered. It is certain that in the course of years Lassalle's metaphysical and purely Hegelian views had been replaced by a more historical outlook. At the same time, the book provides a comparatively faithful picture of Lassalle's scientific life in his early youth. The " Philosophy of Heraclitus the Obscure " is a study in Hegelian style, a study in the history of philosophy. Lassalle was inevitably and powerfully attracted to the philosophy of Hegel, which was paramount during his earlier years, by something in his disposition, by the dialectical tendencies of his nature, and his yearning to find some key or picklock to open the way to that understanding and knowledge which imply power. Vast indeed were the promises which Hegel's philosophy made to its disciples. The fact that Lassalle paid special attention to Heraclitus may probably be ascribed in the first instance to his passionate inclination to make trial of his strength in the face of appalling difficulties. From the days of early antiquity Heraclitus had been known as the Obscure, and such of his writings as remain consist of few and scattered fragments ; the task of completing these and making them intelligible implies a knowledge of the whole of classical literature. Thus the enthusiastic disciple of Hegel obviously discovered some pleasure in depicting a mind which seemed to him a distant forerunner of Hegel himself, and who might be thought, simply on the ground of his relationship to

32

the modern master, to have missed due appreciation. Finally, the young and vigorous apostle of his age may have been attracted by the great figure of antiquity, many of whose traditional characteristics will be found to correspond with the instincts and tendencies which Lassalle felt at work within himself. Heraclitus is also said to have " banished all peace and quietness from the world, which became for him only absolute motion." With what satisfaction does Lassalle assert in one passage : " We see that Heraclitus was far removed from that apathy which inspires the ethical-political arguments of the Stoics with such profound monotony. His nature was one of storm."[1] Almost all of Lassalle's writings contain some protest against the habit of considering separate sciences or departments of knowledge in irrational isolation, and in this point the inherent width and universality of his outlook may be seen. Similarly this work begins with an emphatic assertion that since history is now no longer considered to be a mere collection of interesting or farcical incidents, and since the idea is regarded as a historical product, and the history of philosophy as the uninterrupted development of thought, so the time cannot be far distant when the history of philosophy will no longer be treated as an isolated department of knowledge, any more than the history of art, constitutional history, or the history of social forms of life. The emphasis which is here laid upon the fact of historical development should not, however, lead us to suppose that Lassalle in this work adopted an attitude less Hegelian and more modern than he actually assumed. The Introduction, which lays such particular stress upon the historical mode of treatment, was undoubtedly one of the parts of the book last composed. In other respects his attitude is entirely speculative. The scientific idea is certainly here termed a historical creation ; but at the same time, the forms under which the idea is conceived are regarded as eternal, transcendental realities, producing history by their automatic movement and by the revulsions which they create. Philosophers are not historically arranged in order according to the stage of development which their general intellectual life has attained, but according

---

[1] Lassalle, " Heraclitus," i. 51 ; ii. 443.

to the place which is occupied in the system by the conceptions which they represent. Heraclitus corresponds to Becoming, Parmenides to Being ; hence it is *a priori* obvious that Parmenides must be regarded as preliminary and inferior to Heraclitus, however superior his intellectual powers may have been.[1]

By this we are very far from implying that Lassalle did not understand Heraclitus. The contrary is the case. The metaphysical method of Hegel was, indeed, an admirable instrument for securing comprehension of a thinker whose strength and chief characteristic was his almost hair-splitting dialectic. I would not rely solely upon my own judgment in this matter, but a well-known authority in this department, Professor Steinthal, of the University of Berlin, returned the following significant reply when I asked him how far he considered that Lassalle had understood Heraclitus : " Certainly he understood him. A normally gifted scholar will not, and, indeed, may not, understand Heraclitus, but there is no denying that Lassalle understood him, and that his book is an excellent and capable piece of work."

Lassalle's conception and statement of Heraclitus's metaphysics betrays the hand of the accomplished Hegelian : the essential unity of the great contraries, Being and Not-Being, the concept of Becoming which forms the transition from Not-Being to Being, is the Divine law itself. Nature herself is but the visible promulgation of this law which forms the essence of her being, the law of the identity of contraries. Day is but the impulse to become night, night but the impulse to become day ; sunrise is but uninterrupted sunset, etc. The cosmos is but the visible realization of this harmony of contraries which pervades and governs all existence. Heiberg himself could have carried Hegelianism no further, and could have displayed no greater pleasure in the technicalities of this school of thought than is apparent in the Hegelian explanation of the origin of Heraclitus from the Eleatic School : " Their pure universal Being is thus Being in itself, Not-Being: for all real Being is but definite and qualitative Being ; the removal and negation of all real tangible Being is Not-Being. . . . The reconciliation of this contradiction, the self-existent Not-

[1] Lassalle, " Heraclitus," i. 35. *Cf.* Lazarus and Steinthal, *Zeitschrift für Völkerpsychologie und Sprachkunde*, ii. 333.

Being, is the kernel and the whole depth (*sic*) of his philosophy. Thus far we may say, that this philosophy is contained in the one phrase, only Not-Being exists."[1]

Heiberg was a Privy Councillor when he died, and if in the next world his feelings were not outraged by his agreement with so notorious a revolutionary, he might well have joined hands with Lassalle in approval of such an exposition as we have outlined.[2] Lassalle then explains with entire correctness why Heraclitus, in spite of his transcendental principles, none the less drew names for his fundamental concepts from the material world. He conceived " Not-Being and its unity with Being as operative, but also as invariably existing objectively, and as positing and perfecting itself objectively. He did not consider it as reflected upon itself, as existing only for itself as a subjective idea ; and as his principle so far was nothing more than Not-Being in objective existence, he could only speak of it as such—that is to say, in terms of outward and objective existence. Not-Being, however, as existing objectively, is fire, water in motion, war, harmony, time, necessity, universally ruling justice, and *Dike* limiting action, etc."

The method employed by Lassalle in this metaphysical and philosophical investigation is purely Hegelian. On the other hand, it is equally clear that the chief interest in the subject of his researches was for him the fact that Heraclitus anticipated his own great master. If Hegel had been born in Asiatic Greece, at the close of the sixth century before our era, he would have become Heraclitus. Even in antiquity it had been observed that while Heraclitus posits contraries as the origin of the world, he does not recognize the fundamental principle of the contradictory. Heraclitus had already adopted a position comparable to the deification of Nature by Spinoza

---

[1] Lassalle, " Heraclitus," i. 25, 35.

[2] Lassalle was never able entirely to abandon the use of Hegelian dialect. In his tragedy, " Franz von Sickingen," Charles V. speaks of his objects, and says in true Hegelian manner :

> " If you could make
> My purposes the content of your will—
>   Then, Franz—
> Then mightest thou rise."

In his last important work, " Capital and Labour," he speaks of the " revulsions " (*Umschlagen*) of conceptions . See also his " System of Acquired Rights," ii. 9, for the dialectical activity of the concept.

when he explained that to God everything was beautiful and righteous, but that man had named one thing righteous and another unrighteous. In Heraclitus may be found the philosophical inclination, which was so predominant when Hegelianism was at its height, to use every possible opportunity of making assertions hopelessly unacceptable to the so-called common sense. Lassalle himself observes : " Modern philosophy was careful repeatedly to emphasize the fact that the most simple and ordinary matters which everyone thinks he knows by instinct are precisely those about which least is known, and whose nature is utterly incomprehensible to the thinking intelligence. But in fact Heraclitus was the first to announce a truly speculative idea, and consequently he was also the first to make this same assertion concerning the impotence of non-speculative thought and of the subjective intelligence."

The ethical system of Heraclitus, says Lassalle, is contained in the single idea, which is itself the eternal and fundamental concept of morality—" surrender to the Universal." This statement is both Greek and modern, but Lassalle cannot deny himself the pleasure of a special exposition, showing how this idea of the old Greek philosophers coincided with the political philosophy of Hegel. " In Hegel's philosophy laws are alike regarded as the realization of the universally existing will, though this definition has not the smallest reference to the formal will of the subjects or to their number. Similarly, the Universal of Heraclitus is far removed from the category of empirical totality."[1]

Stress is laid on this feature, not only on account of the similarity with Hegel, but also because it coincided with Lassalle's most cherished political views. From his earliest youth he had regarded the idea of the State as the realization of morality, right, and reason. His enthusiasm for this idea, and his belief in the destiny of the State, not only as a protective force, but also as a positive stimulus to right and culture, runs through all his writings. The idea may be traced in his scholarly and scientific researches, as in this case of his " Heraclitus." It is more strongly expressed, though appearing only incidentally, in his great legal work (" The System of Acquired

[1] Lassalle, " Heraclitus," i. 36, 92, 119 ; ii. 276, 431, 439.

Rights," i. 47 ; ii. 603 *et seq.*) ; eventually it is proclaimed in his political and economic pamphlets, with passionate attacks upon the doctrine of the Manchester School, and with all the warmth of conviction which made Lassalle so popular and so formidable as a speaker and a writer.

The contrast between Heraclitus and Lassalle in this respect is simply as follows : From the political teaching of the Greek thinker it becomes quite obvious that, notwithstanding his reverence for the Universal, he must have been in the bitterest opposition to the rule of the masses which prevailed in his town of Ephesus ; it is much harder to understand how Lassalle could have advanced from kindred and Hegelian conceptions of the State to practical conclusions, which remind us much rather of Rousseau than of Hegel. But his attractive personality betrays an inward inconsistency which is often noticeable in the case of prominent intellects. By instinct, and as a result of his first principles, Lassalle was a worshipper of intelligence, of reason, and a passionate opponent and scorner of public opinion and of numbers. On the other hand, by conviction, and as the result of his political and practical principles, Lassalle, as everyone knows, was a most decided champion of popular power, a persistent and successful supporter of universal suffrage, and a pioneer in the service of democratic power such as history had never yet seen. An intellectual aristocrat and a social democrat ! The human heart may contain yet greater contradictions than these, but not without loss can they form part of a man's disposition. The phenomenon that here meets us is, in the world of thought, precisely that contrast which was outwardly apparent when Lassalle, in his dandified clothes, his fine linen, and his patent-leather boots, spoke formally or informally among a number of grimy, horny-handed mechanics.

If, however, in this respect a certain contradiction existed between Lassalle and the Greek philosopher he admired, on the other hand a similarity is apparent when we read his description of Heraclitus's character, with its incredible self-confidence and scorn of humanity. Great must have been the appreciation of his own importance possessed by anyone who, like Heraclitus, could repeatedly assert that " mankind for the most part is unintelligent, and that he himself alone possessed knowledge, while all others acted as though they were in their sleep." He could also say of his fellow-citizens, speaking in general terms, that " they deserved to be hung, for the masses only feed themselves like cattle," and in reference to a particular case, the expulsion of his friend Hermodorus : " The Ephesians ought to be strangled as they grow up, without exception, and the State should be left to the children, for they have driven out the most excellent of their number, Hermodorus, saying no one shall be the most excellent among us, and if anyone holds that position, then let him be excellent somewhere else and among other people."[1]

We can hardly doubt that these words must often have occurred to Lassalle in the years immediately before his death, when he saw himself everywhere calumniated and slandered, menaced with years of imprisonment, persecuted by the authorities and the Press, and received with indifference by the greater number of those whom he wished to help and for whom he sacrificed his peace of mind. In my opinion, no more striking counterpart can anywhere be found to the despairing self-assertiveness of Heraclitus, the bitterness and scorn of which reminds us of Timon of Athens, than the sad but wonderfully written meditation with which Lassalle concludes his work, " Capital and Labour."

" To think of this general descent on the part of the middle classes in the land of Lessing and Kant, Schiller and Goethe, Fichte, Schelling, and Hegel! Did these intellectual heroes merely sweep above our heads like a flight of cranes ? Of their vast intellectual work, and of the influence which they exerted upon the progress of the world, has absolutely nothing reached the nation at large ? Does German nationalism merely consist of a series of isolated individuals, each faithfully taking up the inheritance of his predecessors and pursuing his lonely labours, which to the nation are fruitless, in bitter contempt of his contemporaries ? What is that curse which has disinherited the middle classes, so that from the great work of civilization which has been completed among them, and from all this great atmosphere of culture, no single drop of refreshing

[1] Lassalle, " Heraclitus," ii. 269, 281, 442.

dew has ever fallen upon their steadily decaying brains ? They celebrate the festivals of our great thinkers because they have never read their works. If they had read them they would burn them. They rave about our poets because they have seen or read a few lines of their work, but have never been able to appreciate their views of life."

The last point of coincidence between Heraclitus and Lassalle consists in the passionate desire for fame and glory, for praise and the admiration of others, which they felt in spite of their self-consciousness and their pride ; it was Heraclitus who uttered the oft-quoted saying : " Greater fates obtain the greater lot " (i.e., the greater reward). Another saying of his puts this sentence in the proper light : " The masses and those who think themselves wise follow the poets of the people, and ask the laws for counsel, not knowing that the masses are bad, that few of them are good, and that the best choose one thing instead of all, the ever-persisting reputation of mortals."[1] Fame to Heraclitus was, indeed, the greatest reward that the greater fate could obtain. His love of honour did not spring immediately and instinctively from his nature, but was also founded upon reflection and philosophy. " Fame," says Lassalle, " is, in fact, the most opposite of all things, most opposite to the category of immediately real Being and its several objects. Fame is the Being of mankind within the sphere of his Not-Being. It is pure persistence amid the decay of material existence, and is therefore the immortality of man obtained and realized." He adds the enthusiastic remark : " This is the reason why fame has ever exerted so powerful an attraction upon great souls, and has lifted them beyond all petty and limited things. It is the reason why Platen sings of it that it comes only ' hand in hand with the angel of death that puts men on trial '; it is also the reason why Heraclitus regarded it as the ethical realization of his speculative principle."

This estimation of fame and glory may be in complete harmony with the metaphysical system of Heraclitus, but the fact remains that it is sheer logical contradiction to unite this desire for outside admiration with deep scorn for the judgment

---

[1] Lassalle, " Heraclitus," ii. 434, 436.

of other people ; but the smallest knowledge of the world will show that things logically incompatible may coexist without difficulty in the human soul. Hence we may observe even in Lassalle a pride which is never cast down or despondent, in close connection with an irresistible desire to obtain praise and compliments, and to secure the admiration or the applause of others. I am anxious not to be misunderstood. Nothing is more natural or human than to enjoy the approval and the praise of the best men. Anyone who is indifferent to applause of this kind could hardly become an author or take a leading part in any direction ; indeed, we may go further, and say that to the author and the orator a certain amount of recognition is an absolute necessity, and is in certain respects the very breath of his nostrils ; but if the stream is against him, or he is forced to struggle against it, as was the case with Lassalle, he can content himself with private manifestations of respect, and to such private testimony he should appeal only reluctantly and at rare intervals during the period of his public unpopularity. But Lassalle was unable to withstand this temptation, against which his pride was not adequate to defend him. He appeals to private approval inopportunely and with want of tact. In his case there is more than the orator's polemical attitude ; it is something wholly natural to him. I am not referring to the fact that he occasionally expresses with overweening self-consciousness that which was the simple truth, and, in view of the lies and perversions which were poured upon him, was well worth mention—namely, the fact that he was no mere amateur, but a great and, indeed, a supreme scholar, who had produced works of permanent value, including one important masterpiece. I am referring to his unfortunate preference for the froth and fury of reputation, for the drums and trumpets of fame which he required or claimed for himself, even upon occasions of small importance. For instance, he boasts before workmen of having attacked in a literary satire the mediocre historian of literature, Julian Schmidt—"amid the tumultuous applause of the great scholars and thinkers of Germany, who are congratulating me by letter and by word of mouth."[1] The publica-

---

[1] Lassalle, " The Festivals, the Press, and the Meeting of Frankfort Deputies.'

tion of the pamphlet in question, an extremely clever and presumptuous production, became, in his opinion, a high intellectual achievement. The depth of this characteristic in him can only be realized when we observe its emergence in Lassalle's free poetical compositions, in his favourite hero, Ulrich von Hutten, in the drama " Franz von Sickingen." With a pathos drawn from the depths of Lassalle's heart, Ulrich describes his feelings when " the gloomy tyranny of dogma " again raised its head in Germany, when the closed columns of the obscurantists revolted against the rise of science, and Cologne, " the German capital of priestcraft," proclaimed Reuchlin and his writing as heretical. The opening passage is excellent ; the roar and thunder of delivery is entirely appropriate ; but eventually we reach the unfortunate cry for applause :

And now I knew the purpose of my birth,
Why I was welded in the forge of woe.
And, as the billow foams upon the deep,
As the wild breakers roar upon the shore
Back-beaten, so with eyes aflame in wrath,
Trembling with passion and the keen delight
Of battle, did I plunge into the strife—
The battle-axe of anger and the club
Of keen-spiked satire whirled I then aloft
And crushed the enemy beneath my feet,
Europe re-echoing with wild applause
And scornful laughter, as their wretched lives
That strutted in their tinsel finery
Were pilloried and put to open shame.
Then rose the hatred of an angry world
Encircling me, and thus I ever strove
Combating, breast to breast, until the death.

The foregoing analysis will perhaps somewhat lessen the astonishment, which we might at first be inclined to feel, that Lassalle should have devoted so large a part of his youth to the study of a mind so remote from us in point of time and civilization. It will be obvious that the Greek thinker, not only by his logical tendencies and his dialectical method, but also by his doctrine of duty, with its high appreciation of the State and of sacrifice for the general welfare, and by his characteristics, virtues as well as vices, coincided in a very special degree with the character of his youthful admirer, whose conquest he made some thousand years after his death, in virtue of the same law which made Sören Kierkegaard so passionate a disciple of Socrates.

CHAPTER V

I HAVE already mentioned that the period of Lassalle's life which was occupied by his studies upon Heraclitus and by the case of Countess Hatzfeldt also saw his first appearance as a politician, and its consequences.

A few months after his trial at Cologne we find Lassalle once more in the dock, on this occasion at Düsseldorf, and, to use his own expression, " no less battered with criminal prosecutions than the armour of a warrior with arrows." The great social and constitutional movement of the year 1848 had suddenly diverted his attention from his own private struggles. Notwithstanding his youth, he was one of the most influential and active members of the Republican party which was then very numerous in Germany. Young as he was, he was one of the leaders. He gathered political meetings and spoke before them ; he arranged for the exhibition of posters at the street-corners, calling for armed resistance when the Prussian Government, by a breach of the Constitution, declared the National Assembly dissolved. Hated for his share in the Hatzfeldt affair, feared on account of his determined and undaunted attitude, he was thrown into prison as soon as the counter revolution secured the upper hand, and by legal quibbles of every kind his period of detention during the preliminary investigation of his case was protracted over more than half a year.

The speech which Lassalle then delivered before his judges is, in my opinion, one of the most remarkable examples of youthful virility and eloquence that history contains. Unless we were aware of the facts, no one would suspect that the speech was delivered by a young man in his twenty-fourth year. On this occasion Lassalle was magnificent. He felt himself inspired and inwardly enlightened by the noblest and purest sympathy which can fill the human heart, and no one for a moment can doubt the genuine nature or the depth of his feeling. His oratorical blade is wielded with a vigour and an art, a dexterity and a force, which cannot be surpassed, and yet is never used for the sake of mere display. For the first time he comes forth, handsome and radiant, at the height of his powers. The speech has the fresh colouring of early youth, and yet is never marred by youthful bombast or presumption ; but to describe a political speech, a knowledge of which cannot be presumed, is impossible, the more so as its strength is equally distributed over every part of it, so that only by a knowledge of the whole can an estimate of its value be formed. We can, and we must, give a few quotations, but quotation gives but a feeble idea of the nervous vigour of the speech. A bucket of water gives no idea of the depth of the well.

The exordium of the speech is very characteristic. Lassalle does not propose to deal with the defence as such, for this the defending counsel has already done, but with the charge which the orator will hurl against the case which has been strained against him, and the *corpus delicti* of which is to be found in the documents of indictment.

Still more characteristic is the following explanation : Lassalle says that he will always be ready to admit that his own convictions have led him to adopt a revolutionary attitude, and that he is a " revolutionary from principle." He will not, however, conduct his defence from this standpoint, which the Government would naturally decline to recognize. It is impossible, he says, to come to grips with an opponent or to wound him, if one adopts a materially different standpoint from the outset. The opponent is then out of range, and blows fall upon empty air. It is, indeed, possible to overthrow the opponent by adopting a precisely opposite standpoint and exposing the erroneous nature of the opponent's fundamental ideas ; but in that case he cannot be put to shame, and it is impossible to demonstrate his inconsistency, his betrayal of the principles to which he declares adherence or which he is forced to support for the sake of appearances. " In the interests of attack, and to promote the vigour of my onslaught, I will therefore descend to take up the position which the State Attorney himself must at least make a show of assuming, as an official in a constitutional State ; I will adopt a strictly constitutional standpoint, and conduct my defence only upon that ground."

A moment's consideration should be devoted to the expression " revolutionary by principle," which repeatedly occurs in Lassalle's writings, has been often explained by him, and has been as constantly misunderstood, for in a sense it is the central point of his political and social views as a whole.[1] Whenever he has been called a revolutionary, he replies that, in the uprightness of his heart, he has admitted the truth of the accusation time after time, wherever it has been brought against him, in public, in his books, in his speeches, and even before courts of law ; but it is important to understand the sense in which he uses the phrase. In his speech before the Court of Assizes he emphasizes the fact that the Government have lost the support of " the weak and rotten crutch of legal title," and he goes on to say : " In national life legal title is a bad position to assume, because law is only the expression and the will of society reduced to writing ; it is never the master of society ; when the will and the necessities of society have changed, the old legal code should be relegated to the museum of history, and the new presentation of current needs should take its place." For this reason, in another passage of the speech, he appeals to his judges with the words : " Let the courts of the Rhine openly proclaim themselves revolutionary tribunals, and I am ready to recognize them and to explain myself before them. As I am a revolutionary by principle, I know the kind of justification that can be claimed by a triumphant power when it comes forward openly and without concealment ; but I will never silently endure to see the most bloodthirsty power exercised under the apparently

---

[1] For this expression, compare " Speech before the Assize Court," 1848, 32, 49 ; " Labour Programme," 7 ; " To the Workmen of Berlin," 13 ; " Trial for High Treason," 12 ; " Science and the Workmen," 41.

sacred form of legal right, or to see law stand as crime, and crime as law, under the ægis of the law."

These words may certainly indicate some personal preference for the employment of forcible means ; at the same time, throughout his life Lassalle laid emphasis upon the purely scientific sense of the word "revolution" as he used it. His speeches abound with scornful commentaries upon those who can neither hear nor read the word "revolution" without seeing "pitchforks brandished" before their eyes. Revolution implies reversal, and such a change has invariably taken place when an entirely new principle has been substituted for existing conditions, with or without the employment of force ; for the means of change are of minor consequence. Reform, on the other hand, begins when the principle underlying existing conditions is retained, and is merely developed in milder or more consistent or more righteous directions. Here again the means employed is of minor importance. Reform may be achieved amid uproar and bloodshed, and revolution amid the profoundest peace. The terrible peasant war, which Lassalle persisted in regarding as anything but a revolutionary movement, was an attempt to secure reform by force of arms. The discovery of the cotton-spinning machine in 1775, and, in general, the peaceful development of modern manufacture, was invariably described by Lassalle as revolution upon a great scale. In this, as in so many other cases, the important point is the readiness to understand. No thinking reader can doubt that the cry which Lassalle somewhere utters is the expression of deep feeling.[1]

"What ! Can anybody have struggled, like Faust, with firm and serious tenacity though the philosophy of the Greeks and the system of Roman law, through the various departments of historical science, as far as modern political economy and statistics, and can you seriously believe that the conclusion of this long course of development is to place the incendiary's torch in the hands of the proletariat ? Is our knowledge of science and our insight into its civilizing and humanizing force so small that anyone can believe this result possible ?" This appeal does indeed contain a slight tincture of legal

[1] Lassalle, " Indirect Taxation," 117.

hypocrisy excusable in the dock. It is true that Lassalle's object can never have been fire and sword, but for his friends he did not attempt to conceal that he would not recoil from a reign of terror as a means to secure his end. If we wish to secure a true opinion of his inclination to forcible means, we must gain a closer acquaintance with his leading ideas than we have hitherto attained.

If I were asked what was the leading principle around which Lassalle's ideas centred, or what was the main question upon which his mind worked, I should reply, Might and right. These were the two poles which marked the course of his orbit. The fundamental question which occupied his mind was undoubtedly how right and might stand in the relation of cause and effect. The common misinterpretation of his views is to consider that he put might in the place of right. We shall soon see how remote this belief is from truth, and what it was that gave rise to the misunderstanding. His only poetical production is comparatively valueless, regarded as a dramatic work, but is highly interesting as the unreserved and rhetorical expression in lyrical form of the teeming ideas and the full mental life of its author. The passage occupied by the dialogue between Ökolampadius and Hutten deserves special attention :

ÖKOLAMPADIUS.

Believest thou then that this, our sacred light,
The light of truth and reason, which on high
Has risen for us, could e'er again be quenched
In darkness of unreason, and would fail
Of its own self to spread throughout the world ?

HUTTEN.

Master revered, thy knowledge of the past
Should teach thee better. Reason is its content
Therein thou spakest truly ; but its form
Abides eternal, and its form is force !

ÖKOLAMPADIUS.

Bethink thee, knight. Wilt thou then desecrate
Our loving gospel with the bloody sword ?

HUTTEN.

Master revered ! Think better of the sword !
The sword, uplifted for great freedom's cause,
Is sure the Word Incarnate that thou preachest,
Is God Himself, born for the sons of men.
The sword hath spread the teaching of the Christ,

> The sword in Germany baptized that Charles
> Whom yet in wonder we do call the Great ;
> The sword o'erthrew the heathen and restored
> The tomb of the Redeemer to the world.
> Tarquinius was driven forth from Rome,
> Xerxes was lashed from Hellas' windy shores,
> And art and science born for men to come,
> Through that same sword with which Judge Gideon,
> Samson and David slew their enemies.
> Thus early and thus late the sword performed
> The splendid exploits of the storied past,
> And all the glory that shall ever be
> Will owe its being to the sword, the sword !

In this declaration Lassalle first expresses without reserve his respect for might and for forcible measures, which gives so characteristic and so modern a touch to his genius. Throughout the poem we find expressions in the mouths of the most different people, proclaiming this delight in might as the support of right. Thus, for instance, Balthasar says :

> Then he appeared at Worms, was laughed to scorn,
> Justice was then refused us, so he took
> Certain ten thousand well-considered reasons.
> I with steel head-piece, lady, also went
> With him to Worms, and forthwith supervened
> A demonstration and a disputation
> In such sort as you well may understand.

And, in more exalted style, Ulrich von Hutten :

> Might is the greatest blessing under heaven
> When it supports a great and righteous cause ;
> A miserable toy, when to sustain
> Some tinsel state it cumbereth the hand
> Wherein it rests.

It is often the case that some favourite word or metaphor will betoken the nature of an author's ideal. Lassalle's favourite word is " iron " or " bronze." Years before the words blood and iron became a political cry in Bismarck's mouth, Lassalle had appealed to the " iron lot." He uses no metaphor so constantly. Iron is to him the type of beneficent despotism, the blow which clears the way and removes detriment, the imperial stroke which shortens the painful progress of time and accelerates the difficult birth of the ideal of a new period. Franz von Sickingen praises iron as " the god of man," as the magic wand, the stroke of which brings wishes to fulfilment, as the last resort of the despairing, and the highest pledge of freedom. In a style yet more distinctive and more characteristic of Lassalle, Franz indicates the decision by force of arms, when the Emperor's herald offers him the choice, in his master's name, either of submission with full justice from the Emperor, or of outlawry as a rebel.

> Herald, take hence this answer to thy lord ;
> The time for words is past ; portentously
> The hour of stern decision comes and knocks
> With iron finger at the door of Time !
> Low lies thine empire, quivering in the dust,
> And by no legal patchwork shall the strife
> That rends it e'er be quelled.   Herald, behold !
> See there the ordnance and the mouths of thunder
> Whence for this age of ours resistless might
> Is born into the world.   Within my camp
> I hold the power of the imperial courts,
> A new commandment will I soon enforce,
> And nerve me to an action, such as none
> Of Roman emperors ever dared or dreamed.[1]

As a youth in his first case, Lassalle had asserted that he represented right against might, and, strangely enough, with expressions which he then used in a depreciatory sense but now employed for laudatory purposes. Thus, in his speech before the Assize Court, he scornfully says : " As it had been decided to create right solely and simply by the cannon's mouth, why was not the civic guard simply disbanded without stating any further reason ?" At that time he used expressions which are put into the mouth of Balthasar in his poem to denote admiration, but which he himself employed in bitterest scorn : " If they had no rights, they had something better ; they had in Berlin a state of siege, Wrangel, sixty thousand soldiers, and several hundred guns ; in Breslau, Magdeburg, Cologne, and Düsseldorf there were so many soldiers and so many hundred guns. Those are imperative reasons which anyone can understand." With the eloquence of passion in this strong, proud speech, Lassalle had represented the standpoint of law against that of force : "However, the Assembly was dissolved, and instead of summoning a new Assembly in virtue of the same electoral law, a Constitution was forced upon us— in other words, the whole system of public right was abolished with one stroke. They were tired of slowly breaking the constitutional organism of the country upon the wheel, shattering limb after limb and law after law. They boldly threw the

[1] Lassalle, " Franz von Sickingen," 2, 62, 85, 92, 140, 151, 207.

whole concern into the lumber-room and replaced it with their *sic volo sic jubeo* and with the eloquence of bayonets." Strange is the apparent contradiction to his praises of sword and iron, when he then exclaimed : " The sword is indeed the sword, but it is not legal right. Judges who would stoop to persecute citizens because they wished to defend their laws, on the basis of those very laws the maintenance of which is their sacred duty, judges who impute the defence of their laws to their nation as a crime, I will never consider judges, but can only regard them as the satellites of force, and perhaps the nation will think with me. . . . In my prison cell I will endure whatever menaces the sword may have for me when it has desecrated the forms of right. I shall allow my case to assume a form most disastrous to myself before I will enter counter pleas or fulfil any of the formal processes of law, for the purpose of playing any part in the legal farce which force is pleased to perform." These and many similar expressions show a keen consciousness of legal right and a no less keen hatred of brutal force, when usurping the place of right.

But the mind of this young orator, who had thus early reached maturity and practical power, was also dominated by a conviction no less keen that ideal right was powerless if it was not represented by active minds and strong wills, capable of taking the right measures and using the proper means for the realization of this right. This was a fact that must have stirred the observation and the feeling of a young genius, whose deepest characteristics and inclinations were practical, when he lived through the miserable failures that marked the progress of the German Revolution of 1848. Behind a forehead which expressed energy so strongly, it was impossible that thought should not be active, when right was seen to be miserably overthrown in consequence of some idealist abhorrence of other weapons than those of words, in consequence of an hereditary fear of armed authority, in consequence of personal cowardice in one case, want of counsel in another, conjoined with frivolous prating and a hesitation worthy of Hamlet. Anyone who has read Fr. Engel's treatise, " The German Imperial Constitutional Campaign " (the revolt in Rhenish Prussia and Baden), which appeared in Karl Marx's

Neue Rheinische Zeitung of 1850, will understand that this helpless generation, with its lack of discipline, was necessarily followed by a generation firmly resolved to clothe its ideals in adequate armour, and to give them a mighty sword—a generation which regarded the noble metal of right as incapable of becoming current coin unless it was consolidated by the alloy of might. Eventually both the noble and the base metal was almost entirely amalgamated under the eyes of this generation —a generation which realized that the dice of iron were the hardest and the best, and which, like Brennus of old, threw the steel into the scales.

Read Lassalle's lamentations in that speech, over the failure of the National Assembly to create a real citizen force at the right time for the protection of the Constitution. Read his murderous sarcasm upon the invitation of the National Assembly to begin a course of " passive resistance " against the attacks of the Government : " Passive resistance, gentlemen—and we must concede that our enemies have appreciated the fact—the passive resistance of the National Assembly was certainly a crime. Choose one of two alternatives—either the Crown was within its rights when it issued those measures, and in that case the National Assembly was a band of rebels and outlaws when it opposed the legal rights of the Crown and brought discord upon the country, or the measures of the Crown were illegal acts of force, in which case the freedom of the people was to be vigorously protected with their persons and their lives, and the National Assembly was bound to call the land to arms. In that case the strange device of passive resistance was a cowardly betrayal of the people, and of the duty of the Assembly to protect the people's rights. . . . The individual, gentlemen, if he suffers ill-treatment from the State or from a body of men—if, for instance, I were condemned by you—could honourably offer a passive resistance. I could shelter myself within my rights, and utter my protest, as I have not the power to make it effective. . . . The nation can be subdued by force, as Poland was subdued, but the subjugation was not effected until the battle-field had been besprinkled with the blood of her noblest sons and until her last forces had been mown down. . . . Then, when all strength has been broken, the body of such a nation may content itself with passive resistance—that is to say, with protests to secure their rights, with endurance and toleration, with anger in their hearts, with silent hatred repressed, waiting with folded arms until some moment of salvation brings redemption. Passive resistance of this kind, *after* the event, after every means of active resistance has failed, is the highest degree of enduring heroism ; but passive resistance *before* the event, when not a blow has been struck, when not the smallest appeal has been made to the forces ready to hand, is the profoundest disgrace, the most supreme stupidity, and the greatest cowardice which could ever be attributed to a nation. Passive resistance, gentlemen, is self-contradiction incarnate ; it is tolerant resistance—a resistance that does not oppose or resist. Passive resistance is like Lichtenberg's knife which had no handle and the blade of which was lost, or like fur which must be washed without making it wet. Passive resistance is the inward will without the practical action, and passive resistance is the product of the following factors : a clear recognition of duty imperatively urging resistance, and personal cowardice declining resistance. These two factors during their abhorrent embraces on the night of November 10 begot that consumptive child, that hectic offspring, passive resistance."[1]

Can we be surprised that the man who could inveigh against weakness and impotence with such emphasis at the age of twenty-three should praise iron as the god of man ten years later ?

This relationship between might and right is a problem that always occupied Lassalle's mind. He penetrates more deeply into the conditions of their interaction, and studies ever more zealously their dependence upon one another.

In 1862, amid the Prussian constitutional struggles, he gave a lecture in Berlin upon the nature of constitutions. He attempts in this lecture to define the idea of a constitution or of a fundamental law, and in analyzing the term "fundamental law" he finds, firstly, that such a law must lie deeper than ordinary legal decision ; so much is shown by the word "fundamental." Secondly, that as it is the basis of other laws, it must

---

[1] "Speech before the Assize Court," 16, 26, 33-35, 48.

preserve an active and operative influence upon them. Thirdly, that these conceptions are necessary and inevitable, for the idea of fundamental contains the idea of operative necessity and active force.

If the constitution thus forms the fundamental law of the land, it must be defined as an operative force, necessarily making all other laws and legal institutions in any country what they are. Lassalle then proceeds to ask whether there is in reality such an operative force. " Yes," is the answer, " there is indeed such a force—namely, the actual conditions of force which exist in any given society. These actual conditions of force are the living power which so determines all the laws and legal institutions of a society, that they cannot be materially otherwise than they are."

To explain his meaning, Lassalle employs an example for illustration. " Suppose," he said, " that some gigantic conflagration destroyed all written law in Prussia, and that the land by some such calamity was deprived of all law, with the consequence that the difficulty could only be solved by the promulgation of new laws, are we to suppose that in such a case the legislator could go to work as he liked ? Could he issue any new laws he pleased ? Let us see. Suppose people said : ' The laws have perished ; we are compiling a new code, and on this occasion we decline to give the royal power the position it had previously held, or we prefer to give it no position at all.' In such a case the King would simply say : ' The laws may have perished, but, as a matter of fact, the army obeys me, and will march as I order it. As a matter of fact, again, the commanders of the arsenals and barracks will send out their guns at my orders, and the artillery will march through the streets, and, relying upon this practical power, I will not permit you to assign any other position to me than that which I choose to take.' " Lassalle then concludes : " You see, gentlemen, that a King who is obeyed by his army and his artillery is part of the constitution." Developing his argument in similar fashion, he goes on : " A nobility which has influence at Court and upon the King is also an element in the constitution.—Now let us suppose that King and nobility agreed in virtue of their full powers to introduce the mediæval system of guilds; for instance, that the calico printer should employ no dyers, and that no master in any branch of handicraft should be allowed to have more than a certain number of workmen ; in other words, that production upon a large scale should be impossible. What would be the result ? In such a case the great manufacturers—men like Borsig, Egels, etc.—would close their works, and even the railway directors would dismiss their workmen. The whole mass of workmen crying for bread would then invade the streets, incited by the whole of the middle classes, and a war would break out, in which victory would not inevitably belong to the army ; and thus you see, gentlemen, that such men as Borsig, Egels, and great manufacturers in general, are also elements in the constitution. In virtue of the Government's need for large monetary resources, the great bankers and the Stock Exchange in general are likewise elements.

" Let us now suppose that the Government should think well to issue such a law as exists in Japan, to the effect that if anyone committed theft, his father should be punished ; we then discover that general opinion and culture as a whole within certain limits are also elements in the constitution. Let us further suppose that the Government should deprive the citizens of less importance, and the working classes not only of their political but also of their personal freedom ; that it made them serfs and slaves; and we can see that in certain extreme cases even the common man, without the support of the great manufacturers, becomes a part of the constitution.

" Having thus seen what the constitution of a country is —namely, the several forces existing within it, we proceed to ask what is the relation of these forces to the legal constitution, and we can easily see how this constitution has been brought about. The actual conditions of force are reduced to writing, and are given documentary expression, and when they have thus been written they are no longer actual conditions of force, but have also attained legal force, have become legal institutions, and those who act in opposition to them are punished."

The explanation concludes with a proof that any change in the actual conditions of force (the power of the nobility, the prosperity and progress of the towns, the relations between the inhabitants of the capital, and the size of the army) is invariably accompanied by some corresponding change in the constitution. When too wide a discrepancy exists between the written and the actual constitution, and when this discrepancy leads to oppression, a conflagration occurs in the form of actual revolution. The conflagration which we proposed as an instance had occurred in March, 1848, but—and here Lassalle returns to his old complaint in the speech in his defence delivered in 1849—the triumphant people, instead of creating a strong defensive force from the lower classes and the proletariat, and thus altering the actual situation, were so foolish as to draw up in *writing* a new and powerless constitution, which therefore proved absolutely useless. " If, gentlemen, you have an apple-tree in your garden, and hang a ticket on it bearing an inscription, ' This is a fig-tree,' has the tree then become a fig-tree ? No, and even if you gather together the whole of your household, or all the inhabitants of the country, and make them swear loudly and solemnly, ' This is a fig-tree !' the tree remains what it was, and the following years will show that it will bear apples, and not figs."

" Constitutional questions," concludes Lassalle, " are, therefore, in the first instance, not questions of right, but questions of might. The actual constitution of a country has its existence only in the actual conditions of force which exist in the country ; hence written constitutions have value and permanence only when they accurately express those conditions of force which exist in practice within a society."

This analysis, incredible as it may seem, was immediately interpreted by the Liberal newspapers as a declaration that might should precede right. Even Count Schwerin said in reference to the subject, amid the applause of the Chambers, that in the Prussian State right preceded might. Newspaper after newspaper, in the hope of silencing Lassalle, refused to accept a short article upon the facts of the case, entitled " Might and Right," in which he explained the misunderstanding, and he found himself obliged to publish the article in pamphlet form. In it he says with admirable truth and emphasis : " If I had created the world I should very probably have made an exception at this point in favour of the wishes of the *Volks-zeitung* and of Count Schwerin, and have arranged that right should precede might. Such an arrangement would be quite in harmony with my own ethical standpoint and desires. Unfortunately, however, I have not been entrusted with the creation of the world, and must therefore decline any responsibility, any praise or blame, for the nature of existing arrangements."

He then explains it was not his intention to analyze any ideal conditions, but to state the facts as they exist, and that he was not writing a treatise upon ethics, but a work of historical investigation. The result is, that while right certainly ought to precede might, might none the less takes precedence of right without exception and until right can gather sufficient power behind it to overthrow the might of injustice.

He analyzes the course of development by which the Prussian Constitution since 1848 had been formed by continual breaches of right, and says : " What is the meaning, then, of the complacent satisfaction with which the Chamber received the declaration of Count Schwerin, that right precedes might in the Prussian State ? The statement is nothing more than a pious expression of hope. Any deeper meaning than this it could only have for men who were determined to make might inferior to right. No one in the Prussian State has the right to speak of ' right ' except the democracy, the old and real democracy, for that alone has invariably clung to right, and has refused to humiliate itself by any compromise with might."

The question of the relationship between might and right was to Lassalle a question of facts and reality. His observations upon this subject are entirely true, and his position is impregnable. He realized and apprehended better than anyone else in what cases right is supported by might, and in what cases it is not, and when also might can become right, and when it becomes wrong.

It was not merely with reference to practical life, but also with reference to the deeper question of constitutional right, that he examined and appreciated the interaction between the force of the old right which the Conservatives championed, and the right of the new intellectual force, as represented by the Radical parties. The old right is an acquired right ; the new might is the new consciousness of right. What, then, are the relations of the new right to the acquired right ? The new consciousness of right will both confer and assume rights, but how far may it go in this latter respect ? What rights have been properly acquired and are inviolable ? If all old rights have this character, progress is at a standstill, and the past will slay the life of the present. If, on the other hand, no one can base his position upon an acquired right, the present will slay the past. Thus we reach the conception of acquired right with which Lassalle's chief work, " The System of Acquired Rights," deals.

CHAPTER VI

THE task which Lassalle proposed to himself in this work is, as he observes in the preface, nothing less than an exposition of the political and social idea which has predominated throughout the whole of our period. " What is it," he asks, " that forms the principle inherent in our political and social struggles ? The conception of acquired right has again become a point of dispute. In the legal, political, and economic spheres, the conception of acquired right is the mainspring and impulse to all further development, and even where legal rights as related to civil law appeared to be separated from political rights, they are none the less even more political than political rights properly so-called, for they form the social element."

The fact that Lassalle thought it necessary to refer to this point shows the superficiality, in his opinion, with which the conception of political right was understood by the leaders of the Liberal middle classes.

The title-page explains the object of the work as an attempt to reconcile practical jurisprudence with the system of natural right. The standpoint adopted by the author in this respect, when compared with his standpoint in "Heraclitus," shows that he has made a great advance. He is now less definitely bound to Hegel. He certainly describes himself as an adherent of Hegelian principles, nor would any other statement have been in accordance with truth ; but this does not prevent him from criticizing with the greatest freedom an important part of Hegel's system and of his school. It soon becomes obvious that he is upon the point of introducing a modification which is indicated in his preface to " Heraclitus." This modification,

57

which Hegel's French disciples afterwards adopted, tends to change a system of philosophy which dealt more than any former system with the Unconditional, to a philosophy of the Relative, and to remodel as an historical system a view of life which was more metaphysical than any other. The divergence between this position and that of a thinker who desires to apply the methods of the experimental sciences to jurisprudence is in appearance inconsiderable, but Lassalle's loyalty to Hegelian dialectic and the tendency of his mind, which was rather inclined to soar boldly aloft than to advance with patience and care, and to prefer systems and hypotheses based upon pure reason, also removes him from the scientific methods in force at the present day.[1]

In Lassalle's opinion Hegel had merely indicated the general logical outline for the work, and as the Hegelian school, with their usual hesitation to go to the heart of the matter merely re-echoed his teaching, constitutional philosophy and practical jurisprudence remained as widely separated as natural philosophy and natural science. Hegel's philosophy of mind, indeed, can only be evolved from his system at the price of some sacrifice of logic. In Hegel's time the term " natural right " would have been regarded as implying a right existing from time immemorial, universally valid, and agreeable to reason. Such an idea was related to positive or historical right, as the first draft of a general idea is related to its execution in practice ; and people failed to see that natural right is also a matter of history and is historical. Thus the fundamental conceptions of philosophical jurisprudence were regarded as eternal and unconditioned and as categories of the logical concept ; hence Hegel failed to apprehend the nature of historical right, and retraced it to lack of reason, arbitrary dealing, and force. But the work of mind in history is ever a process of becoming ; consequently, in a philosophy of jurisprudence, it is impossible to speak of *the* property, *the* wrong, *the* family, *the* right of succession, *the* civil society, or *the* State. On the contrary, it is necessary to examine the historical conceptions of the Greek,

---

[1] Compare, for instance, with Lassalle's views a small treatise by Giuseppe Saredo, a high Italian legal authority, " Dell' applicazione del metodo sperimentale allo studio delle scienze civili e giuridiche."

Roman, and Germanic minds, and to develop from thence Greek, Roman, and Germanic ideas of property, etc. Hegel adopts a very different position in his philosophy of religion. What would have been the result if, instead of studying different religions, he had spoken of God, dogma, the future life, etc. ? The important point in this matter is that the historical, and not the metaphysical, method should be used. In dealing with the philosophy of jurisprudence, Hegel's pupils have merely followed the misleading traces of their master. The most capable of them, Gans, in his work upon inheritance, straightway introduced our modern conception of heirship, and then proceeded to regard this conception as a logical category of universal validity. Three years later, during a period of most violent agitation, in his work " Capital and Labour," Lassalle analyzed the economic conception " capital " and the legal conception " property," and showed that these conceptions are by no means eternal and unalterable, but are of historical growth and beset by historical limitations. Similarly in this work, with reference to all legal ideas, Lassalle has applied the same historical point of view in the second part of the book with special reference to the right of inheritance.[1]

Not less old than law itself is the reluctance to adopt retrospective legislation. The question of acquired right and the question of the retrospective action of law coincide. The reason of this reluctance is apparently to be found in the apprehension that man's freedom might be infringed, retrospective legal action involving an arbitrary extension of the idea of responsibility. Proceeding from this fundamental idea, Lassalle, in divergence from all previous investigators, succeeds in defining acquired right in its relation to the retrospective action of law in the following way :

1. No law may have retrospective force if it affects the individual only through and in virtue of his voluntary actions.

2. Any law may have retrospective force if it affects the individual without the intervention of any such voluntary act,

---

[1] " System of Acquired Rights," i. 68, 70. *Cf.* " Capital and Labour," 165, note.

and therefore affects him immediately in respect of attributes which are involuntary, common to humanity, or transmitted to him by society, or if it affects him only by producing an organic change in social institutions.

Lassalle proves in considerable detail that the modern reluctance to adopt retrospective legislation is entirely non-existent among peoples and at stages of civilization in which no clear conception has arisen of the human mind as possessing consciousness, freedom, and responsibility. The Chinese pass a new law denoting as criminal an act which has been previously performed in entirely good faith in reliance upon existing law, and punish the act unmercifully as criminal. Even the Jews in antiquity had not attained to the reverence for acquired rights which exists among enlightened nations. In the case of the daughters of Zelophehad (Num. xxvii. 1-11), where the God of Israel delivers a legal decision, He undoubtedly performs a piece of retrospective legislation in civil affairs without any apparent consciousness of the fact; but, then, He was an eastern God who had not studied Roman law, and was certainly not a product of Greek culture and art ; in other words, He was the God of a nation which had come to no high consciousness of their humanity, as expressed in personal rights by Rome, or in perfect beauty by Greece.

Lassalle's logical point of departure is thus primarily the idea which he expressed in earlier years, in his first speech before the Court of Assizes—the idea that law is a means of expressing the national consciousness of right, and that the whole body of legal right is merely a definition secured upon one occasion by this national consciousness, which is in continual process of change. Hence every new definition which proceeds from this national spirit immediately affects the individual with the same right as preceding changes. The individual, therefore, can only regard as securely his what he has upon some one occasion by legal means and by his own will and action diverted from this stream and so made his own. The individual cannot stake out a claim within the territory of right, and declare his independence within that sphere for all time and against all future and preventive legislation. The analysis of the whole range of jurisprudence in the light of this idea occupies the first volume of the work. The exposition is clear and most incisive, but hardly ever polemical. Only with Stahl, the well-known romantic reactionary writer, does Lassalle pick a serious quarrel. He shows that Stahl's doctrine leads him to regard the whole of the existing social order as inviolable and sacred, as this order, according to Stahl, together with all the rights that arise from it, must form the acquired right of the individual. Stahl proclaims that no age is ever summoned to sit in judgment upon the past and to recognize or to destroy the rights which the past has produced, according to its own views of their suitability. "Certainly," replies Lassalle; "but just because every age is autonomous, no age can be subject to the domination of another, and no age is bound to permit the continuance as right of anything that contradicts its own consciousness of right, or seems to it to be wrong." With his usual penetration, he then discovers Stahl in the act of contradicting himself upon several occasions, and cannot deny himself the pleasure of demonstrating that his adversary has been influenced by "the unavoidable breath of Jacobinism, which every dabbler in modern philosophy inevitably and even involuntarily receives from it."

The most interesting section of this instructive first volume, as illuminating the mental growth and the political standpoint of the author, is undoubtedly that in which Lassalle treats the question of retrospective legislation with regard to the great French Revolution. Here the designation, which we have before mentioned, "revolutionary by principle," appears in a new light, and remarkable confirmation of his doctrine is forthcoming. Here at length we see that Lassalle was guilty of no empty boast, but spoke the bare truth, when he cried to his judges: "Do you know the real thread of connection running through the history of the French Revolution, gentlemen? I know it to its minutest fibre."[1]

The ancients—Cicero, for instance—held that everything which was regarded as established by the moral consent of a nation, even if it had been reduced to no legal form, might

---

[1] "System of Acquired Rights," i. 61, 197, 200-214, 449 ff; "Indirect Taxation," 116.

be regarded as an element in the national body of rights. If it became a law, this new law could only be regarded as an exposition of the content of that body of rights. Hence, in the opinion of the ancients, such a law could reasonably have a retrospective effect. Against this doctrine Lassalle emphasizes the fact that it could only hold good with the men of antiquity, among whom alone such complete moral unanimity can be said to have prevailed. For modern times the claim must be maintained that only such elements in the universal consciousness of right should lay claim to realization in the form of law as have already found some form of expression, either direct or tacit. The question then arises, When can it be said that such expression has been found, and what does this conception imply? The conception obviously implies that the elements of a nation's legal consciousness need not necessarily be stated in words, but can be just as well realized and made effective by national action.

The French Convention determined by its law of the 17th Nivôse, in the year II., that the succession to any inheritance after July 14, 1789, should be subject to the terms of this new law. During the reaction of Thermidor the regulations respecting this matter were regarded and stated to be obviously retrospective. At the same time, it certainly was not the intention of the Convention to infringe the rule against retrospective legislation. The statement of the principles which the law was to express denied that any retrospective action took place, because the law merely developed the principles then proclaimed by a great people, and the further phrase was added : retrospective force would only begin at the moment when these limits were overpassed. None the less, as we have said, this so-called retrospective force was afterwards cited as a proof of the atrocious acts of the French Convention ; but on July 14, 1789, with the capture of the Bastille, the French nation had certainly displayed a consciousness of right which rejected privileges and monopoly rights. It cannot be maintained that this action gave rise to any legislation developing this national consciousness of right to some practically new form ; but the state of affairs was materially changed when the content of the new right amounted only to a demand for the abolition of previously existing privileges. Hence, only such laws as the Convention passed from this point of view are to be referred to July 14, 1789. " Thus we see," says Lassalle, " that this philosophic assembly declared its legislation concerning inheritance to contain only the formal declaration of those principles which the people themselves had proclaimed by storming the Bastille, and had thereby established as rights, and in two ways history has justified the Convention. In the first place, the principles of hereditary succession, laid down in the law of Nivôse, which were transferred to the civil code, remained undisputed under the First Empire, during the Restoration, under the July Monarchy and under the Second Empire, and have thus most clearly shown that they were a necessary and integral portion of the consciousness of right that became predominant with the Revolution. In the second place, all historians, French or German, reactionary or revolutionary, whether writing philosophical works or mere manuals, date the French Revolution from July 14, 1789."

Apparently, it was not without a sense of inward triumph that Lassalle stated these instructive facts, for they displayed not only the demonstrated validity of laws which are brought forth by a revolution, but the no less definite validity of retrospective legislation, which was conceived as adequately justified by a reference to " unwritten law," and to a new and entirely revolutionary consciousness of legal right, expressed in a piece of forcible or violent action which Lassalle regarded as profoundly justified. Very characteristic is the absence of any reference in his words to the fact that the Bastille at the time of its capture was almost an empty fortress used for the confinement of actual criminals, and of any reference to the much more important fact that the garrison consisted of brave *invalides* who were anxious to spare the assailants, while the attacking force was composed of a ruthless and bloodthirsty street mob. Lassalle regards the capture of the Bastille only as a typical action, denoting the fall of an arbitrary despotism.

It should be clearly noted that there is no question here of defending any popular rising or any retrospective law issued by authorities temporarily in power, nor is there any want of a criterion by which revolutions justified upon Lassalle's principles may be distinguished from unjustifiable and purposeless risings. Lothar Bucher wrote a colourless preface which bears the stamp of his official position as an introduction to the second edition of Lassalle's great work in 1881. In this he points out the difficulty which any observer who stands too close to events must feel in deciding whether at any definite point of time " a people has become conscious of its rights." He asserts that not every destruction of a building, though such action be styled typical, is equivalent to a storming of the Bastille, with all its consequences. But these observations are applicable to Lassalle only in the very slightest degree.

Again, Rodbertus Jagetzow thought he had struck a blow at Lassalle's doctrine by proposing the question : " How am I to learn the intentions of the national consciousness of the present day, and how am I to discover whether a national consciousness rejects the whole content of previously existing right, or merely certain forms of that right ?" Only in the latter case, upon Lassalle's system, can any claim to compensation exist, and Lassalle was correct when he replied that this question had not the smallest connection with the doctrine of retrospective legislation. The question, " What are the intentions of a national consciousness at the present day, or what will its intentions hereafter be upon any subject such as marriage, the State, the monarchy, hunting, mining, newspapers, or property, is a question concerning the *content* of the consciousness of an age to which no answer can possibly be given by formal rules. The theory of retrospective legislation can do and is expected to do nothing more than to establish the logical sense of right. Whatever may be the content of a national consciousness now or hereafter, the logical sense of right expresses the consequences which result from the application of this consciousness to existing conditions. The content of national consciousness itself must be presupposed as known.

In thoroughly characteristic style, displaying his nature both as a thinker and a leader, Lassalle writes to Rodbertus in a private letter under date February 17, 1863 : " You are naturally quite right when you say that it is impossible to discover the intentions of the national consciousness at any one time either by a decision of the majority or even by a plebiscite. How do I then discover these intentions ? My opinion simply is that what you can demonstrate as correct to yourself and to the age by means of reason, logic, and science, the age will inevitably demand."

CHAPTER VII

THE second part of Lassalle's great work is exclusively concerned with the law of inheritance, and especially with Roman law testamentary. The chief object of the book is to break down the difference between the historical and the dogmatic treatment of jurisprudence. Hence this portion of the work is intended to show by a magnificent example how the dogmatic element in a department of law can only be understood by a comprehension of its historical meaning—that is to say, by means of the definite historical position in which any legal institution may find itself at any one time.

Lassalle now makes the very considerable claim that not only particular details in the Roman system, but that the whole of this system of testamentary jurisprudence has been uncomprehended and misunderstood until his own time, and has remained an unsolved riddle.

This assertion is based upon an unsatisfactory interpretation of a difficult passage in Gaius concerning the idea of the *familiæ emptor*. In accordance with his idealistic conceptions of history, and using Hegel's audacious method as an instrument, Lassalle proposes a theory of Roman testamentary law which modern science has rejected. The only point with which I am immediately concerned is to give the reader a full and true impression of the close and comprehensive thought, of the penetration and scholarship, with which Lassalle has conceived and developed his main ideas. I then wish to isolate the purely psychological elements apparent in his method of treating the subject, and to use his conception of Roman testamentary law for the purpose of providing the reader with

66

a view of the author's intellectual procedure, and of displaying the main impulses which determined, unknown to himself, the manner and object of his investigations. We shall see that even when he is buried in pandects and commentaries future systems of evolution or revolution are continuously before his eyes in the course of his work.

Lassalle brought together a large amount of material to prove his fundamental idea, which is that an heir in the Roman sense originally inherited only the intentions, and not the property, of the dead man. For this reason the objects and the interests of the Roman law of inheritance, and also its historical origin, do not belong to the subject of testamentary jurisprudence, for, according to Lassalle's conception, this law of inheritance does not imply any conveyance of property, but a conception transcendental in its nature, which is in direct contradiction with the natural idea of an heir. The idea of eternity and of the infinite life of the soul in Christianity is preceded in history by another idea, the purely material continuance of the existence of the subject—the infinity of the personal will, which is related to, and can act upon, the outer world. Quintilian naïvely says that there seems to be no other consolation for death except the will which can persist beyond death. In this passage Lassalle sees a proof of his central idea that Roman immortality consisted in testamentary disposition.[1]

A testament must invariably provide for an *institutio heredis*, the formal institution of an heir, and any provision in the testament which simply concerned the division of property was null and void unless provision were made for the direct institution of an heir to carry out the will of the testator. Further, this institution was bound to precede all other provisions, in particular the mention of legacies, and must form the beginning of the testament ; finally, if the heir died before entering upon the inheritance, or if he declined it, the whole testament was usually annulled, and the legacies became invalid. Hence it is clear that the existence of the heir is necessary to the existence of the testament, and that it is the heir whose existence guarantees and provides legal existence

---

[1] This view is supported by Maine, " Ancient Law," 1861, 188, 190.

for the intentions of the testator.   In consequence, only when
the intention of the deceased has been transferred to the heirs
as existing after his own death, can his intention be regarded
as still existing, and as securing execution in his testament.   If
there be no one to continue the testator's intentions, those
intentions become what they actually are—dead, null and void.

Hence the conception of inheritance is bound up with the
continuation in practice of the intentions of the testator.   The
interests, therefore, of the testator are concentrated, not upon
the future position of the heir, but upon his future action
and upon his action in accordance with the desires of the
testator.   According to Roman ideas, the triumph of the
testator is to secure that the heir should act in accordance
with his will ; but as long as the heir is both in possession and
in action—in other words, as long as he receives and takes
over the inheritance—so long is the situation ambiguous ; for
the possibility always remains open that his own interests
and his own selfish desires, instead of continuing the intentions
of the testator, may absorb or nullify these.   There is but one
effective method of neutralizing this possibility—namely, to
give the heir no advantage whatever, and even to place him
in direct opposition to his own selfish interests.   The heir who
receives nothing and yet remains an heir, and none the less
acts according to the intentions of the testator—the disinherited heir, in other words—is an irrefragable proof of the fact
that the will of the testator still exists by continuance in the
heir.   The heir without inheritance is the highest triumph
of these intentions, and the fullest enjoyment of the continued
existence with which these intentions can provide themselves.

Is this ingenious explanation probable ?   Is it conceivable
that such a nation as that of Rome, which even by its language
is distinguished as practical, matter-of-fact, and acquisitive
in a high degree, should have failed to sanctify the property
interests of the individual, and to deify the conception of
possession, and should have developed the conceptions of
inheritance on the basis of a religious idea, conceptions with
which the conveyance of property has nothing whatever to
do ?   The thing seems impossible from the very outset, and if
our sources of information are examined, our doubts are but

confirmed. These sources provide no satisfactory explanation. The most important original source, a short statement in Gaius, can be explained in different ways, while at the same time an important passage in his text, which has only been preserved to us in one manuscript of Verona, has been badly mangled by the copyist. The so-called *testamentum per æs et libram* originated in Rome from two earlier forms of testament. With reference to its employment and the form of its statement, Gaius says that the testator, by means of mancipation, left his estate, a quantity of personal property, according to the views of time, to the care of a friend, and indicated to him, the so-called *familiæ emptor*, to whom he was to give portions of the estate, and what each person was to receive.

This mancipation is what Lassalle regards as a cession of personal authority to the friend, in virtue of which the friend has full disposal of all that was previously subject to this authority. As a proof that such personal authority is indicated by the words *familia* and *patrimonium*, Lassalle quotes the use of the term *patrimonium* in the phrase " things which are outside our *patrimonium* " ; he understands the phrase to imply that an object is unable " to fall within the property sphere of private will."

This remarkable interpretation of the Latin term cannot be defended. The conception of property includes dependence upon the will of the possessor ; it is therefore impossible to speak of the property sphere of private will. We may speak of the sphere of private property or the legal sphere of private will. To say that objects can come within the legal sphere of private will is simply to say that they can be objects of private property, for property rights imply the complete and full legal dependence of an object upon the will of an individual. The Latin phrase, " Things which lie without our *patrimonium*," is thus not used to denote simple personal authority, but a special nature of this authority, property rights.

The central point in Lassalle's theory is the fact that he regards as the heir the friend to whom the inheritance was transferred for division, the man whom we should call the executor. He asserts that Gaius himself referred to the *familiæ emptor* as an heir. But the passage in Gaius, correctly interpreted, has a different meaning. It runs as follows : " But those two former kinds have now become incapable of use. Only the kind which is brought about *per æs et libram* has remained in force. It is, indeed, otherwise constituted than in the days of old, for formerly the *familiæ emptor*—in other words, the man who receives the inheritance from the testator by mancipium—took the place of the heir, and for that reason the testator indicated to him what he wished to be given to each man after his death ; but now one man is appointed heir by the testament, and another, for appearance' sake, is called in as *familiæ emptor*, in imitation of the old legal custom." It was only a strange mistake in translation that enabled Lassalle to interpret this passage as meaning that the *familiæ emptor* was regarded as the heir.[1]

Hence this passage provides no proof that the *familiæ emptor* was originally identical with the heir, nor can this identity be proved from the testamentary dispositions of later times, as Lassalle believes, for the reason that a *familiæ emptor* and an heir coexisted. At this time the persons who were dependent upon the *familiæ emptor* could not act as witnesses, but persons who were dependent upon the heir could so act. The reason for this, in Lassalle's view, is that the *familiæ emptor* was originally the former heir, whereas the heir of later days was originally no more than a legatee. The domestic position of the former, in contrast to that of the latter, incapacitated him for the position of witness, for the simple reason that the former was a party to the mancipation, while the latter was not. So much is obvious from the fact that in the later form of will by mancipation the household of the mancipant were unable to act as witnesses. Here the fundamental idea seems to be that, in the case of a mancipation will, the witnesses were the representatives of the Roman people, and that the people could not be represented against

---

[1] " Sane nunc aliter ordinatur quam olim solebat, namque olim familiæ emptor, id est, qui a testatore familiam accipiebat mancipio, heredis locum obtinebat, et ob id ei mandabat testator quid cuique post mortem suam dari vellet ; nunc vero alius heres testamento instituitur, a quo etiam legata relinquuntur, alius formæ gratia propter veteris juris imitationem familiæ emptor adhibetur."

Lassalle did not understand the construction *alius . . . alius*, but connected *alius* with *heres*, and translated, " another heir."

any single individual by those who belonged to his household and were in his power. Even later, when the *familiæ emptor* came forward only as a matter of form, the custom was continued of incapacitating those subject to him from acting as witnesses.

In other words, the case stands as follows : In early times the *familiæ emptor* received the estate of the testator as his own property in virtue of the twofold legal process, neither part of which could be omitted. It was then his business to distribute the estate among those to whom the testator had left bequests. He was thus the executor of the testator's intentions, and not the continuer of those intentions in Lassalle's sense of the word. He was not an heir ; for the succession of an heir is founded either upon a will—that is to say, upon a one-sided and revocable appointment on the part of the testator, or upon law, or upon hereditary tenement. The position, however, of the *familiæ emptor* rests upon none of these three foundations, and obviously upon neither of the first two. Nor, again, is he in the position of one who inherits under a contract, for in that case the heir must come forward to secure the succession, whilst in virtue of mancipation a *familiæ emptor* becomes possessor of the estate without further ceremony. Finally, he is not an executor in the modern sense of the word, but occupies an entirely unique position.

Lassalle explains the circumstance that no one before his time had adopted the views upon testamentary law which he formulates, by the fact that previous writers upon Roman law had made Justinian the starting-point of their researches, where legal developments are found in their latest form, instead of going back to their origins. He explains the earlier history of the law of inheritance as follows : Gaius informs us that a very frequent occurrence in the earlier years of Roman history was the refusal of the person instituted as an heir to accept the inheritance, as it was open to every testator to exhaust the whole of the estate by legacies, and so to leave the heir nothing but the empty title. To meet this abuse, he goes on, the Furian law was brought forward about 183 B.C. This law provided that, with the exception of particular persons, no legatee should receive more than a thousand asses—a small

amount ; but, continues Gaius, even this limitation failed of
its object, as estates continued to be exhausted by legacies.
Hence the Voconian law was passed about 169 B.C., which
provided that no one in the position of a legatee should receive
more than the heir. This law at least provided a certain
prospect that the heir would obtain something. It proved,
however, ineffectual ; for by dividing the estate into a large
number of legacies, it was possible to leave so small a portion
for the heir that he regarded the advantage as far too inadequate
a compensation for the task involved by the whole burden of
the inheritance. In consequence, the Falcidian law was passed
about 40 B.C., which prohibited the bequests of legacies
amounting to more than three-fourths of the estate and secured
to the heir at least one-fourth of the inheritance.

Gaius, at whose time, according to Lassalle's view, the old
metaphysical theory of inheritance was no longer understood,
regarded these successive provisions merely as so many efforts
to improve clumsy legislation. Lassalle, however, regarded
these three laws which were passed within a period of 150
years as evidence of a long and weary struggle which the
Roman spirit had fought out with its own inherent views.
This civil war was not carried on, as at one time was supposed,
between the heir and the legatees, but between the testator
and the heir. The legatee is merely the whipping-boy on
whose back the heir delivers the blows intended for the testator.
So much, says Lassalle, is clearly obvious from the nature of
these successive laws. The starting-point is provided by the
Twelve Tables, which place the legatee in the most favourable
position. His position suddenly becomes most unfavourable
in consequence of the Furian law, and is then materially
improved by the Voconian law, under which the legatee can
then receive a full half of the estate. The Falcidian law still
further improved his prospects, as a legatee under it could
receive three-fourths of the estate. This development, when
compared with the parallel situation of the heir, which also
became most favourable after the last law, seems inexplicable
if we assume that the struggle was carried on between the
legatee and the heir. Lassalle regards the struggle as entirely
different in nature ; it is the struggle of personal interest and

sound human understanding against the religious and transcendental views of life and death which had dominated the whole of the national spirit. As long as this national spirit in Rome was left firmly rooted in its foundations and free from attack, the personal interests of heirs could not initiate any revolt, for the reason that inheritance represented the most binding and sacred principle in this national spirit, its idea of immortality. Only after lapse of long time can the heir venture to declare as a principle that he desires to receive something, and something unconditionally for himself, independent of his relations to the legatee. Such a development was bound to come about, as sound human reason declines to be shut out of consideration. The Falcidian law implies a clear recognition of the fictitious nature of the principle on which the whole system of inheritance is originally based ; hence with the *lex Falcidia* the downfall of the whole Roman system of inheritance definitely begins. Yet even at this point the Roman national spirit finds a chapel within the temple of testamentary law in which it can preserve its most sacred object. The *lex Falcidia* was promulgated under Augustus, and under the same Emperor the law appears concerning the *fidei commissum* form of inheritance, which opens a new refuge to the testator. Anyone who is an heir upon the basis of this voluntary fidelity to the national spirit and its sacred traditions, neither can nor should make any use of the new influence which the heir could exert upon the testator by virtue of the preceding law, and cannot claim the advantage provided by the *lex Falcidia*.

As long as the sense of Roman nationalism was in existence, it strove to cling to the truth of the fiction which concerned the continuance of the testator's intentions and the identity of intentions between himself and the heir. History during its course of development stamps the fiction as false ; Roman nationalism attempts to save its existence, in however reduced a form. The testament is, therefore, to the Roman people a cult of the national existence, for it is the highest form in which the national spirit can appear as operative, and every act in which the people manifests the public spirit which pervades, it is worship or is of a religious nature. Hence wills are made, not only in popular assemblies and in the presence of the priests, but also in *comitia* expressly summoned for purposes purely religious. Thus, the intentions of the Roman, which during his lifetime were his private affair, became a matter of public concern after his death. It has often been said that the Roman testator, in view of his unlimited freedom of action with reference to the system of intestate succession as established by law, can be compared with a legislator ; but this is an under-statement. It was customary in Rome for the testator to threaten a monetary fine if his tomb were sold or hired or mortgaged—a regulation inserted not only in the testament, but also in the inscription on the tombstone, which was often erected during his lifetime. These fines were invariably payable to the Vestal Virgins, the high-priests, or the public chest. A testator was not obliged to repeat this injunction in his testament. Whence did he acquire the power of inflicting a fine ? According to the usual conceptions of Roman testamentary law, it was only the heir that he could thus threaten, but the penalty is made applicable to the outside purchaser as well as to the seller. This burial-right has a twofold nature ; outwardly it is not a formal testament, but in reality it is practically testamentary ; in other words, it is a final expression of intentions with reference to the maintenance of individual personality—an idea most clearly proceeding from the conception of a testament and the underlying significance of that conception. The Roman at death obtains a right which he never possessed during his life ; death raises him to the glory of a legislator. The dying man, according to his own ideas and in his own interests, must thus rise to a legislative power, for he has now to express his intentions as a permanent, enduring, and definite part of his environment. They must therefore appear as law. He must, and he can, assume the attitude of a legislator towards other persons in law, and can invade their spheres of right, for, compared with the transcendental interest which the spirit of nationalism feels in him, other persons in law who are merely private individuals in comparison with him—the dead man— are of no account. Thus, during the history of the Roman Empire a transition slowly took place from this metaphysical conception to the conception of property, and the person continuing a dead man's intentions is transformed into the heir to his property, until eventually under Justinian, by the introduction of inheritance *sub beneficio inventarii,* the heir regards the acquisition of property as the main point and as the only point which concerns his relationship to the testator. The process of detrition here ends, and with it disappears the national character and the Roman national spirit.[1]

Such is Lassalle's theory. We have seen that Roman jurisprudence did not originally recognize any testamentary executor. However, the need of such an institution had already been felt, and attempts were made to satisfy it by other methods. Thus it was possible to make the heir himself an executor by depriving him of the inheritance while laying upon him the burden of its administration. The testator had the right to exhaust the whole of his property in legacies, until this right was limited by the Furian, the Voconian, and the Falcidian laws. The reasons which provoked the Falcidian law were concerned with political taxation. Under the second triumvirate inheritances by will were subject to taxation, to cover the expenses of the war against Sextus Pompeius, and it was therefore necessary to secure the due execution of testaments, for the legal heirs, who were really nothing more than executors, often preferred to decline the inheritance, and thus to nullify the intentions of the testator, for the estate was then administered as though in case of intestacy, and the legatees received nothing. Legislation therefore attempted a compromise in the interests of those concerned by securing to the heir a fourth of his inheritance. Thus the testator was less free than before to dispose of his property by will, but at the same time the execution of his testament was secured, as the payment of the sums representing his bequests was now certain.[2]

Shortly after Lassalle's "System of Acquired Rights" appeared, Ihering objected to his speculative treatment of Roman law upon no scientific grounds, but in the name of normal human intelligence. He deals in a particularly humorous

[1] See especially "System of Acquired Rights," ii. 21, 62, 72, 77, 101, 105, 179-184, 233, 486.
[2] Hermann Deutsch, "Die Vorläufer der heutigen Testamentsvollstrecker m Römischen Recht," 3-17.

way with the statement that the Roman questions of inheritance in no way turned upon the transmission of real property. From Lassalle's theory he draws the sarcastic conclusion that Roman testamentary law is a region of speculative thought realized in fact. Everything that it defines or does not define, contains or does not contain, can be deduced by philosophical argument, and if not a word concerning the whole business had been preserved to us, Lassalle could none the less have discovered it *a priori*. He illustrates Lassalle's theory by the following amusing parody : Two baby twins are left without parents ; one of them dies, and the other inherits his estate *ab intestato*. The case may then be assumed to develop as follows : The testator, anxious to secure immortality for his intentions or the continuity of them, has, by a silent act of will, instituted his brother as " the person continuing the existence of his own will." Having in this way " overcome mortality, though with the help of the general will," and casting a thankful glance upon the future executor of his intentions, who is nestling at his side and performs his responsibilities through a representative, he gently falls asleep and returns with a sigh of satisfaction to his cosmic dust.[1]

As in Lassalle's view the whole Roman system of inheritance was based upon certain religious and metaphysical theories, he attempted to carry his foundations as deep as possible, and for this purpose studied from the philological side the origin of the conception to which his legal studies had brought him. To discover this origin, he goes back to the prehistoric age of the nation. The origin must be religious in character, for religion invariably preserves a deposit of the earliest recollections of a people. Lassalle then finds that this conception was intellectually rooted in the ancient worship of the Manes and Lares. The Manes, or spirits of the departed, were regarded by the Romans not as the dead or as those who had passed away, but as those who remained. The idea of the Manes as remaining is seen in the word *manere*, to remain ; the correctness or incorrectness of the derivation is of no account, as it was the derivation current in antiquity. The

---

[1] Ihering, " Scherz und Ernst in der Jurisprudenz," 32 ; and " Geist des Römischen Rechts," ii. 2, 533 *et seq.* ; and iii. 1, 247 and 295.

Manes are and remain what they were—spiritual individualities, so far agreeing with the Roman conception of individuality ; persons able to will, with objects of will in the outer world. The Romans did not originally burn a dead man, but buried him in his dwelling upon the scene where his will had been exerted, and only after the custom of cremation had been introduced was the Lararium, or house chapel, regarded as the abode of these spirits. The Lares thus become protecting gods, the watchers and guardians of the house, and so long as the same family continues to inhabit the house they are family divinities, but they are bound to the house and not to the family. They are not ancestral but local divinities, and do not remain in possession of the family if the family removes. The Lares are those in power, the powerful ones (*potentes*). The Lar protects the place of his abode, but not as a household god. He guards the house only as the particular sphere subject to his power. Obviously, therefore, his relations with a new owner will not be of the most friendly nature, as an incomer is an intruder within his sphere of power. For the purpose of appeasing the Lar and the goddess Mania, human sacrifice was customary in Rome at the earliest times. The new owner of a house sacrificed his own child upon the altar to avoid damage to the family. As early as the period of the Kings this worship was forbidden in Rome. Tarquinius, who was an Etruscan, and therefore closely connected with religion, reintroduced the worship. Junius Brutus put an end to it by ordering that the oracle should be satisfied by cutting off garlic and poppy heads ; in other words, this barbarous custom, which originated in the Pelasgic period, was suppressed by the Republic. The Pelasgic spirit becomes the Roman spirit. The true religion of the Romans is law. Religion is but a pre-historic point of departure, and is therefore preserved by the Roman as an element alien to himself and his national spirit, but as an element which none the less fills his mind with reverential awe, as being the foundation of his nationalism. While all other peoples have their religious ceremonies performed by their own priests, the Roman entrusts them to a foreign nation, and this nation was the nation of his origin— the Etruscans. The Haruspices, who demand the death of

Curtius as an atonement to the Manes, are of Etruscan origin. Etruscan also was the art of augury. The reconciliation between the dead and the living, between the Lar and the new owner, which is brought about by the Roman national spirit, or rather is not brought about, but exists, took place within the region of law. The appointment of a testamentary heir is the outward sign of this reconciliation. Such an heir represents the continued existence of the deceased, and undertakes to continue the deceased's will. But a deeper and more essential necessity now brings it about that law is forced to reflect the inherent breach and contradiction between the dead and the living, which was a fundamental element in religion. Thus upon the basis of a reconciliation already effected there arises once more the old hostility between the Lar as a permanent force of will and his successor, in the form of the mutual antagonism between the testator and the heir. This dissension was bound to reappear, for the same national spirit which became obvious at the lower or religious stage of development now asserts itself when a higher stage has been reached. All previous developments fall into a new and wider perspective in the light of this relationship, and so far as the sense of Roman nationalism is concerned, its development in the sphere of law now only becomes entirely clear. All nations have laws, for all nations give practical expression to their intellectual conceptions. What the Roman has here brought to reality is the conception of personal will as unending ; in other words, he has expressed the idea which is the basis of all law. Hence it is the law, and not any one form of law, which thus becomes the real expression of his being. The transition from the original Pelasgic people to the Greeks and Romans is the transition of the infinite ego, from the essential imaginativeness of religion to the higher form of art among the Greeks and to the higher form of law among the Romans. Behind these two intellectual forms religion remains in the case of Greece as the form of art, in the case of Rome as the religious and transcendental foundation of law.

The weak side of this great poetical and philosophical explanation of legal ideas as originating from religious conceptions seems to lie in the parallel between the household god

and the new owner on the one hand, and between the testator
and the heir upon the other hand. Closer critical examination
in this case can find nothing but indications and no real
parallel. The household god did originally demand human
sacrifice, but on this we cannot lay stress, for all gods originally
did the same. This is too common a relation to be explained as an early state of antagonism to the heir, in which
the Roman testator of the theory is said to have existed.

After this ingenious investigation of the nature of Roman
hereditary law, Lassalle turns his eyes to the Germanic system
of inheritance, and thus reaches the main point of the work,
which is in no respect open to the objections above stated.
His conclusion is that not a word in his explanation of Roman
law has any application to the wholly different system of
inheritance in force among the Germanic races. In this latter
case it is a fundamental rule that on the death of the testator
the inheritance immediately passes to the heir. When the
Germans appeared in history, their only institution of the kind
was intestacy, the right of inheritance when no will has been
made ; and there is a vast difference between intestate inheritance, which in Rome was only an emergency means
employed when the testator had not pronounced his individual
intentions, and intestacy as the sole form of inheritance,
excluding any divergency in the will of the testator. The
Germanic form of intestate inheritance is thus that which the
Roman form has been wrongly styled—simple family right.
The moral identity of persons resting upon the tie of blood
forms in this case the conception of the family. If an anti-
thetical form of statement is desired, we might say that Roman
hereditary right stands to the Germanic system as will stands
to love. The unity between the testator and the heir is in this
case undoubtedly identity of blood. The property, according
to his ideas, is regarded as the common family possession. It
is acquired by the heir as soon as he is begotten, and his
acquisition becomes practical upon the death of the testator.
Thus the rights of a possessor to his property are confined to
his lifetime. Hence testamentary dispositions are unknown
among the Germanic peoples. When they come in contact with
the Romans, they certainly borrow from them the custom of

making wills in a purely formal manner, without any comprehension whatever of the underlying meaning. They regard
the Roman testament as what it is in its outward material
form—a means of bequeathing property. As such they use it
because it flatters their sense of individual freedom, but they
understand its real meaning so little that for a long time they
regard a testamentary bequest as equivalent to a presentation
between living men, proceeding from the idea that a transaction
in property cannot possibly be conducted when one of the
parties to the business is dead. This erroneous view can be
described as logical. It is a mistake which contains more truth
than its rectification upon that basis.

Even when the legal character of the Roman testament has
been reconstructed within the Germanic system of inheritance,
it is divergent from those fundamental conceptions in which
alone its inner meaning and its possibility of existence were
rooted. It is transferred purely in outward form to an environment of ideas with which it is in every respect contradictory, and in one respect inherently incompatible. The
testamentary law of the Germanic nations is thus a vast
mistake, a theoretical impossibility, and this is a statement
based upon no arbitrary and personal criticism of the testamentary system, but upon practical criticism supported by
history itself.

The great mistake of modern writers has been to suppose
that the testament is part of natural law. The Roman, however, was very far removed from regarding the capacity to
make a will as natural to the individual, and therefore as part
of natural right. On the contrary, he was so impressed with
the natural incapacity of the individual to exert his intentions
after his death that the conjunction of two intentions, the
amalgamation of the dead man's desires with those of one
living who made the desires of the dead man his own, was
thought necessary in order that the deceased's testament
might reach execution. The whole system of the Roman law
of inheritance indicates a mighty effort to secure that a man's
desires shall not become inoperative with his death, but shall
be maintained for ever by the maintenance of his personality.
The system might thus be described with truth as the dogma

of immortality in Roman form. A right has been interpreted as a natural right which never existed anywhere, either in Roman or Germanic law, in any people or at any time.

Here again Lassalle adds his laudation of the philosophical and legal insight displayed by the French Revolution :

" Only now are we able clearly and intelligibly to understand how it was that at a time when, as Hegel says, the world was placed upon its head—namely, reason—the French National Convention abolished all possibility of bequeathing property in a direct line by the law of March 7 to 10, 1793. The reaction against all empirical tradition gave rise to a return of the national spirit to its own vital substance, and deprived it of an element of Latinism. This reaction, however, did not imply immediate retirement to the forests of Germany. An heir by intestacy obtained no right to the property of a testator during his life, and he could only inherit when any property remained after death ; but he could not claim that any part of his property should be transmitted by inheritance. The idea of individual freedom as against the Germanic system of law had developed so far that the owner had now become the sole and unconditional owner. Property was thus no longer family property as such, the common possession of which is only dissolved by death. For this purpose it would be necessary that, even during the lifetime of the possessor, the intestacy heir should have a right limiting the possessor's powers of alienation. Property, on the contrary, was now purely individual property ; yet the owner who has children can only give his property away within certain limits during his own lifetime. Upon what principle, then, is intestate succession here based ? As we have seen, it is not based upon any claim to the property peculiar to the heir by intestacy, as such a claim must also have been in existence during the testator's lifetime. As, again, the testator cannot make testamentary dispositions, such rights cannot be based upon his presumed will. It is therefore clear that the claim rests upon nothing else than the general will of the State, regulating questions of bequest. It rests, indeed, upon the family, as it qualifies the family only for inheritance, but not upon the family as inheriting by its own right, nor upon the family as called to inherit by the presumed

6

will of the deceased ; but upon the family as a State institution. Even when testamentary freedom exists within a quantitative limit, as is for the most part the case with testamentary rights at the present day, the character of the testamentary right is that of the development which we have described up to the point when this *quotité disponible* is involved. Much as we may be surprised or shocked by the fact, the fact remains, when truthfully examined, that the majority of modern systems of inheritance—such, for instance, as the Code Napoléon—in their fundamental nature and up to the point where the *quotité disponible* is involved, simply represent a regulation of testamentary dispositions by society."

The great philosophers of earlier times, when considering the law of inheritance, did not go to work historically like Lassalle. The conception of hereditary right, as based upon the moral identity of the members of a family which finds outward expression in the necessarily common possession of property, is due to Hegel. He, however, was mistaken, and regarded as the idea of testamentary law in general what was merely the particular historical idea peculiar to Germanic law. Thus he only succeeded in producing a theory of intestate succession, and was unable to arrive at any permanent theory of the testament. The only great philosopher, apart from Hegel, who attempted the question is Leibniz, whose penetrating genius was upon the point of developing the idea of Roman hereditary law by a process of deduction, notwithstanding his entire want of historical knowledge. He says : " Testaments would have had no importance whatever as law if the soul were not immortal, but as the dead still live in reality, they remain masters of their property, and the heirs which they leave behind must be considered as their representatives."[1]

But while in Roman testamentary law a testator continues his existence in his heir, who is himself the continuation in life of the deceased, this idea cannot be considered as supported by the spirit of Christianity, which believes that the individual

---

[1] " Testamenta vero mero jure nullius essent momenti, nisi anima esset immortalis ; sed quia mortui revera adhuc vivunt, ideo manent domini rerum ; quos vero heredes reliquerunt concipiendi sunt ut procuratores in rem suam."

continues his life in a totally different position and under quite different conditions than in his finite will, which he abandons when he abandons all mortality. If it is true that the testament depends for its significance upon the presupposition of personal immortality, this only holds good when immortality is regarded as it was in ancient Rome ; for in the Christian sense it is the soul that is immortal, and this possesses no earthly property ; hence it cannot remain the permanent master of property in any relationship of agreement with its representative. Finally, the institution of the testament could only be preserved by this means at the cost of destroying the whole conception of property. As Adam was the first testator, so he would be the only possessor.[1]

It has been by no means easy to compress within the space of a few paragraphs an exposition which occupies more than six hundred pages in Lassalle's concentrated style. Nevertheless I hope that I have given the reader a correct and adequate conception of the characteristics and leading ideas contained in the second portion of the work. The ultimate issue of it is obviously the view directly expressed by Lassalle in one passage of the book, that " a stricter conception of the theory of the State is the source from which all progress that has been made in this century has been and will be derived."[2]

Beyond this statement there is no syllable or further hint in this direction. The book is strictly confined to theoretical considerations, and not a line of it indicates a desire to translate the theory into practice. More than this, the book, as a scholarly, historical, and philosophical investigation, not only contains no single hint in the direction of practice, but throughout the rest of his life, even during the most passionate agitation and the most violent persecution of his party by middle-class organs of opinion, never did Lassalle indicate by any single sign that he would care to rouse an agitation in support of a practical system corresponding to his theory. In private life Lassalle was often wanting in

---

[1] *Cf.* " System of Acquired Rights," ii. 400-604 ; and also Von Sybil's criticism of Lassalle's chief work in " Doctrines of Modern Socialism and Communism " ("Lectures and Essays," 81 *et seq.*) ; and F. A. Lange's reply in his book, " The Labour Problem," 399.

[2] " System of Acquired Rights," i. 47.

proper self-command, but in public life he was so entirely master of himself, and was of so eminently practical a disposition, that he invariably devoted his efforts only to the object immediately before him. Often and obstinately did he call for agitation to attain such immediate objects as direct and universal franchise, and often did he speak on behalf of workmen's industrial enterprises to be supported by the State, the institution of " productive unions " based upon State credit. But in all his pamphlet writings not a line or a syllable touches upon the question of inheritance rights. Lothar Bucher concludes the preface to his edition of the " System of Acquired Rights " with a quotation from Lessing, which he says he provoked Lassalle to utter one evening during a party at his house : " At all times men have lived who were able to form a correct estimate of the future, but were unable to await its arrival. They desired that movements for which history requires the space of centuries should come to maturity within the short space of their own lives."

The reader has seen that these words are applicable to no one so little as to Lassalle, and in no respect can they be applied to him in a less degree than as the author of the " System of Acquired Rights."

It was in the year 1861 that he published this book, which is his chief work, and was dedicated to his father on the latter's sixtieth birthday. He repeatedly expressed his intention[1] of making this work the foundation-stone of a connected system covering the whole range of mental philosophy, which he " would perhaps complete some day, provided," he adds very characteristically, " that the period of leisure for theorizing never ceases for us Germans." In the year 1859 he had sent his " Heraclitus " into the world with regrets that the struggles of practical life had postponed its publication for so many years. Only two years later his chief work upon law is accompanied with a further regret that the prevailing political peace provided him with leisure enough to elaborate this book. Deeply as he was able to bury himself in theories, his desires and ambitions were directed to the work and influence of practical life.

[1] Preface ; *cf.* ii. 586, note.

CHAPTER VIII

To avoid interrupting the connection between certain ideas propounded by Lassalle, we have followed his work down to the year 1861. A retrospective glance now becomes necessary.

Berlin had become impossible as a residence for Lassalle in consequence of his participation in the Revolution of 1848. His life in Düsseldorf was a kind of forced exile from the capital of his country, where he must have wished to live for many reasons. Ten years of his life were spent on the Rhine, and his house and purse during that period were ever open to political refugees or to impoverished democrats and workmen. Many years later, in one of his agitation speeches to the Rhenish workers, he reminded them of this period of his life with the following striking words : " You know me. For ten years I have lived among the working-classes of the Rhine. With you I spent the period of revolution and the time of the white reign of terror in the fifties. As your address truly says, you have seen me in both of these movements. You know what house was the undaunted asylum of democratic propaganda, the asylum dear to the boldest and most determined supporters of our party, notwithstanding the white terror of Hinckeldey and Westphalen, notwithstanding the wild lawlessness of that time, even to the last moment of my stay in the Rhine Provinces."[1] At the same time Lassalle was yearning for Berlin, and his wishes were known to his friends. Dressed as a coachman he entered the capital in April, 1857, after long years of absence, and attempted from his hiding-place to secure permission through his patrons to remain. No one exerted himself so zealously on his behalf as the old

[1] Lassalle, " The Festivals, the Press, and the Meeting of Frankfort Deputies." Hinckeldey, chief of the Prussian police ; Westphalen, Prussian minister.

and influential Alexander von Humboldt, whose house had ever been open to him. The authorities had little or no objection to Lassalle's residence in the capital, but the influential family of Countess Hatzfeldt desired at any cost to prevent this lady from living in the neighbourhood of her relations. It was regarded as inevitable that she would take up her abode in Lassalle's house, and attempts were therefore made to keep her at a distance by preventing any arrangement of the kind. The Prussian authorities thus employed against Lassalle a procedure precisely opposite to that which the Austrian authorities had pursued against Byron in Italy, when the whole family of the Guiccioli were banished from Ravenna because they were convinced that Byron would follow the young Countess.

One evening Alexander von Humboldt happened to be sitting near Hinckeldey at a large dinner-party, and urged him to give Lassalle permission to reside in Berlin. A member of the company who heard the conversation told me that he had plainly heard Hinckeldey's answer : " Readily, so far as I am concerned ; I have no objection to him. It is a matter of total indifference to me, but the King will not hear of it." " Is that the only objection ?" replied Humboldt. " I will undertake to persuade the King." He kept his word, and Lassalle remained in Berlin.

Berlin, the town to which he belonged, in which he had studied philology in his youth and had absorbed the ideas of Young Germany, provided precisely the environment which he required in maturity ; the town of work, the great factory in which ideas are forged and sharpened, the great smithy in which plans are welded into action, the great storehouse in which learning is gathered and from whence it is disseminated, the point of contact from which Germany's spirit sends forth its illuminating beams ! So indeed the anagram runs :

Berolinum—lumen orbi !

Berlin ! Populated by inhabitants of mixed blood whose intellects have gained the clear and decisive imprint of France from the descendants of refugee Huguenots, and whose wit has been so polished by well-to-do and well-bred Jewish immi-

grants that it glitters in a thousand facets ! Berlin, the city
of Prussia over which the dominant spirit of Frederick still
hovers, even as his bronze figure on horseback towers above
the flowering linden-trees ! Berlin, the town of Frederick,
with a trace of Voltaire's smile still playing in the air !

In 1859 Berlin was not the great city with millions of inhabitants which, as Germany's capital, it has since become. It
was a town of moderate size, in which an individual of distinguished powers was not lost in the crowd. It possessed
neither new and splendid public buildings, nor many of the
fine new streets in the west ; but if its architecture was poor,
its natural beauties were rich. The nearer part of the Thiergarten had not yet been sacrificed to the necessities of city
extension. Lassalle settled in the pretty quarter in the
neighbourhood of the Thiergarten. From 1858 onwards he
lived at No. 13, in the fine and beautiful Bellevuestrasse,
a street in which there are no shops, with splendid rows of
chestnut-trees which seemed to be connected with the Thiergarten, into which it opens. At the end of the year before his
death he moved house to another No. 13, in the Potsdamer-
strasse hard by.

Berlin was still the town of Frederick William IV.—the town,
that is, that had revolted against him. Beyond, on the other
side of the Thiergarten, from *In den Zelten*, the revolution of
1848 had proceeded. Its spirit was subjugated and repressed,
but not dead. Its weak breath still inspired the whole world
of scholarship and the whole of the upper middle-classes, in
the most distinguished houses of which all the leaders of the
yet undivided opposition met. All the opponents of the prevailing and antiquated system met as allies in these circles,
careless of their different shades of opinion, held intercourse
with the leaders of science and art, and formed the good society
of that time.

Lassalle, with his brilliant personality, his reputation as a
scholar, and his obvious power of conquest, of inspiring enthusiasm and of domination, found little difficulty in obtaining
a footing in these circles. There were indeed salons, including
many of aristocratic character, which were closed to the "cash-
box thief," but access to houses thus limited can have had no

great value for him. With such an income as that of which Lassalle could then dispose, a citizen in Berlin was not only comfortable, but almost rich. In his house, which was decorated with elaborate splendour, according to the ideas and conditions of that age, he enjoyed the pleasure of gathering an ever-increasing circle of highly educated, clever, and cultured men, free from prejudice, many of whom were far-famed, and of beautiful, vivacious women, in many cases celebrated for their wit and talent ; and among the aristocracy of mind were to be found numerous members of the aristocracy of birth. Lassalle kept a French cook, and did not care to drink wine at less than twenty or thirty marks a bottle. " Why should we leave all the good wine for William the Just ?" he was accustomed to say ; and the numerous parties which he gave in Berlin were enjoyed no less on account of the admirable food and wines than they were famous for the perfection of their social tone and their cheerfulness, and also for the unrestrained and ideal freedom of conversation which visitors to the house involuntarily adopted.

At his house were to be met, not only men of the generation to which Lassalle himself belonged, but also many distinguished members of the earlier generation, men whose experiences, studies, works, and deeds, made their conversation delightful. There was old Varnhagen, whose acquaintance Lassalle had made through Heine ; there was Boeckh, born in 1785, who had been the first to define classical philology as the knowledge of antiquity in its totality and as the comprehensive reproduction of ancient culture, a man who was able to fulfil the demands laid down by his own definition. It was Boeckh who replied, when the beautiful wife of Professor Diderici exclaimed at a party, " Lassalle is the handsomest man that I have ever seen " : " The handsomest man ! I can offer no opinion upon that, but he is the cleverest and most learned man that I have ever met."[1]

Förster, the historian, was there, born in 1791, the poet and connoisseur who had ridden in his youth by the side of Körner among Lutzow's volunteers. In 1817 he had been brought before a court-martial to answer for his treatise upon the

---

[1] Helene von Rackowitza, " My Relations to Ferdinand Lassalle," p. 46.

constitution of Prussia, and since then had been living in private life with a distinguished reputation as an author. There was old General von Pfuel, born in 1780, with whom Lassalle was in constant intercourse for many years, Minister of War and Prime Minister in September, 1848. He had entered the army in 1797, had travelled through Europe with his friend Heinrich von Kleist, had gone through the campaign as a member of Blücher's General Staff in 1809, had entered the Austrian service after the peace, and the Russian service in 1812, and had commanded the advance guard in the Battle of Ligny in 1815. It was there that he mounted all his drummers and sent them forward against the enemy drumming loudly, so that the enemy imagined a powerful force was in their neighbourhood, and did not venture upon any movement until Pfuel was relieved by reinforcements. In 1815 he was in command in Paris, and in 1847 in Berlin ; in 1848 he had suppressed the revolt in Vienna. He was a man who had seen history made, and had helped to make it.

In Lassalle's house were also to be found men of his own age—scholars, authors, lawyers, energetic democrats, and men of the Progressive party, most of whom are still living, and have remained faithful to their youthful convictions, with the exception of Lothar Bucher, who has changed his views.

Lassalle found favour with many women. He desired to make an impression, and it is a fact that he was often successful. In his relations with the other sex he was, so to speak, desirous of conquest, inconstant, carried away only momentarily, rather anxious for the triumph of pride than amenable to the influence of the one woman. The earliest and deepest feelings of his life had been devoted to Countess Hatzfeldt. To her he remained faithful, because on this point he remained faithful only to himself. The Countess had believed in him when he was a nobody, had placed her fate in his hands when he was young, unknown, and powerless ; nor could he ever abandon the woman who had been the first to say to him, " I believe in you." But his feelings were those of friendship, gratitude, and pride, with, perhaps, at most, a few grains of love at the outset. At a later time he certainly had love-affairs, but was at no time deeply in love, while he was loved as such outwardly imposing and dominant men usually are. Women who are admitted to their intimacy are often the most brilliant members of their circle, as a rule the most unimaginatively gifted, and their powers are generally obvious at the first glance. Who does not know the remarkable ring of female forms which invariably surrounds genius and becomes a small and exclusive world of strangely composed elements? I doubt whether Lassalle regarded women with other emotions than those aroused by a somewhat crude sense of beauty, or with other desires than to find wit and intellect and to receive admiration. Between 1870 and 1880 I occasionally met old ladies in Germany who were said to have been in close intimacy with Lassalle. To the eyes of a younger generation these ladies seemed in no way particularly impressive. There was a sharpness, a dry intelligence, and a certain virility in all of them, and they spoke of Lassalle with the quiet admiration which is customary in such cases.

Meanwhile, in the winter of 1858 and 1859, those Berlin families who had taken Lassalle to themselves were put to a somewhat severe test. His " motherly friend," the Countess Hatzfeldt, arrived in Berlin, as was to be expected, settled there permanently, and proceeded to exert her old rights over her former protector. Her existence had been almost forgotten in Berlin. Male conversation knew her only in caricature, and though tolerance was then the order of the day, the respectable middle-class families would have been glad to exclude her ; but on this point Lassalle was inexorable. The reception and recognition of the Countess was regarded by him as a cabinet question. He declined intercourse with those who would not know her, and, when confronted with this alternative, hesitation disappeared, for society neither could nor would be deprived of him. The much-discussed lady was found to be generally pleasant and amiable, and her attitude towards Lassalle was that of a mother. She acted as hostess at his table, though they did not live in the same house. She never betrayed any trace of jealousy, however zealous his attentions to other younger or more beautiful ladies. Though now fifty-four years of age, her splendid figure and her beautiful shoulders, which she was careful not to hide, gained her such enthusiastic admirers as Marx and Rüstow; nor was she indifferent to the admiration which she aroused. The smallest knowledge of the world will enable us to understand that the proximity of this lady and the irregular and ambiguous nature of her maternal attitude towards Lassalle considerably injured his social prospects. With her painted eyebrows and lips, with all the art and industry which she expended upon the preservation of her beauty, she brought a note of false and almost ridiculous colour into his life and his household.

Lassalle's life in Berlin was divided between study and distraction. Public attention did not lose sight of him, and he had certainly no objection to publicity. Rumours of his extraordinary whims and of the luxurious entertainments which he gave spread abroad in Berlin. Distorted accounts of them even appeared in the descriptions given of him by the daily Press.

Thus, in the collection of " Contemporaries," a story may be found to the effect that he was accustomed to intoxicate his guests with hashish and to play similar senseless tricks. The incident which gave rise to this story occurred only once, when Lassalle and a few of his guests, as one of them has told me, amused themselves by sitting in the smoking-room, which was fitted up in Turkish style, wearing Turkish dresses which he had brought home from the East, and trying the effects of hashish. Lassalle's conduct at this time also caused a scandal of no importance, which none the less roused some painful feelings. A gentleman whose eyes had been sharpened by jealousy, conceived himself insulted by Lassalle and boxed his ears at a large party when he was with a lady who was certainly more interested in Lassalle than in the gentleman concerned. Lassalle, who had invariably asserted that, as a member of the Democratic party, he would not fight a duel, had shown strong disapproval of the duel between Twesten and Manteuffel ; and though he was a good fencer and a good shot, he possessed sufficient self-command to decline the ensuing challenge. The next day, however, his insulter with a friend waited for Lassalle as he was taking his usual walk, and came upon him in the neighbourhood of the Brandenburger Thor ;

but Lassalle gave the two men so sound a thrashing as obliged them to abandon their warlike intentions. This trivial and unpleasant incident is of interest because it shows what a height of passion Lassalle must afterwards have reached when he sent the double challenge which became the cause of his death. On the occasion of this attack Förster presented him with a Robespierre stick, the handle of which was a model of the Bastile in wrought gold. The transference of such a stick to such hands was a remarkable coincidence.

Though Lassalle was strong enough when bodily exertion was in question, his health was by no means invariably good. As his first speech before the Court of Assizes proves, he had suffered from a troublesome and chronic malady from earliest youth, and when he was in the prime of life his health had been undermined. He was therefore obliged to undergo long and wearisome courses of cure.

While undergoing some such course he was once forced to keep his room for some weeks. Ernst Dohm, from whom I have this information, one day received a note in which Lassalle asked him to come and see him. " I want to show you something with regard to which I require your help and advice. You will probably laugh at me, but please come." My informant found Lassalle at work on the drama "Franz von Sickingen." The first act was completed. The astonishment of the friend may be understood at the idea of Lassalle, who was certainly the most unpoetical of men, trying his powers as a poet. " I know what you will say," said Lassalle hastily. " I know as well as you that I am no poet ; but Lessing also wrote dramas with the full consciousness that he was not a poet. I have no wish to compare myself with Lessing, but I do not see why I should not try my hand," etc. He required the help of Dohm for details of stage management, which he did not understand, and upon matters of metre, in which Dohm was an expert. Dohm began by advising Lassalle to write in prose, nor could he have given better advice. Even if the prose had been oratorical, it would have been excellent of its kind ; while Lassalle's incapacity to produce a harmonious verse in correct metre is quite astonishing. It cannot be said that he had no ear, for he read metrical translations of the

Greek poets aloud with good taste, and enjoyed them, but his own lines form very amusing evidence of the uncertainty of his sense of metre. Iambics of six feet appear in his drama, and produce a most harsh and discordant effect among the five-foot lines, while the emphasis in these halting verses is left to fall where it may. " The scientific redecorator " sounded to Lassalle a good iambic line in five feet. None the less, or, more correctly, precisely on this account, Lassalle could not be induced to give up verse as his chosen form, as it coincided with the theories of tragedy which he had adopted from the Greeks and from Hegel. Thus " Franz von Sickingen " received its present form. As a work of art the drama possesses, apart from its interesting plot, practically every defect of form that a poetical work can have. It abounds with lapses from good taste ; the scenes drag painfully, and are without central point or climax ; naturally the work would never bear production on the stage. At the same time it is impossible to assert that this drama, which is full to the brim with Lassalle's glowing energy, produces an unpoetical effect. The deep political insight into an age which was stirred to great movements, and the stormy pathos which thence proceeds, certainly have their poetical value. As we have it, this drama is certainly a most valuable gold-mine for anyone who wishes to study the mental life of its author. Whichever of Lassalle's works we may have at hand, the drama rises continually to recollection, for it contains everything ; it displays the strongly marked characteristics of Lassalle's natural and individual personality, and it provides manifold and numerous indications which enable us to understand how he formed his ideas of the world, and how his views of history, of foreign and domestic politics, arose. The production is necessarily not a uniform whole, and must not therefore be considered as providing a complete description of Lassalle ; but for purposes of illustration it can be used at every point.

We now glance at the personal description of Lassalle which the work contains. I propose to quote the most important passages, giving a prose version of the poetry, which is often dreadfully poor, and quoting only a few significant passages in metrical form.

Ulrich von Hutten describes his miserable life since his excommunication by the Pope. He relates how Town Councils, in fear of difficulties with the Pope or the Princes, have not ventured to grant him a refuge within their walls. " Still," he says, " if they had offered me shelter I would have promised to remain quiet," but

> I cannot hold my peace ; I cannot buy,
> At price of silence, safety for myself ;
> The spirit drives me on to testify :
> I cannot stanch the mighty stream within.

" The general need," he says, " rises higher, so that everyone confines himself in his house, as in a time of plague, or steals noiselessly by anyone he meets. All the more am I driven by the power of the Spirit to oppose this devastation and to attack it the more vigorously, the more menacing its appearance. Oh, that I had a thousand tongues ! With every one would I now cry aloud to the country. I would rather wander from village to village like a hunted animal than keep silent and abandon my vocation for truth-telling. Praise me not for it, Franciscus ; many have blamed me bitterly for it.

> And yet, when I perpend, I do not deem
> Censure nor praise to be my rightful meed ;
> A heart of ruth was set within my breast
> Which feels the general woe ; the common pain
> Stirs me more deeply than the heart of man
> Is wont to feel : how can I help it, sir ?
> 'Twas set within me !

He describes the attitude of his friends. Some are delighted to see him again, but many shun him in the cowardice of their hearts. " Some openly declared that I was a burden to them ; others would not so openly admit it, but I felt it none the less. Others, again, who had been consoled by my voice in times of trouble, whose sheet-anchor I had been in many a storm, told me that they would gladly continue as my friends in secret, but could not be seen with me again in public, as they could not afford to quarrel entirely with Rome.

> To suffer this from friends,
> This, sir, from friends, to whom I did devote
> Myself with ready service and with love
> Unbounded, this is hard !

Ulrich is warmly received by Franz von Sickingen, and wins the love of his daughter Marie, to whom he replies : " Before you surrender yourself to this love, Marie, learn the nature of the curse which drives me on. It is the most powerful and the most inevitable of all that God, in the anger of His love, can cast upon mortal head. For ever the old story remains true. When an abyss yawned wide in Rome, and plague and destruction threatened the State, the oracles said that the gods could only be appeased if the most precious thing that the State possessed were cast into the gulf ; and then on horseback, decked in full martial array, Curtius sprang into the abyss, devoting himself to the gods of the lower world. The best men must leap into the open jaws of a vengeful age, and only over their bodies will the abyss close."

Franz thinks as Ulrich does, and as Lassalle also thinks. He says : " We owe our lives to those great purposes for accomplishment of which generations are sent into the world as workmen. I have done what I could. I feel relieved and happy like one who has honourably paid his debt."

But of all the utterances in the piece there is no better or more complete characterization of Lassalle's mental life than the following, which shows his condition when his powers were strained to the utmost amid threatening dangers, and his strength of will was derived from an inexhaustible source within him. At this point he attains real poetic power, for here he has felt so deeply that the words rise from these depths in lyrical form. The difference between an artist in language and a poet consists in the fact that the rhetorician has others before his eyes while the lyric poet is alone with himself ; and Lassalle is alone with himself when he utters the following outcry :

Look thou not earthwards, Balthazar, look up !
Only in danger's hour do we men learn
All that a man may be.   Then shrink away
The pale and coward fears that, earthly born,
Would fetter him to earth.   From out the wreck
Of well-schemed counsels and the overthrow
Of vain devices, rises to its height
His spirit pure, untrammelled, undismayed.
Then to the infinite almighty will
That sleeps within him doth he turn for strength,
And with closed eyes he drinks vitality,
New inspiration from himself, and stakes
His life and fortunes on a single cast ;
Then springs to action, casting care aside,
And strikes the blow which, like the lightning flash,
Shall change the face of all material things.

These words, in my opinion, display the real and the ideal Lassalle as he was in his most characteristic moments, and surely at such times he was indeed himself. What result can be gained in the case of great minds by counting all the hours in which they were not truly themselves and judging them thereby ? How much time have they not been forced to concede to their bodily wants and the claims and distractions of daily life ? How many hours have they not wasted in illness, sleep, personal needs, and the claims of others upon their attention and sympathy ? And all that may be said of these hours definitely lost for the mental life, may be said almost as entirely of the similar periods in their inward life absorbed by uncontrolled passions, restless ambition, voluptuousness, or weakness. Can we not forget, and ought we not, as far as possible, to forget these moments when we wish to know what the individual was in the depths of his heart, and is it right or sensible to dwell continually upon the weaknesses of a great soul ? In any case, it will be understood that the artist who insists upon laying no less weight upon the negative than upon the positive characteristics is not likely to produce a picture of the man, whatever else he may make, for it is certain that no one is capable of painting a portrait if he attempts to represent the original as he might have been in all situations, and if he has not a certain ideal of the personality in question before his eyes. The important point is not idealization, but the power of seeing, with a keen eye for reality this ideal figure in its essential expression and activity, or, in other words, the person in his main characteristics as he revealed himself more or less completely to his contemporaries ; and such an ideal picture of his nature Lassalle has given in those lines.

The play also contains a premonition of his sudden death. Marie asks Ulrich, when she sees him despondent with regard to his future, whether he does not believe in some higher Providence which defends the cause of good. He replies :

> The universe indeed may build thereon,
> Wrapped in its own mysterious purposes,
> Advancing ever to its mighty goal,
> It wanders not from its appointed path.
>
> *　　*　　*　　*　　*
>
> Each single man doth build upon the force
> Of chance, which, like a powder-mine, explodes,
> And hurls his shattered fragments high in air.

These words contain a true and bitter philosophy of life ; a philosophy with truth and consolation for a nation, with truth and bitterness for the individual, but with greatest truth for those who, like Lassalle, dig their mines and storm barricades that have been undermined.

Any student of the writer's personality will feel that these almost autobiographical features of the play are closely connected with those revealed by Lassalle's fundamental views of history and politics. Even in his speech before the Court of Assizes Lassalle had described how the inward movement of men's minds really determines the course of historical development, and cannot be subjugated by measures which can only affect the outward manifestation of feeling : " Long before barricades can be raised in the outer world, the citizen in the world of mind must have dug the pit which will swallow up the forms of government." In conformity with this idea Franz von Sickingen tells the Emperor Karl, in words of much importance, that he should not overestimate his own power, which " can only accelerate, but cannot retard, can only modify, but cannot suppress." The principles of Lassalle's historical faith are here seen transformed into a political principle. Every theoretical conviction immediately assumed practical form in his case. It was upon this conviction that a definite and irresistible influence runs through history that he based his dislike to the petty arts of diplomacy, to half-measures, and to dissembling of any kind. When Karl wishes to negotiate with the reformation, Franz replies : " There can be no negotiation with truth ; you might as well attempt to negotiate with the fiery pillar which went before the people of Israel." Afterwards, when Franz summons a levy of his troops in the neighbourhood of the town of Trèves, with the object of secretly collecting an army which he can use as a trump-card in his struggle against the other Princes, Balthasar, the keen-sighted politician of the piece, tells him the foolishness of this policy. " Whom are you deceiving ?" he asks. " Not your enemies ; for however much a man may misrepresent himself, his enemies will always suspect his thoughts and desires. The vital instinct in a threatened man becomes speedily suspicious of the intentions of any who threaten him with destruction. There-

7

fore you have not deceived the Princes ; with infallible instinct they see in you the enemy of their order, and put no credence in the story of this petty feud. Only your friends have you carefully deceived and fooled, for they trusted your word. To them this feud implied only the petty possibility which you represented it to be, and they do not support you. Now, if you wish to break loose, it were better for you to rise openly against the Emperor Karl, to inscribe the reformation of Church and State broad and wide upon your standard ; better that, in virtue of the rightful character of your object, you should proclaim yourself Emperor of this realm, and unchain the fettered forces of the nation ; better this than play hide-and-seek with your friends without deceiving a single member of your enemies.

> Oh, thou art not the first, nor shalt thou be
> The last, who practised cunning in affairs
> Of moment, to the loss of his own life.
> For in the market-place of history,
> Where only by thy harness and thy arms
> The motley throng shall know thee for thyself,
> There is no reason in disguise.—Put on,
> And boldly wear the colours of thy flag,
> Yea, wrap thyself therein from head to foot.
> Then, in the shock of conflict wilt thou prove
> The vigour and the power given by truth,
> Wilt stand or fall, thyself in all thy might.
> To fall is not the worst ; but overthrow
> With strength unconquered, power unimpaired,
> This is the worst that heroes can endure.

The political views expressed in this speech are those which Lassalle maintained and followed throughout his later life. These views he continually urged upon the Progressives at the time when this party, during its struggle with the Government, fondly imagined that the Ministry could be induced by continual importunity to concede its faithfulness to the Constitution and therefore to prove it. " You wish," he cries out," to hoodwink the Government ; but all real success in life and history is only to be obtained by real reform and remodification, and not by hoodwinking." When Bismarck came to power, and the air was full of curses against him, Lassalle's views immediately enabled him to see in Bismarck the coming man, and to predict directly what Bismarck would do. Accused of high treason on the charge that he wished to overthrow the Constitution by his

agitation in favour of universal suffrage, he said to his judges :
" Well, gentlemen, though I am but a simple individual, I
can tell you that I will not only overthrow the Constitution,
but shall perhaps have done so within the space of a year !
Possibly in less than a year universal suffrage will be granted.
Bold games, gentlemen, can be played with cards thrown on
the table.   The strongest diplomacy is that which does not
require to surround its calculations with any secrecy because
they have been founded upon iron necessity, and I therefore
tell you in this solemn place that in less than a year, perhaps,
Herr von Bismarck will have played the part of Robert Peel,
and direct and universal suffrage will be granted."

As is well known, Bismarck fulfilled this prophecy, after the
war with Austria, with reference to the newly-formed North-
German Federation, and afterwards to the German Empire.

We have now seen the general political principles which this
drama contains—principles deeply characteristic of its author.
This is not the place to dwell upon the specially German nature
of its policy. I will only observe that that policy is now in force
to an unlimited extent—the policy of passionate opposition
to all petty Princes and to the principle of petty States.
" The breath of history," says Franz, " cannot pass through
such tiny particles."   Of similar character is the deep exaspera-
tion at the retention of priestly rule, with its benumbing effect
upon the people, while the immediate object proposed as a
remedy is a Protestant Emperor at the head of the German
Empire.

In the autumn of 1860, while Lassalle was staying at Aix-la-
Chapelle to take a course of the waters for his malady, he
made the acquaintance of the young Russian lady who in 1878
revealed to the world in three languages the fact that Lassalle
had wooed her and had been rejected.   The edition in which
Lassalle's letters were published in their original language,
French, bore the title " Une Page d'Amour de Ferdinand
Lassalle. Récit—Correspondance—Confessions."   So far as
we can judge this incident from the matter published, it is a
strong proof of Lassalle's weakness of judgment where women
were concerned.   After a few days' acquaintanceship with the
father and the daughter in Aix-la-Chapelle, he seems to have

conceived the idea of marrying the young lady. In the French text she is stated to have been twenty years younger than he, or fifteen years of age, while the Russian text gives her age as nineteen. We may safely conclude that she was young, and, though she was far from beautiful, and by no means wealthy or distinguished, she seems to have been a lively and enthusiastic character. To her Lassalle offered his hand and heart with astonishing precipitation.

The most original feature in Lassalle's autobiographical love-letters is the circumstance that in them he details his disadvantages, uninterruptedly and with the utmost care relates everything which could produce disinclination to a union with himself, and concludes by asking the girl whether, in spite of all these defects, she is bold enough to unite her fate with his. She can bring him no dowry, but he states that this is a matter of total indifference to him, not because he is too simple to know the value of money in this world ; for he admits with the greatest openness that he would perhaps have married a woman even if he had not loved her, provided that she brought him a dowry of three or four million thalers, for so large an amount is in itself a power which he could have used for artistic, scientific, or political purposes. But as things are, he is in love with her, can look only at herself, and dismiss pecuniary matters from his mind. He tells her the amount of his income, which would in the course of time increase by about three thousand thalers yearly, and informs her that she will not be able to live on this sum as she might have been accustomed to live in Russia on her father's estates (which had long before been sold), but that she would be forced to undergo some privations. He further adds that she must not expect that he will ever add a single halfpenny to the amount of his income. His work is purely intellectual, and it is entirely against his principles to write for money, which he calls " the most unworthy and unnatural of all proceedings." This is the attitude of intellectual exclusiveness which Byron also adopted in his youth, but speedily abandoned. Lassalle's hatred of journalism induced him to confuse justifiable literary business with the trade of writing for pay where the writer is obliged to deny or even to combat his own convictions, a phenomenon of daily occurrence. But as things were at that time in Germany, a man with such capacities as Lassalle could gain nothing worth mentioning by his pen unless he held a definite position as a journalist; and though Lassalle felt no scruples in basing his economic existence upon the income derived from the Hatzfeldt property, he none the less had such a horror of journalism that he regarded it as impossible under any circumstances to increase his income by literary work.

The lady has attempted to preserve her anonymity. Her name was at that time Sophie Solnzew, and is now Arendt, of Simferopol, where she is lady superior of an asylum. Her father was a Russian official, deeply in debt, the Vice-Governor of Witebsk, and the family had a bad reputation for many reasons. It is clear that the Russian lady had succeeded in impressing Lassalle with the idea that she was of royal blood. Those about her knew that she derived her origin from no less an ancestor than the ancient Vladimir who introduced Christianity into Russia; but the derivation was based only upon similarity of name, and not upon any genealogical tree. Vladimir received from the people the additional name of Solnze (the sun), the addition of " w " to which produces Solnzew; no derivation could be simpler. The lady was far from noble, and was herself obliged to admit that her father was not acquainted with any language but his own—a most unusual circumstance among the higher classes in Russia. How the father was able to excite Lassalle's admiration to the high degree betokened by the letters is quite inexplicable, as the two men were unable to converse. The letters are undoubtedly genuine. Their tone and style are entirely Lassalle's, and even the solecisms which they contain are some evidence of their genuineness, as they are mistakes which could only be committed by a German writing French. But it is impossible to discover the contents of the letters which are said to have been lost, or what omissions, alterations, and so forth may have been made. Equally impossible is it to decide how much coquetry and what overtures the lady employed; her own account represents her as encircled with a halo of innocence, and therefore it is hopeless to gain any clear idea of the character of this intimacy.   Sophie Solnzew shortly afterwards made several attempts, which remained fruitless, to make a name for herself as an actress and a singer.   The part which she played to win Lassalle's attention seems to have been that of a young and enthusiastic disciple, whose life and thoughts were devoted to the welfare of the poor in her own country. The letters show that Lassalle's infatuation disappeared as rapidly as it had arisen.   It was but a transitory whim, which left no trace behind it.   The only certain fact is that Lassalle's choice upon this first occasion, as afterwards, fell upon an object hardly worthy of him.   It is also noteworthy that the two girls whom he desired to marry were actresses of moderate ability.[1]

[1] From Russia I have received a considerable amount of information concerning the lady who edited the letters.   In the light of this information it seems very doubtful that her description gives an accurate account of the intimacy between Lassalle and herself.   I have seen two photographs of her, one taken in early youth and one at a later date.

It is noteworthy that the Russian and French edition are entirely discrepant, wherever she speaks in her own name.   Many circumstances which in other respects bear the stamp of truth are given in the Russian edition, though the author has seen good to withhold them from her non-Russian readers.   Conversely, in the Russian edition a passage from Lassalle's long letter to her is left out immediately after his declaration : " I will begin by saying that I will not marry you unless I am completely cured of my illness." The omission runs as follows : " For you need a man of full bodily vigour and strength, as I was a few months ago."   The reason for the omission is clear.

The real cause why Lassalle's proposals were rejected is not plain.   The lady's sudden attack of homesickness, her yearning desire to devote herself to the education of Russian peasant children and the wish to teach, which she asserted of herself in the Russian edition, are hardly more credible than her royal origin.   Did the father think the match too unsafe ?   Was he afraid of losing his office if his daughter married Lassalle ?   Did he in return show unusual friendliness to his daughter's lover ?   How are we to explain this outburst of admiration on the part of Lassalle : " What I admire as much as the generosity and delicacy of your sentiments is your account of your father's attitude.   He is a man above all that I have seen in my life ; indeed, he is prodigious !   What a man he is !"

In the social democratic newspaper, the Vorwärts of September 25, 1878, the following statement is to be found : " Although doubts were felt on our side also at first concerning the genuineness of the said letters, it afterwards appeared—and Countess Hatzfeldt supported the statement—that the letters were written by Lassalle himself."

No such evidence on the part of the Countess has been published, but it can easily be seen that such a statement in no way guarantees the genuineness of the letters in any particular point, and still less their completeness.

The answer by the head of the firm of Brockhaus to one of my friends, whom I asked to put a few questions to him as the publisher of the letters, runs as follows : " On the other hand, I can return an equally definite negative to the second question, whether we have felt any doubts concerning the authenticity of the letters since their publication.   We had no doubts as to their authenticity previously, either upon internal or external evidence, otherwise we should not have undertaken their publication. Since that time the originals of the letters have, in part at least, come before our eyes, and have convinced us that they are in Lassalle's well-known handwriting."

It is very remarkable that the firm of Brockhaus should have undertaken the edition without previously seeing the original letters and testing their genuineness by experts, and it is still more remarkable that this firm should only have succeeded in seeing a part of them since that time, apparently after these questions had induced them to make inquiries. The reason cannot have been any fear that the firm might betray the name of the editor, for this name had been communicated to the firm as a business secret, as Herr Brockhaus expressly states in the above-mentioned letter.

CHAPTER IX

PRECISELY at the moment when Lassalle sent his " Franz von
Sickingen " into the world he was induced, for the first and last
time in his life, to expound, under the cloak of anonymity,
against his usual practice, his views concerning the foreign
policy to be followed by Prussia. War with Austria had been
declared. Europe was shaken by a great wave of national
feeling, and the national liberal middle-class in Prussia were
excited, and had lost their bearings. They were calling for
war upon Louis Napoleon, to punish his attack upon Austria,
which it was thought should be supported at any price as a
land of German nationality. The righteousness of Italy's
cause and the political interests of Prussia were lightly abandoned in favour of an evil policy of sentimentality. This state
of things induced Lassalle to cast upon the world his pamphlet
entitled " The Italian War and Prussia's Task : A Voice from
the Democracy." Here he shows first that the democracy
could not trample upon the principle of free nationalities,
unless it broke with its own programme. He then explains
that it would be foolish to allow mere hatred of Napoleon III.
to dictate an attack against him at a point when he had
undertaken, no matter for what reason, an enterprise which
must and would be most dangerous to himself. He then
proceeded to show that Napoleon was even then tottering,
that his Councils were divided and distracted, that, allied
to Victor Emmanuel and supporting the Pope, he was
fighting for national freedom in order to strengthen his
own despotism. In consequence, he was not nearly so dangerous to the democracy as Austria, for Austria was then

" a thoroughly firm, consistent and consequently reactionary principle." Eventually he strikes the point by clearly demonstrating that the political results of the Italian war could only be to the advantage of Prussia and Germany. The reason was that the defeat of Austria would compensate for the obstacles which stood in the way of German unity, the obstacles upon which the revolution of 1848 and the German efforts for unity had so miserably made shipwreck. To what purpose had the revolution of that time dissolved the German Federation, which, with strange simplicity, the people regarded as the cause of disruption? This movement did not remove the real and inherent cause of disruption—namely, the balance of power existing between the two great German States. Division was due, not to a defective Constitution, but to the actual conditions of power. The Italian war, assuming that France was victorious, would inevitably deal the first blow overthrowing the balance of power between the States. " On the day when Austria is destroyed as a State of the German Federation the colours upon the toll-gates of Bavaria, Würtemberg, and the other countries will pale." On that day German unity was founded and secured for Lassalle, and with prophetic insight of surprising depth, which was really derived from his profound understanding of all existing conditions, Lassalle proceeds to prophesy, undisturbed by the very divergent dreams and inclinations of the national spirit, unmoved by the forebodings and menaces of opposition newspapers, and states everything that would come, and, indeed, has come, to pass : that France would annex Savoy and Nizza, and that Italy, against Napoleon's wish, would become an independent State. Involved in the usual German prejudices towards Denmark, he demands in the name of the principle of nationality that Prussia should declare war against Denmark, and annex Slesvig and Holstein ; that she should then exclude Austria from the German Federation, and finish her work by the foundation of the German Empire.

When the peace of Villafranca had been concluded, Lassalle undertook a journey to Italy, stayed with Garibaldi at Caprera for several days, and is said to have attempted to persuade him to undertake a freebooting expedition in Austrian territory, with a view to forwarding German unity by this means. To accomplish something for his own country akin to the achievements of Garibaldi for his Fatherland was, strangely enough, one of the dreams for the future which Lassalle perhaps entertained in moments of hope. For the present, when calm had descended upon the political world, he retired to his study, and elaborated his " System of Acquired Rights," with which, in 1861, he had completed two great works of theoretical speculation. He was now in the prime of life, at the age of thirty-six, and a spectator by necessity of the few events proceeding in the outer world. It was a year before Bismarck took up his post as Minister of Foreign Affairs, and the field of foreign policy lay fallow. The social problem which filled the mind of the young scholar in preference to any political question had disappeared from public discussion in Germany since 1849 ; the old democratic party had ceased to exist. With the enthusiasm which distinguished Lassalle in everything that he undertook, he now penetrated more deeply into the complications of political economy with which he had been occupied from his earliest youth. Only by the thorough study of this subject, which appealed to the practical disposition of his temperament, was he able to lay the coping-stone upon a series of scientific investigations, the starting-point of which lay in the metaphysics of a remote antiquity, and which opened a deep-cut road through history and philosophy to politics and statistics of the most modern character.

With fierce impatience, he saw superficial and officious charlatans persuading public opinion to tinker with the great social question. He saw honourable, but unscientific and unimportant people attempting to satisfy the crying necessities of the moment with the most inadequate and often the most mischievous measures. Deep sympathy was burning in his heart, and capacities yet undeveloped lay dormant within him. Though a born public speaker, it was now more than ten years since he had spoken. He was provided with all the gifts necessary for dealing with the case before him—a confident bearing, presence of mind, determination, the power of leadership, and a rare capacity for organization. Yet, with a world of unsolved problems before him, he was obliged to fold his hands and rest. He had attempted to arouse those in power by his words, and perhaps for a moment he had hoped to see Prussia stirred to action, and to accomplish by the methods which he had indicated that which he regarded as the task and inevitable object of his country. He had attempted, *flectere superos*, to move those in high places, but his voice had been drowned amid the outcries of many others. His social position and his past precluded for ever any possibility that he might himself attain to power, and thus perform something to forward his own ideas and the welfare of the people. Thus the thought must have continually recurred to him that it might be possible to organize and to prepare for political action the masses who had been excluded from politics for the last twelve years. Much might be done by working from below. As the line in Virgil runs, " If I cannot move the gods, I will stir the lower world to uproar."

Then came the period of political struggle in Prussia. The dispute concerning military organization placed the Government and the Chamber in deadly opposition, and the majority thought that the result would be a war, with absolutism or democracy as the stakes. For a moment Lassalle seems to have hoped that the middle classes would take energetic action through their representatives. In 1861 several members of the Liberal party, in conjunction with the Democratic party, which had reappeared after the election of Waldeck in December, 1860, had coalesced, and formed the Progressive party. Lassalle approached the Committee of this newly-founded party with a request to support his candidature, but his rejection, and the attitude of the Chamber upon the whole matter, finally convinced him that the middle class had ceased to be a force in politics. Their conservative interests inevitably led them to prefer the loss of their freedom rather than to call in the dreaded fourth estate for the protection of it. Thus the working classes once more became a power ; they alone had no reactionary interests, but were by nature the supporters of national freedom. For a Government which found itself in a life-and-death struggle with the middle classes, no other resource remained, in Lassalle's opinion, than to appeal to the workmen as a class. Lassalle was entirely excluded from all immediate influence upon the Government, and therefore upon the development of society in the State. He stood upon the farther side of the great gulf formed by the obscurantism of the petty nobility and revolutionary Radicalism. But Lassalle was by no means excluded from exerting influence indirectly, if he were able to avoid creating unnecessary enemies for himself by attacking the Monarchy in general, or the reigning dynasty, or the Government, or national sentiment, or religion, or hereditary right, and could raise the so-called fourth class from its political impotence, and rouse it to a struggle properly conducted by lawful means, for the purpose of securing social and political equivalence (not equality) with the other classes. This seemed no impossible purpose. No wonder, therefore, if Lassalle, pondering like Achilles in his tent, mentally repeated to himself for nights and days the burden of Virgil's line :

" Flectere si nequeo superos, Acheronta movebo."

PART II

LASSALLE AS AN AGITATOR

IT was as an agitator that Lassalle came forth from his tent. The word seems to have been made to describe him. An agitator in the full sense of the word is a man who has the power to inspire dead masses with the life of his spirit, and simultaneously to vivify and to lead them. The agitator's art is to electrify and to inform with one and the same shock, and for this purpose supreme will is no less necessary than supreme intellectual power. An agitator must be simultaneously an orator, a writer, a guerilla chief, and a general : he must appear, now here, now there, make his influence felt at once over many scattered points, and yet keep all the strings of action well in hand. But for intentional and sudden action of this kind, electrifying by unexpected shocks, Lassalle had ever been destined. What was the chief requirement for such a destiny ? In every case strength of will, and strength of will to him was life. The expression of will at sudden moments, yet continuously, was needed, and this was his calling. I say his calling, for strength of will describes his inmost nature. At the first glance it seems as if Lassalle's life had hitherto shown but scanty traces of those characteristic and unconscious elements in a man's nature which go to compose what is known as his calling. He belongs rather to those who choose than to those who are called. A chance occurrence meets him on his way ; he chooses to pursue it with the whole passion of his soul, and thus makes it an actual necessity for himself, but such occurrences cannot be regarded as necessities imposed by Nature.

It was by chance that Lassalle became a lawyer, in order to help Countess Hatzfeldt, and spent nearly ten years of his life upon a department of learning which was not his profession. For years he devoted himself to the most difficult problems of classical philology, but never made the study of classical antiquity his special province. Upon occasion he was a poet ; he investigated modern and ancient law from the standpoint of theoretical jurisprudence, but in none of these cases do we feel that he was obeying a definite call. He selects an object, and pursues it to the end. But ultimately he has no desire to be a learned jurist, or a dramatic author, or a classical philologist, or a practical solicitor. Hence the observation of F. A. Lange concerning Lassalle is profoundly appropriate, when he says " that the legal matter contained in his chief work has been elaborated with extraordinary ingenuity, but none the less was elaborated merely for the purpose of this particular achievement."[1] It is impossible to characterize in better terms an object arbitrarily chosen by an act of will, as distinguished from objects imposed by definite call ; but, as we have already observed, the truth is that Lassalle's will was in itself a call. Lassalle's acts of will invariably betray something of the agitator in their nature, taking the term " agitator " in its widest and fundamental meaning, and not in the ordinary sense. The concept *agitare*, in contrast with *agere* (to act), implies the constant pursuit of new points of departure—the repeated, restless, energetic and unchecked desire for further action. The agitation which he carried on in public was but the outward sign of the uninterrupted mental agitation in which his will existed. This inward tumult was his life, and became his death. Only in his will did he find full life, as Goethe, by his own confession, found life only in the creations of his intellect, and it was this will which made him invincible in practice—that is to say, when he directed himself to great and important objects ; but, considered abstractly, in other words, when his will subordinated everything to the one object of gaining his desire, his will became his fate, his curse, and eventually his death. This will was his strength as long as it repelled or overpowered the desires, temptations, impulses, or

---

[1] F. A. Lange, " The Labour Problem," 248.

distractions which rose around him, and might prove in the youthful mind so many obstacles to the studies and plans which he proposed. This will became his misfortune when it was stirred to passion by resistance in the course of his last love-affair, and eventually destroyed love, reason, the sense of moderation and proportion, and some of the best impulses of the mind. But for the moment this will raised its own memorial by its restless work of creation.

CHAPTER I

THE years 1862 to 1864, the last two years of Lassalle's life, embrace the whole of that part of his work which has made his name known throughout Europe. He almost seems to have concentrated the exertions of ten years within these two, and what he performed in this space of time is astonishing. Between March, 1862, and June, 1864, he wrote no less than twenty works, three or four of which, both in their extent and their contents, may be considered as books, and most of which, in spite of their brevity and the popularity of their style, contain a wealth of thought, and are written with a scientific regard for logic which very few great books display.[1]

Apart from this, at the same time he delivered numerous speeches, was constantly negotiating with deputations of workmen, emerged from the entanglements of some ten political lawsuits, founded the General Union of German Workmen, carried on an enormous correspondence, and organized the conduct of the Union. He seems to have had some premonition of his approaching death, which led him to put forth almost supernatural exertions.

The most remarkable criticism of Lassalle's general activity

[1] The order of his writings is as follows :

1862. " Herr Julian Schmidt, the Historian of Literature," " Constitutional Theory," " The Workmen's Programme," " Fichte's Philosophy," " Science and the Working Classes," " Criminal Trial, the Court of Second Instance."

1863. " Indirect Taxation," " Might and Right," " Criminal Trial, the Court of Third Instance," " Open Letter of Reply," " The Working-Class Problem," " The Workmen's Handbook," " The Festivals, the Press, the Frankfort Deputies' Meeting," " To the Workmen of Berlin."

1864. " Herr Bastiat-Schultze von Delitzsch ; or, Capital and Labour," " Prosecution for High Treason," " Reply to a Criticism," " Speech at Ronsdorf," " Criminal Trial on June 27."

during this period, which was offered after his death, is the accusation that his work is lacking in originality. This statement is based either upon misunderstanding or upon an inadequate knowledge of the writings which are criticized. During his lifetime his enemies boldly denied the truth of the historical facts and the economic laws which he asserted. After his death they adopted an opposite form of procedure, and repeatedly emphasized " astonishing lack of originality," as characteristic of the evidence which he adduced, the truth of which is now indisputable. But so far as the economic facts are concerned to which Lassalle continually returns in this period of his life, he by no means proclaims himself as their discoverer, but, on the contrary, passionately asserts that they are truths long before recognized by science. Statements which have passed from handbook to handbook for centuries have been made the bases from which his conclusions were drawn, and are treated by his opponents as inventions of his own. He never reproaches his adversaries with the fact that they shut their eyes to his discoveries, but with the incredible ignorance, as he considered it, which they displayed when they accused him of making new and unheard-of assertions (*e.g.*, his arguments concerning indirect taxation).[1] No scholar has yet ventured to complain that the author of the " System of Acquired Rights " was lacking in scientific independence and originality. With regard to questions of pure political economy, or, more correctly, with regard to the great theoretical questions concerning the fundamental points of contact between political economy and law, there is but one earlier thinker of importance, to whom Lassalle, and Marx in an equal degree, owes a distinct debt. This was Rodbertus Jagetzow, whom Adolf Wagner has called the Ricardo of economic Socialism. That the existence of this debt is in no way derogatory to Lassalle as a scientific thinker is obvious, and is in addition stated by Wagner. With regard to the points upon which Rodbertus and Lassalle differed in their conclusions, the

---

[1] " Scientific men have shouted themselves hoarse for centuries, and their cries have at length reached the ears of the Government. One state counsel and one court of justice have remained unmoved by the general outcry, have stopped their ears with wax as Odysseus stopped his ears to the Siren's song, and for this reason I am to go to prison ! How unreasonable ! " (" Indirect Taxation," 95).

above-mentioned distinguished economist, who is still alive, proclaims his preference for the latter.

The theoretical foundations upon which Lassalle's agitation was based are not entirely characteristic of him, though the manner of their development is characteristic enough, but in this respect he claims no honours which were not duly his. His main point of view was that generally adopted by the German democracy, properly so called, of 1848. This democracy, which must not be confused with the opposition constitutional party, called itself sometimes Socialist and sometimes Communist. The manifesto of the Communist party, issued anonymously, but composed by Marx and Engels, and almost a mere translation from Victor Considérant, contains in compressed form and drastic expression the ideas which Lassalle afterwards propounded and developed in a style at once the most definite and the most politically prudent. This old Socialism of 1848 is the basis of the whole of Lassalle's activity, and for reasons of prudence he does not immediately refer his ideas to it, though at the very last—indeed, not until his last speech of all, and then with considerable reluctance— does he admit that he might be called a Socialist. Where he bases his theory upon Marx in one individual point, in his explanation of the nature and formation of capital, and modifies the doctrine of Marx only to a very small extent, he is careful to state the fact with the fullest possible acknowledgment.

Throughout the period when Lassalle was thus active, Marx kept silent, but after Lassalle's death asserted with some bitterness that he had borrowed his own economic doctrines. Marx might have added, without too great a concession to the dead man, that his special characteristic as an agitator consisted, and must consist, not in theoretical elaboration, but in practice, in method and in form. Lassalle himself often asserted the fact that while a theoretical work is all the better in proportion to the completeness with which it deduces the very farthest conclusions from its principles, practical agitation, on the other hand, is powerful in proportion as it is concentrated about one cardinal point upon which all others turn. There is, therefore, no opportunity in this case for displaying originality in point of theory. The art of attaining practical results consists in concentrating one's strength upon one point, looking neither to right nor to left. The only theoretical requirement in such a case is that this point should be theoretically on the highest plane, so that all due conclusions can follow from it in practice and in course of time. The special nature of Lassalle's movement consists in the conjunction of two circumstances—its deep scientific truth and its popular character. As it was easily intelligible, it was able to influence the great majority of the uneducated ; and as it was scientifically profound, it was also able to influence the little band of highly cultured thinkers among the educated classes.[1] Regarded from a literary point of view, the originality of the movement consists in the clarity with which the agitator was able to compress the last and highest results of scientific investigation, and make them comprehensible to audiences in whom no scientific knowledge could be presupposed. In other words, Lassalle was original by reason of the tangible and definite form which he impressed upon every one of his utterances.

[1] " Open Letter of Reply," 31 ; " Capital and Labour," 174, note ; " Trial at Düsseldorf," 21 ; " Trial for High Treason," 33.

CHAPTER II

ANY writer who takes himself seriously has a twofold and difficult problem to solve. He must ask himself, " How can I maintain the creative freshness of my mind day by day, when the facts of life are continually intruding upon my inmost thoughts ? How, again, can I induce some thousand fellow-citizens to whom my person, my life and my interests are absolutely indifferent, to read my prose or—an almost preposterous supposition—to buy my book ?" But this twofold difficulty is as nothing compared with the countless obstacles against which an opposition leader in Lassalle's position is bound to fight.

An author can, within certain limits, promise his reader some amount of pleasure. What prospect can the leader of a new opposition party—an opposition which he must himself create —hold out to his adherents ? Troops can be induced to advance under fire when the happy fields of Italy are promised for their plunder. How can an agitator induce his adherents to advance, when all that can be honourably and certainly promised for their attainment within a reasonable time is the persecution and hatred of those about them, the loss of their money and reputation, passionate complaints of their behaviour in the newspapers, and a thousand obstacles in the way of their future progress, supposing that their progress be not immediately cut short ? The leader of a rising opposition party has no reinforcements upon whom he can rely. Generals and Ministers need not be men of outstanding capacity ; they have but to give their orders, and to direct the strength of the masses where they will. The founder of an opposition party must do the same, without any outward or practical authority, by the mere inward force of his personality, by his power for inspiring enthusiasm and attracting, and by his capacity for convincing and rousing others to fanaticism.

To have courage for oneself is no great art. In hours of depression a man may fold his arms and wait till the crisis is past, or he may allow the waves to pass over his head in the consciousness that he will rise to the surface hereafter, or he may clench his teeth and force a way through difficulties in obstinate silence. But when he may not be silent, must ever be speaking and giving counsel and consolation, and pointing the way for others, the case is very different. Very different is the necessity of finding courage for twenty others who lose their heads and their nerve at every moment, and ask their leader to inspire them with that confidence in a fortunate issue which he does not himself feel. He may show no sign of weariness, unless he is prepared to see the whole band fling themselves down and remain lying in the road. Tired to death is the burden of Lassalle's closing letters to his friends.

Ten or fifteen letters must be answered daily, apart from letters which can be destroyed when read. At every post the bell rings, and a bundle of letters is brought in ; more drudgery, more questions, fresh matters which must be considered and decided on the moment—announcements of new disasters.

With the letters come the newspapers ; fresh attacks, mis-representations, accusations, insults from anonymous and known writers. The hostile Press—and at the outset the whole Press is necessarily hostile—utters its cries of fury morning and evening ; and even if this uproar frightens no man, at any rate it works unconsciously upon the nervous system. Lassalle may indeed write : " Such a daily concert of bankrupt musicians I never heard before ; I could die of laughing." Whether a man dies of laughing or frets himself ill is a matter of indifference, if the last word in either case spells illness or death. It is indeed ridiculous when such a writer as Max Wirth discovers that the law of wages to which Lassalle appeals " is a very antiquated standpoint "; when a Faucher discovers that Lassalle knows nothing whatever of political economy ; when

the Workmen's Union of Nuremberg declares that he is a
"paid tool of the reaction"; or when Schultze writes his
"piteous answer." But what does it profit the subject of
these remarks, if no one but himself can appreciate the
humour of the situation, and if the public regard the cater-
wauling of newspapers as the voice of morality and true
science ?

Then the agitator feels the necessity for dealing some great
blow, and the need of victory becomes for him the firm consciousness which produces victory. In such a frame of mind
Lassalle writes to Rodbertus, after determining to deliver a
speech in Frankfort : " You are quite right in saying that
public disputations of this kind produce no result, but upon
this occasion I need a disputation. The Berlin Press has been
turning the recent workmen's comedy here to account, and as
we have no organ in which we can express ourselves, I feel the
necessity for some display which will force the middle-class
Press to serve my purpose ; so I must go, and I *must* be triumphant. I feel the want of a triumph. The people there
are unanimously against me, and have only invited me out of
politeness, but I shall stake everything upon this throw, and
the old war-horse will shake his revolutionary mane. Things
will be bad if I do not conquer. The general knowledge of
the fact that these unions are collectively against us will
increase the triumph of our victory, and will deprive defeat
of its sting, if defeat should come to pass."

In Frankfort he was triumphant, but hundreds of triumphs
of a very different character were necessary, for disappointment
followed disappointment. Then, according to the law of consciousness, the everlasting illusions of good fortune and success,
of the influence which he exercised, and of the support which he
found, rose afresh before his mind. The following words are
from an unpublished letter, and reproduce the feverish haste
and pressure in which the agitator's life was passed :

" DEAR M.,
" Thank you for your letter. You will receive herewith
for distribution gratis three hundred copies of my address (to
the workers of Berlin). It has an enormous effect here, and

we think it likely to bring over the Berlin workers in a body. *At last* I am making way here ; at last !

" As regards the other pamphlets, you may distribute anything gratis that you have from my pen ; the rest do not belong to me, but to the publisher or to the Union.

" Now a point of the greatest importance. We *absolutely must* have a plenipotentiary in Königsberg. This is most important. Wherever merely one such official is stationed, a community rises automatically. Experience has shown this to be true everywhere ; so appoint master-mason Schmidt to be our plenipotentiary in Königsberg. Write him an *urgent* and imperative letter, representing his acceptance of the post as a duty incumbent upon him and demanding an immediate statement of his choice, and send me within the next week official notice that you have appointed Schmidt as plenipotentiary for Königsberg.

" In a week I shall be publishing the recent new appointments which I have proposed for the different parts of Germany, and I should be *extremely glad* if I were able to announce at the same time the appointment carried out by you to Königsberg.

" This would make a very good impression. I count unconditionally upon your readiness to fulfil my desire at the right time."

The italicizing of words here betrays passionate emphasis. We feel the words trembling on his lips, " I demand, I order, I will endure no refusal." We feel that he is then forced to remember that he can only request, and we see how he compensates for this restriction by making his request an imperative demand.

The addressee to whom this letter was sent writes to me : " You will see from this letter under what illusions Lassalle still laboured in October, 1863, as regards the strength of the movement which he had aroused among the working classes. I was unable to fulfil the desires expressed in his letter, because in Königsberg, as in the whole province of Prussia, scarce a man was to be found with any adequate knowledge of the question or any readiness to take part in the agitation."

And yet he did not lose courage. Amid all these disappoint-
ments and this disquietude, he went on preparing his speeches
—often out of humour, weary, hoarse, and overstrained, obliged
to show himself in public and make a display of invincible
power. He must concentrate his mind with his faculties undisturbed and unimpaired by the daily waste of time expended
upon current business, direct his thoughts to a rough and
surging assembly of partly hostile hearers, and elaborate in his
study the phrase that can strike home and arouse enthusiasm—
the effective and convincing argument, the immemorable
oratorical form.

CHAPTER III

A CONSIDERATION of the agitation in its outward form implies an estimate of Lassalle as an orator.

It might be thought that he was not specially gifted by Nature for this purpose, and that his best qualification was his very unusual memory. He told one of my acquaintarces that in his youth he knew the whole of the " Iliad " and " Odyssey " by heart, and he delivered his long lectures, which were never improvised, word for word as he had written them, without a manuscript before him. In ordinary conversation his voice was high and shrill, and he spoke with a lisp ; but as soon as he appeared in public these defects disappeared, and his voice sounded strong and attractive. His literary work had trained him for oratory, and seems, indeed, to be the best of schools for this purpose. In ancient Rome it was generally asserted that oratorical readiness could only be gained by speaking ; but Cicero, whose authority is indisputable in all that concerns eloquence, most vigorously attacks this view (" De Oratore," i. 33). " It might as well be said," Crassus asserts in Cicero's dialogue, " that the power of speaking badly would be most easily attained by bad speaking. No," he continues, " the great point is to write as much as possible. Writing is the best school and the best means of education for the coming orator." I believe this to be the case when it is necessary to make a speech which can afterwards be read with profit. If the speech is to make but a momentary impression, previous literary training is hardly required. Gambetta's speeches, for instance, which exerted so powerful an influence, owing to the fiery nature of his temperament, and the beauty of his voice, make no great impression when they are read. They provide a momentary solution of the question at issue, but are far too lacking in depth of thought to rivet attention for any lengthy period, nor is their expression stamped by any definite literary character. The wide point of view from which all questions are regarded, the keenness and novelty of his ideas, the great foundation of scholarship suspected by the hearer, but not displayed by the orator, together with the brevity and strength of his style, give the best of Lassalle's speeches permanent literary value.

Ancient writers—for instance, Quintilian—divided eloquence into the Asiatic and Attic styles, or the flowery and the dry styles. If we adopt this principle, Lassalle's eloquence undoubtedly belongs to the dry and nervous style. But in one single and important point Lassalle is very far from the Attic style, and this is his preference for superlatives. The delight with which he strides along the highest summits of the adjectival forms is incredible, as also is the enthusiasm with which he devises and heaps together such expressions as " the immense," " the horrible," " the gigantic." In this one instance the admirable phrase of Metternich, " the superlative is the mark of fools," is not confirmed ; but such heavy artillery remains no less unwieldy, even when worked by a man of talent. The German author who has studied Ferdinand Lassalle with deeper intelligence than anyone else, uttered in my presence the sharp criticism of him : " He had no taste at all." This is somewhat exaggerated, but it can justly be said that his taste was very uncertain. From French literature he learned astonishingly little, though considerable parts of it must have been known to him. I have already mentioned that he did not shrink in his drama from making Ulrich von Hutten describe his own greatness in the purest bombast. When he speaks of the considerations which forbade him to unite the life of a beloved woman with his own uncertain and perilous existence, he speaks as if he could shatter the earth in pieces, and uses such expressions as :

When in my wild career athwart this globe
Of earth I crash confounded, hurtling wide
In manifold disruption.

And again, when he describes his greatness and his ill-fortune, he says :

> Then in a Baltic haven I embarked ;
> The vessel could not bear me and the planks
> Beneath my feet did part incontinent.

This is rhodomontade in utter lack of taste. While he was thus entirely wanting in a sense of humour, his speeches do not, at any rate, reach such points of exaggeration as we find in his poetry ; but it happens occasionally that the metaphors by which he attempts to attract the attention of his hearers are ridiculous enough to arouse laughter. In his first speech before the Court of Assizes he speaks of the " Erinnys of the murdered basis of right." In " Science and the Working Classes " he says : " The proud and lofty tree of scientific knowledge has been transmitted from age to age with holy reverence."[1] The murder of a legal basis and the transmission of the tree of knowledge are pictures somewhat too highly coloured ; but a masterly painting is not ruined because a line here or there is out of drawing.

I said that Lassalle's style was of the dry type ; the metaphors are therefore rare and short. The use which he makes of them is, generally speaking, all the more remarkable.

Lassalle never uses metaphor for purely decorative purposes. His metaphors always contain a logical explanation of the true nature of the matter at issue, and are therefore logical continuations of his arguments, while they serve at the same time to crystallize his ideas, and to arouse the enthusiasm of his hearers. For instance, in his speech before the Court of Assizes, Lassalle was obliged to deal with one difficult point : he had appealed for armed defence of the overthrown Constitution, which, among other things, had contained provisions for universal suffrage. He proved that the Government, by the *coup d'état*, had outraged and scorned the manifest desires of the people ; but the people, by taking part in a new election conducted upon the law of December 6, which provided for the three classes of electors, recognized the Constitution that

---

[1] " The Erinnys of murdered legal right. . . . But that which has grown more powerful than them all . . . transmitted from age to age with holy reverence, is the proud and lofty tree of scientific knowledge " (" Science and the Workmen," 3).

had been forced upon it, and to this fact the Government appealed.

Lassalle refutes this assertion : " On what erroneous conclusions are these attempts based which would justify the foolish idea that because the people voted to procure means of expression for themselves, and to gain champions by whose help they might recover the freedom of which they had been robbed, they, by this very action, have recognized the robbery as legal? I will take the first example, gentlemen, which occurs to me. Supposing a robber, while I am asleep, snatches from my side a precious Damascus blade, and leaves me his clumsy club in its place : when I start up and seize the club for the purpose of pursuing him and recovering my property, have I, by the act of using the club, admitted the justice of its exchange for my Damascus sword ?"

Whether this analogy was really the first that came to hand, or whether it was elaborated by careful thought, I regard it in any case as a model of what a simile should be. The picture by no means interrupts the course of the description, and not only illuminates the business under discussion, but also removes a difficulty which could only have been explained away by a much longer political argument in logical form. It is no mere rhetorical decoration, but gives vigour to the speech.

On some occasions Lassalle succeeded in so compressing his thoughts in a simile of this kind that it passed from mouth to mouth as representing the quintessence of his ideas. For instance, in his " Workmen's Programme " he develops the connection between the ideas of the working classes and of the time, and thus exclaims : " The high honour in the history of the world which this determination implies (the desire to become the ruling class) must claim all your thoughts ; not for you are the vices of the oppressed, or the idle distractions of the thoughtless, or even the harmless carelessness of the unimportant ; you are the rock upon which the church of the present is to be built." Similarly, he characterizes the political philosophy of the Manchester school in realistic fashion : " Thus the middle class conceives the moral object of the State. This object consists simply and solely in securing the personal freedom of the individual and his property. This is the night-watchman theory, gentlemen, for this conception can regard the State only under the form of a night-watchman whose duties are confined to preventing burglary and theft."

In Cicero's times (De Oratore, ii. 28) the orator's task was formulated as follows : it was threefold—the orator must instruct his hearers, win their sympathy, and urge them to action. " To win their sympathy," says Cicero, " a man's personality must be attractive "; and he adds, with some childishness, " the orator will not find this difficult if he is an honourable man." He need only consider the views and inclinations of his hearers. We know to what resources the orator in ancient times turned, in order to win the public to his point of view, and we know with what similar sentimentalities —the production of children in tears, etc.—our juries can be moved at the present day.

Lassalle, when confronted with his judges, not only despised such surreptitious methods of securing their sympathy, but invariably adopted so proud and unbending an attitude that one can only suppose him to have been desirous of gaining the approval of those upon whom his fate depended, by means of the calmness and greatness of heart which he displayed in the face of his judgment. I have given examples of his power of crystallizing his thoughts and informing his audience by means of metaphor. Here is an instance of another kind, when he attempts to win approval with the help of metaphor : " Upon a man," he says, " such as I am, who has devoted his life to science and the working classes, even the condemnation with which he may chance to meet will produce no other effect than the bursting of a test-tube would make upon a chemist absorbed in his scientific experiments. With a slight frown at the difficulties which the properties of matter raise in his path, he will continue his investigations and his work as soon as he has cleared away the damage. But for the sake of the nation and its honour, for the sake of science and its dignity, for the sake of the country and its legal freedom, Mr. President and Councillors, I call upon you to pronounce for my liberation."

Finally, when Lassalle is not concerned with instructing or attracting his hearers, but with urging them to action, his style and his metaphors become entirely martial. His preference for similes drawn from battle and war is preponderant. In one place he concludes :

" In this case let us not be carried away by conciliatory sentimentalism, gentlemen ; you have now seen by fully adequate experience what the old absolutism is. Let us, then, have no fresh compromise with it, but overthrow it with our thumbs in its eyes and our knees upon its breast." In another place he appeals to the working classes of Berlin to join his union, and his summons is couched in the style of a bulletin.

" The most important centres of Germany have been won ; Leipsic and the manufacturing districts of Saxony are for us ; Hamburg and Frankfort-on-Maine are marching under our banner ; the Prussian Rhine Provinces are advancing at the charge. Reinforced by Berlin, the movement will be irresistible. Will you, workmen of Berlin, take upon yourselves the responsibility of delaying by your attitude this great German movement and this triumph of your common cause ? Will you, workmen of the capital, whose duty it is to take the lead, bear the reproach of being the last to join the movement ?"

Such expressions as " smashing blows," " review of the troops," " battalions," " the iron hand," " the iron grip," " iron law," and others of the kind, are metaphorical expressions which constantly recur in his speeches. He was invited by the Progressive party to speak before their own workmen's union in Frankfort, and succeeded in two successve speeches in winning over an audience originally hostile. He relates his success as follows : " I defeated the men of progress in a two days' conflict with the troops which they had themselves brought against me." When he was accused of attempts to begin a revolution, he describes the revolution which he was not desirous of producing, but which he was certain would arrive, by the following metaphor : " The revolution may occur in all legal form, and with all the blessings of peace, if the government is wise enough to resolve upon its introduction in proper time, or it will break upon us, within a period unknown to me, with all the convulsions of force, with hair wildly streaming and iron sandals upon its feet."

The chief object of Lassalle's warlike outbursts and of his most impetuous attacks is that organ which is both the servant and the master of the middle classes at the present day—the Press. Anyone who studies his style when he " calls for action "—to use the phrase of the ancients—must be particularly impressed by his war against the newspapers. It extends through almost all his writings. As an instance of the tone and style of Lassalle's compelling rhetoric, I will quote a few sentences from one of his most important pamphlets upon this subject : " The series of personal concessions which the journalists have made to the Government, purely in the interests of their own business, naturally could not be granted as concessions by those concerned. . . . Thus, the only alternative was to represent these concessions to the public as so many new points of view which the public mind should adopt, and to impose them upon newspaper readers by representing them as developments and salutary compromises in the interests of the national welfare. Thus it was possible to emasculate and to dilute the national spirit to the point at which the continuance of the lucrative newspaper business could be guaranteed. . . . If anyone wishes to earn money, let him manufacture cotton or cloth, or gamble on the Stock Exchange ; but daily to inject spiritual death into the nation from a thousand syringes for the sake of some contemptible gain is the most criminal proceeding of which I can conceive. . . . Much as I regret it, I have no hesitation in telling you that if we do not shortly see a complete transformation of our daily Press, and if this plague of newspapers rages for another fifty years in its present form, our national spirit will be destroyed and brought even to the dust. The reason is easily intelligible : thousands of journalists, the modern teachers of the people, with their countless voices, are daily inoculating the nation with their crass ignorance, their lack of conscientiousness, their insensate hatred of everything true and great in politics, art, and science ; and the nation, in credulous confidence, stretches out its hands for this poison, under the impression that it is deriving intellectual nutriment from this source. Under such conditions, the national spirit must be ruined, were it thrice as noble as it is. Not even the most highly gifted people in the world, not even

the Greeks, could have survived the influence of such a Press.
. . . I have explained that the corruption of the Press is a
necessary consequence of the fact that, under the pretext of
championing intellectual interests, it is steadily becoming a
commercial speculation in virtue of the system of advertise-
ment. The problem is thus simple enough, and merely consists in separating these two things, which have no connection
with one another. In so far as the Press represents the interests of the national life, it may be compared with the pulpit
orator or the schoolmaster. In so far as it exists to publish
advertisements, it is but the town crier or the public bell-
man, announcing to the public with its countless voices where
a watchchain has been lost, where the best tobacco or the best
malt extract is to be procured. The preacher has nothing to do
with the town crier, and the union of these two functions is a
sad miscarriage. In a Social Democratic State a law must
therefore be passed forbidding newspapers to publish any
advertisements, and confining advertisements exclusively and
solely to the official papers published by the State or community. . . . Grasp firmly and with glowing enthusiasm the
solution which I offer you—scorn and hatred, death and destruction to the ignorant Press ! It is a bold solution, propounded by one man against the thousand-handed institution
of the Press, against which even Kings have fought in vain ;
but as truly as you hang with eager passion upon my words,
and as truly as my heart trembles with pure enthusiasm while
its feelings overflow to yours, so truly am I penetrated with the
certainty that the moment will come when we shall launch the
thunderbolt which will whelm this Press in everlasting night."

I am far from regarding the methods which Lassalle recom-
mended to check the corruptions of the Press as either effective
or practicable, but the scorn which boiled within Lassalle like
molten bronze is here poured out, and has assumed in cooling
the strongest form of words.

I said that although Lassalle was a born orator, he developed
his power of using the spoken word by perfecting his mastery
of the written word. Sparklingly eloquent as he was in society,
the gift of extempore speech was apparently denied to him, nor
did he ever attempt to acquire it. At the same time, he was

so good a speaker that his oratory seemed to be the result of momentary inspiration, while he was so unconstrained that if he was interrupted or obliged to answer an unexpected question, he was able to combine the interruption of the moment in the speech he had prepared with such dexterity that no transition point is perceptible. Cicero says of this gift : " A man who proceeds to the art of oratory after much practice in writing has this advantage—that even when he speaks unprepared, what he says will sound as though it had been written. . . . Even as a vessel in rapid movement continues its progress when the rowers cease their efforts, so, too, in the stream of oratory, when written matter comes to an end, the spoken word retains its impetus, and the speech speeds forward along the path of the written matter." A few examples of Lassalle's presence of mind under these conditions may now be given.

In his speech in his defence (January 15, 1863) he had demonstrated that every point in the accusation was based upon ignorance and lack of intelligence. He exclaims : " How can I help the literary incompetency of the counsel for the State ? How can I be responsible for his lack of acquaintance with every department of progress at the present time—progress already recognized and catalogued by science ? Am I to be the scientific whipping boy of the counsel for the State ?"

The counsel now interrupted Lassalle's speech, and entered a most vigorous demand that he should be refused a further hearing, as this outburst " was the culmination of his mockery of the State counsel." He concluded : " I therefore demand, referring to Article 134 and the supplementary law of May 3, 1852, that the accused should be refused a further hearing, and that he should be removed from the court if he should continue further to reply." (Sensation.)

The President. " The accused is accordingly refused a further hearing, and any further expressions on his part are therefore inadmissible."

The Accused (quickly). " Mr. President, upon this point I must ask for an expression of opinion by the whole court. I demand such an expression, and ask that I should be allowed to speak in justification of this demand."

Counsel. " I must protest against any further speaking by the accused, as the President has already deprived him of a hearing."

The Accused. " This is a confusion of ideas. I have been refused a hearing on the main point ; I have demanded a resolution by the whole court on this question, and the court cannot decide upon so important a matter without first hearing what I have to say about it."

The President. " The accused may speak upon the question whether he is to have a hearing or not."

Counsel. " Then I will at least point out that the accused cannot be heard upon any other subject."

The Accused. " You need feel no anxiety. I will confine myself to the point."

He then proceeded to explain what in any case was obvious, that he could not be said to have insulted anyone by calling himself a scientific whipping boy, and that anyone to whom, for instance, an opponent in a literary quarrel exclaimed, " Am I your scientific whipping boy ?" would be dismissed from any court if he attempted to bring an action for libel against his opponent. Lassalle then proceeds immediately and undisturbed to continue his interrupted speech in his defence.[1] The situation is worthy of Shakespeare. One might almost be reading the scene in which Mr. Justice Shallow holds his Court in " Henry IV."

But the most amusing and instructive instance of Lassalle's gift of rising to the occasion which I can find is the following : in the speech which he delivered at Frankfort-on-Maine at the invitation of his opponents, he demonstrated that one of the literary men who was opposing him had asserted in some book of very moderate merit precisely the statements which he now disputed when they were brought forward by Lassalle.

Lassalle. " You see, gentlemen, a hired workman is, in my opinion, a very honourable character, but a hired writer is something very different." (Cries of " Order !" Great uproar. " Let him speak !" " Put the question !" " No, let him speak !")

The President. " I must ask the speaker, once for all, to avoid personal remarks. On this occasion he has been personal."

---

[1] " Science and the Workmen," 43 ; " Criminal Trial," part ii., 15 *et seq.*

Lassalle. " This is quite a new experience for me, and the scene that has just taken place shows the point that we have reached. Gentlemen, I will not be deterred from open expression of my opinions. (Loud cheers.) Apart from this, I ask you to notice one fact : I have uttered no criticism of anybody in particular, but have merely enounced a general statement. I did not say that Herr Max Wirth was a writer for hire ; no one can have heard anything of the kind ; I appeal to the reporters. . . . The President, therefore, has no right to censure the intention of my words." (Cheers from the hall and galleries, and cries of " Stop !" and " Go on!")

The President. " Are you not aware, gentlemen, that this is a meeting upon which the eyes of half Germany are turned ? Pray do not let it be said that this assembly could not maintain order, because the working class are lacking in Parliamentary tact. I interrupted Herr Lassalle because he used the phrase ' writer for hire ' in connection with Herr Max Wirth ; no one can doubt that fact, although that was perhaps not the phraseology which he used. I am therefore within my right in calling the attention of the speaker to the necessity of avoiding anything of the kind in future."

Lassalle. " I must again remind the President that he may object to unparliamentary expressions, but not to the sense of my speech. Freedom of speech depends entirely upon the possibility of indicating a point apart from expressing it directly—of saying what one pleases, provided Parliamentary language is used. Both freedom of speech and the capacity of the orator are based upon this point. Otherwise, suppose you feel indignation at anything or any man, how do you propose to communicate your feelings to others ? (Loud cheers from the hall and galleries.) I have thus demonstrated that Herr Wirth in his work has stated precisely what I have stated. Possibly in the same book, which I have not read, other passages may occur in which he has stated the opposite. . . . You may wonder how I have been able, as I have not read the book, to point to the crucial passages. On this matter I owe you an explanation. When the book appeared, a copy reached me, but after running through a few pages I discovered that it was an unoriginal compilation, and threw the book aside, as I have no time to waste over worthless compilations of the kind ; but on the present occasion a friend (it was Rodbertus) sent me the book and pointed out that passage. I will make a further observation in reference to the President's objection to my mode of expression. I may use unqualified language, but in that case I am not personal, for I am keeping to my argument throughout. I merely show a lack of refinement, and that is quite a different matter. Unrefined I must, can, and should be, as I will prove to you. Every representative of a great cause must use unrefined methods against all who intervene with falsehoods between him and his great object, and I am resolved to overthrow with the smashing blows of intellect those who come between you and me with falsehoods. In your interests, therefore, I must be unrefined, and I both may and should be so ; for if Herr Max Wirth, who will afterwards have an opportunity of replying to me, cared to show as little refinement towards me, there would, in any case, be an enormous difference between what he says and what I say. For instance, if he wished to call me an unoriginal compiler, as I have called him, he would merely arouse enormous laughter from every scholar who knows me. But when I use the term to him, every expert knows how enormously true it is, and therefore my words come upon his head with crushing force." (Loud applause.)

This passage—in which, by the way, the word " enormous " occurs three times in succession—seems to me a real model of rhetorical vigour and readiness. The special talent of the orator is apparent, not in the veiled personal attack (and the veil here is extremely transparent), though the definition which Lassalle here gave bases the orator's capacity upon his power of veiling his direct attack, but in the manner in which he repels an attempt to reprimand him. His style contains none of those characteristics peculiar to authors who are forced to keep themselves strictly in hand under the pressure either of a Government or of hostile feeling. Such writers appeal chiefly to the power of imagination, which is hampered by direct expression, but rather stimulated by veiled suggestion. The reader who knows the caution which the author is obliged to observe, and the little which he dare express of his real and deepest meaning, reads attentively, and a secret bond of sympathy is formed between him and the author. The one conceals his meaning and the other his comprehension. None of these characteristics can properly be attributed to Lassalle, who utters his meaning straightforwardly and without reserve, up to the point at which he considers the laws against incitement to rebellion or high treason might become applicable. He appeals, in other words, not to the imagination, but to the will and energy of his hearers.

We have given examples of his style and tone, and it is now worth while to consider his speeches on their artistic side, and to glance at their logical construction. The orators of antiquity taught that the supreme law governing the arrangement of matter and argument was to omit no opportunity of making a deep impression. We might say that if this law had never previously been observed, Lassalle would have been credited with its discovery, for he had a special capacity for grasping the opportunity with unusual readiness, and of making it his own. The ancients also said that the first and most important point of all in a speech was to establish the question at issue, *to define the facts of the case, and to give them their true names.* In this respect Lassalle is one of the greatest masters that ever lived. The capacity here required is practical common sense, and in the case of a political orator the term implies political insight. Political insight, in my opinion, may be defined as an *eye for the centre of gravity.* To see the position of this point among conflicting political forces is the *first* condition under which interference becomes possible ; and political capacity, in accordance with this definition, may be further defined as the power of *changing* this centre of gravity. The power of seeing the means by which such a change can be made is the *second* condition under which political action can become effective. The *third* and last condition is that a man should have the means within his power, and understand how to use them.

In full harmony with Lassalle's peculiarity of style, his habit of direct utterance, is his characteristic realism, which induces him to express and to emphasize the bare facts of the case on every occasion. The real and logical point of departure in his conduct of the agitation consists in the revelation and destruction of false appearances. As an instance, I will choose the speech in which Lassalle exalts his own practice to the dignity of political theory. He had been involved in some trouble by a pamphlet in which he asserted that constitutional problems are ultimately and invariably problems of political power. Disseminated during the constitutional conflicts of 1862, the pamphlet had aroused special excitement in the governmental camp. The Minister of War disapproved of it, though in the same breath he uttered its leading ideas ; the President of the Ministry, Herr von Bismarck, made use of expressions which led directly to Lassalle's assertions ; the reactionary *Kreuzzeitung* devoted a leading article to the pamphlet, which it termed in its own dialect, " A Speech delivered by a Revolutionary Jew of whom much has been formerly heard, who has shown a Profound Instinct for hitting the Nail on the Head." In a following pamphlet (" What Now ?") Lassalle considered the means at the disposal of the Chamber for enforcing its will in the face of so determined and so powerful a Government, and showed that the most natural means, a general refusal of taxation, would be quite ineffective. In England, where the army is of secondary importance, the real elements of power are in the hands of the nation. Relying upon this fact, men might refuse, and refuse unpunished, to pay their taxes, and such methods would inevitably produce a result ; but they would be ineffectual in Prussia, where no one would venture to execute the threat. Such a resolution on the part of the Chamber would therefore be nothing more than a beating of the air. What, then, is to be done ? Lassalle considers that there is but one means, as simple as it is infallible, which he defines as follows : " to state the facts." This is the means which he himself employed throughout his career as an agitator. In his opinion, it is the most powerful form of political leverage. As Fichte has shown, it was one of the favourite methods of the great Napoleon, and in our own days has been one of the means most constantly used by Bismarck. Lassalle examines its application to the given case, and shows that the result would be to make absolutism impossible. The prevailing power in Prussia at that time was absolutism,

ostensibly limited by a constitution. Why, then, did absolutism exist in so hypocritical a form ? Because the counter-
revolution after 1848, wherever it reintroduced the arbitrary
system of government, considered that some concession was
advisable to the spirit of the times—in other words, to the
unorganized power of the people. Even Napoleon III. after
the *coup d'état* conceded a chamber elected by the people ;
even Austria, which had originally declared the Constitution
of 1849 invalid, restored the Constitution on its own initiative. Hence Lassalle concludes that Prussia could not afford
to do without a Constitution, in view of the power of its
middle-class. If, therefore, the Government persisted in
their presumption, the great means of bringing compulsion
to bear was to renounce all such outward forms, and this
result, thinks Lassalle, might be secured if the Chamber would
only " state the facts." Supposing, then, that the Prussian
Chamber was to declare : " In view of the fact that the
Government is incurring expenses on its own responsibility
which the Chamber has declined to approve ; and in view of
the fact that the Government has even declared its intention
of continuing in this course ; considering, further, that under
these circumstances it is unworthy of the representatives of
the nation to support the Government in maintaining an outward show of constitutional form—the Chamber resolves to
suspend its sittings for an indefinite period until the Government intimates that it has the approval of the Chamber for
its expenditure." In this case the Government would be
forced to decide either to give way or formally to appear
before the world as that which it really was—a bare absolutism.
Lassalle explains that the Government neither can nor will
adopt the latter alternative. It cannot, because, in Talley-
rand's phrase, " you can do anything with bayonets except
sit on them." Bayonets cannot provide a solid and permanent foundation. Again, the Government will be unwilling
to adopt the latter alternative, for, requiring as it does so
great an annual sum, and incessantly putting its hand into
the pocket of every citizen, it must at least maintain an outward show of possessing every citizen's approval. The
Government would also be unwilling, because in every foreign

dispute it would expose itself to the most insolent and intolerable insults on the part of the other Powers, as a Government which was in open and constant antagonism with its own nation, and therefore unable to hide its weakness from anybody.

As we know, the Progressive party at that time made no attempt to use the means which Lassalle had indicated. Only one member of the Prussian House of Deputies—Martiny, who is now a distinguished advocate in Dantzig—considered that he could best serve his own honour and the dignity of his party by resigning his seat, after delivering a detailed and carefully argued proposal, to the effect that the House should suspend its sittings until the Government recognized its obligation to administer the financial affairs of the State only upon the basis of a budget legally adopted, and ceased to spend money upon objects to which the House refused consent. I have in my possession a printed copy of Martiny's proposal, and also the manuscript of it. The latter is a very interesting document, as Lassalle carefully corrected it, and introduced alterations in blue pencil to strengthen the expression and to emphasize the decisive arguments. Compare, for instance :

MARTINY.	LASSALLE.
Considering that the House, if it continues its functions under such conditions, would not only be exposed to the insult to its honour and dignity implied in the disregard shown to its rights, but would also further the openly expressed intentions of the Government, to make the present constitutional impotency of the House an element of constitutional practice, and so to make the House a party to the breach of the constitution of the country. . . .	Considering that the House, if it continues its functions under such conditions, would expose its rights to the disregard of the Government, and its honour and dignity, together with that of the nation, to the insult which such disregard implies ; considering, further, that this House would simply promote the openly expressed intention of the Government to make its present constitutional impotence an element of constitutional practice, and would support the continuance of Absolutism *under an outward show* of Constitutionalism, and would thus become a party to the breach of the national Constitution. . . .

Naturally, the resignation of one individual produced a moral, but no political, effect. Whether Germany would have been advantaged if this example had been followed, is a question which I shall not attempt to decide. The great army, over the approval of which the parties were quarrelling, was necessary for the accomplishment of Bismarck's comprehensive plans. At the same time, a bolder attitude on the part of the House would have forced him to communicate his intentions to the party leaders, and would have inspired him with a useful respect for the Liberal party in future. No wonder that no indications of such respect are to be found in him afterwards ! The only point now at issue is, whether the means proposed by Lassalle would have been effective, and what their effect in general would be. For my part, I have approved this practice ever since I have been able to think at all. I have always asserted that this simple method, which is within the power of anybody—the method of calling the facts of a case by their proper names—is the only means by which helpless Right can attain to Might. When intellectual Might is impotent, but at the same time is recognized, as it is in all so-called civilized countries, Might,as such, is invariably based upon some outward show or lie, and the most certain method, though it be lengthy, of overcoming brutal Might will always consist in producing such revelations as will oblige Might openly to admit the real nature of its intentions. The important point is to undermine it precisely where it assumes the outward appearance of an intellectual force.

However, the only point with which we are concerned is the fact that this means was the means of Lassalle's choice, and that this standpoint of his, " Down with appearances," is the logical and actual foundation of all his speeches and of the whole of his agitation. In every case these appearances can be more definitely defined—*e.g.*, the pretence that Right and not Might is predominant ; that the German middle-classes can seriously be called democratic ; that indirect taxation is chiefly paid by the property-owning class ; that the position of one particular class has improved in relation to that of others, because it has improved when compared with its position in previous centuries, etc. Similarly, the pretence in question may receive a more definite name, such as " apparent freedom of action," " apparent liberty of thought," " apparent prosperity," or anything else of the kind. Lassalle's invariable point of departure when embarking upon a speech in opposition is ever to rend the veil of outward show.

I regard this point of departure as very happily adopted. I think with Lassalle that apparent freedom is most poisonously destructive to real freedom, and that nothing can be so emasculating and so soporific, for the simple reason that the good object which ought to be attained seems to have been already attained ; consequently, all those whose duty it would have been to struggle on behalf of this purpose at once relapse into complete self-satisfaction. On the other hand, if pseudo-freedom is forced to reveal itself as such, and to display its many consequences inimical to freedom, there is some prospect of attaining the main object at issue in all intellectual struggles. The indifferent may be won over, and as many minds as possible may be induced to feel sympathy with the oppression which others experience. But this can only be done if people like Lassalle, in contrast to the Progressive party, decline to be intimidated by the threats of opponents, and steadily defy them until they are forced either to put their threats into practice—a proceeding which will affect many more men than the one individual concerned, and will disperse the halo of apparent freedom which encircles the head of the persecutor—or until they are forced to give way, whatever their reluctance, in order to retain their fictitious halo.[1] This is a means which, naturally, can lead only those to ultimate victory who are in the right ; for if people seek martyrdom with the errors of centuries upon their side, with the object of appealing to the sympathy of the thoughtless multitude—a policy boldly and cleverly followed in Prussia and Switzerland by the Catholic clergy— their prospects of ultimate victory are not increased. Every falsehood has its martyrs and its apostles, but the assertion of " that which is not," whatever its boldness or audacity, is in the long run the most hopeless policy in the world.

We have thus seen that, in the strictest sense of the word, Lassalle's point of departure was what Cicero calls the decisive point of departure for an orator—to define his facts and give them their true names. Upon this principle the logical construction of his speeches rests, which must be studied in their

---

[1] " What Now ?" and " The Festivals, the Press," etc., 11.

argumentation. I may be allowed one example as an illustration, and will choose his speech upon indirect taxation.

He was accused of rousing the lower classes to hatred and
contempt of the well-to-do, by his assertions upon the
subject of indirect taxation, which he stated were chiefly
paid by the poor. With secure mastery of an important
scientific subject he collects in fifty pages the statements
of great economists, together with statistics confirming the
correctness of his assertions and even the mildness of their
expression. He proves how much greater is the prevailing
extent of poverty than is generally supposed.

" Thus we have 11,400 persons in the whole State of seventeen millions with an income of more than 2,000 thalers, and
44,400 persons (including the 11,400 just mentioned) in the
whole State with an income of over 1,000 thalers. Such is
the condition of our social balance-sheet.

" You would hardly have believed this, gentlemen, or have
regarded it as possible, if the facts were not to be found in
official publications. It is a ridiculously small handful of
people with their families, who fill the theatres, the concert-
halls, the parties, the balls, the clubs, the restaurants and the
wine-shops in every town, and by reason of their ubiquity
assume the appearance of an extraordinary number. They
think and speak only of themselves, imagine themselves to be
the world, and, by controlling all the newspapers and establishments where public opinion is manufactured, they induce
everyone else to share their beliefs and to be persuaded that
these 11,000 or 44,000 are really the world.

" And beneath this scanty handful of people, who alone
live and move, speak, write, perorate, realize and secure their
own interests, and persuade themselves that they pay the
taxes—beneath this handful of men writhe in silent, inexpressible misery the swarming numbers of the poor, the
seventeen millions who produce everything that makes life
tolerable for us, make possible for us the indispensable condition of moral existence, the existence of the State, fight its
battles, pay its taxes, but has no one to think of them or to
represent them.

" Justice, therefore, for this class, gentlemen, and do not

gag the men, in any case sufficiently isolated, who take up the cudgels on their behalf." [1]

Lassalle has thus shown that his assertions concerning indirect taxation rest upon facts, and are irrefutable. He then demonstrates that even the Government which was accusing him had made the same assertions under Manteuffel's Ministry, and had expressed them even more strongly. Manteuffel's Ministry had attempted, by legislative proposals, to lighten the burden of taxation which rested on the poorer classes, but the proposals were a failure. The upper classes roused public opinion against the law with all their might, which was naturally an easy task for them, as all the means of stirring public feeling were at their disposal ; and when the proposed law came before the First Chamber, it was rejected. The Government then declared, with a deep sigh of regret, that the task of reform must be abandoned, as public opinion was not yet sufficiently prepared to receive it. Lassalle further shows that the Prussian Privy Councillor Engel, the Director of the Statistical Office, in a speech a few months previously, had made the assertion for which Lassalle has been accused. With the permission of Privy Councillor Engel, he produces a letter in which the Councillor declares his agreement with Lassalle : " Thus, that which I am proclaiming to you, gentlemen, is practically a State doctrine."

He then shows that the main argument usually adduced in favour of indirect taxation is that the small man under direct taxation knows that he is paying taxes, but under indirect taxation he imagines that he is paying as octroi duties to the town what he is really giving to the State. It is therefore a most useful and politic action to explain the ruinous nature of these taxes to the small man. But, it will be asserted, it is not because such statements are made, but because they are made to the working classes and to uneducated people that they become criminal. Lassalle wishes to know whether these " uneducated " classes have not their share in

---

[1] In confirmation of Lassalle's statement of the scanty numbers of citizens in comparative affluence, compare Lange's calculations upon the Distribution of Meat Foods ; F. A. Lange, " The Labour Problem," 183 *et seq.* Indirect taxation was steadily restricted from Lassalle's death to 1877, but since the change in Bismarck's economic policy has become the most oppressive of burdens.

the legislative power, and whether they are to vote in absolute
blindness, without knowing upon what subject or for what
reason they are voting.   For all the above-mentioned reasons
Lassalle does not hesitate to declare that it is questionable whether the accusation raised against him does not
itself imply a breach of the Constitution.   All that he
desires is to lay the theoretical foundation of a legal and
peaceful agitation for the purpose of advancing the prospects
of universal and direct suffrage.   If it is a principle that
burdens should imply corresponding rights, "why do the
poorer classes have only a third of the vote, when they pay
in taxes five, six, ten, and twenty times as much as the prosperous classes ?"   Lassalle then explains his political principle
in a few eloquent sentences : " Let us have one of two things—
either pure absolutism or universal franchise.   There may be
different and conflicting views upon these two things, but any
compromise between them is impossible, erroneous, and
illogical.

   "An absolute power, removed by its position from all
contrasts of class, standing high above society and all social
interests, might conceivably devote itself to the general
interest—the interest of the vast majority.   Whether and
how far it has done so has depended upon the accident of
personal insight, capacity and character ; it might, at any
rate, have so acted, and was reminded of its duty in this
direction by its position ; and such, in truth, was the motto
of the old absolutism in its best period : ' Nothing by the
people, everything for the people.'

   " This time is past ; the age of constitutionalism has begun—
the age in which society, conceiving that it has reached years
of discretion, desires to decide questions affecting its interest
upon its own responsibility.   Henceforward it becomes a
logical impossibility, a tangible inconsistency and a burning
injustice, to place this decision in the hands of the minority,
in the hands of the prosperous classes of society.   These
classes are not above social interests.   On the contrary,
standing as they do amid the cross-fire of such interests, they
cannot but turn the power of decision to their own social
advantage, and thus sacrifice to their selfish purposes the

general interest—the interest of the vast majority of the lower classes."[1]

It is here worth while to glance at the art of war as practised by Lassalle. His principle is to use every attack delivered upon his previous statements as a means of advancing his parallels a little farther towards the enemy's position.

He had, for instance, to prove the truth of his previous assertion that indirect taxation was paid for the most part by the poorer classes. He first shows by quotations that numbers of economists, who are not writing on behalf of any special theory, are agreed upon this point ; next, that his own description of this abuse is couched in the mildest terms ; further, that the Government which accuses him has made the same statements as himself ; and, finally, that, like himself, they have attempted to remove the evil, but were prevented by popular prejudice.

The point of special importance was to show that the proclamation of such principles before the proletariat was an admissible course of procedure. Lassalle proves that the prejudices which shipwrecked the governmental measures originated among this very proletariat, and that in championing his own principles he was therefore working for the Government and consequently deserved rather a civic crown than a prison. He had been opposed on the basis of the principle that great burdens should bring correspondingly great privileges, and he ultimately proves that the transference of this principle into practice will lead to the introduction of the universal franchise for which he is fighting.

A characteristic common to all Lassalle's speeches in his defence is his habit of accumulating testimony with reference to one disputed point which he maintains with the utmost energy, his practice of adopting the attitude of an accuser, his tactical advance to the attack from a defensive position, and his thorough demonstration of the ill-founded nature of the accusations against him. When criticizing accusers, advocates, and judges, whom he had confronted in the lower

[1] " Indirect Taxation," 50, 110.

courts, he treats all these subordinate intellects as helpless
weaklings and lashes one with another as Vikings lashed
Eskimoes. The presiding magistrate usually plays the same
part during this procedure as the court officials in Shakespeare's "Much Ado about Nothing." When Lassalle has
shown that an accusation is a breach of the law, he exclaims
as if he himself were the judge. *Audiatur et altera pars*, or
he says : "thus the accusation is meaningless ; I will put
it in more direct terms than the State counsel has done ";[1]
or he delivers a personal attack upon the State counsel.
Even in his first speech before the Court of Assizes he read
out a special document, which he had sent to his first accuser,
requesting him most energetically to conduct his prosecution
in person, as he intended to call him to account. Lassalle then
turned to the judge, and added : "You see, I attempted to
lash his sense of honour into life enough to drive him here,
so that he might now be called to account by me. My efforts
were in vain." In his speech upon "Science and the Working
Classes" he gained a triumph by continually quoting statements from Schelling, the famous philosopher, which breathe
a passionate sense of freedom, against the State counsel, who
was Schelling's son. To the amusement of the audience, the
result was a very comical disputation between Schelling senior
and Schelling junior. In short, Lassalle was never so much
in his element as when he was in the dock. This is
the oratorical position which especially stirs his brilliancy and
evokes his capacity for battle ; for his capacities were by nature
military, and were only displayed in their full power under
arms.

During these two years he was, in a metaphorical sense,
continually in the dock. Every word that he uttered or wrote
became a war-cry, rousing the attacks of a thousand voices
and a thousand newspapers. The great connected development of his ideas, which appears in his work "Capital and
Labour," was produced in a most warlike frame of mind, and
was written with bitterness and passion to confute Schultze-
Delitzsch and the moderate school which he represented, with
the result that the book in its present form is comparable to a

---

[1] "Science and the Workmen," 31, 39.

scornful piece of lampooning. But it is perfectly obvious that the penetrating vigour of polemical writing brought one advantage with it, of which Lassalle was entirely conscious, and which is a partial compensation for the poor and noisy tone of his exposition, for its crudity and lack of repose. As he himself said, hundreds and thousands would read this book who would coldly and carelessly pass by a systematic development of his ideas in several volumes.

CHAPTER IV

WHAT, then, were these ideas ? Whence were they derived ? What were their chief sources ? And to what modification did Lassalle subject them ?

These ideas were the traditions of the revolutionary Germany of 1848, as they were proclaimed in the manifesto of the Communist party, which was published in London, in February, 1848, and, in particular, as they appeared in the Socialist writings of Marx and Engels. Their historical source is to be found in the attempts at social revolution which were made in the Reformation period.

Spielhagen, in his book, " In Reih und Glied," has used the traditions of the age of the peasant wars (*die Bundschuh*) as a background for Leo's agitation. The hero grows up amid descriptions of the struggles of that age, and the author's idea is correctly—and, indeed, excellently—conceived ; for as soon as proposals for Socialist reform began to be discussed in Germany about 1848, recollections were aroused of the terrible class struggle to which the Reformation had given rise, and which it had vainly attempted to master. A glance at these intestine conflicts, as they were conceived by the German revolutionaries of 1848-50, is necessary in order to realize in its proper proportions the connection of the modern German working-class movement with an earlier and distantly related event of the same kind, and to understand its position with reference to its historical background.

In 1848 the Radical party held the following ideas of the Reformation period : There were in that age three great camps —the Roman Catholic and Conservative camp, the Moderate

Citizen and Lutheran Reform party, and the Revolutionary
party (the peasants and people), whose demands were most
clearly expressed by Thomas Münzer. Luther and Münzer
were perfect representatives of their parties, both by their
doctrines and by their characters and attitudes. In 1517,
when Luther first attacked the Catholic Church, his opposition
had assumed no decided character, and, though it did not go
beyond the demands of earlier middle-class heresy, it did not
exclude any further line of action, nor could it do so. At the
first moment it was necessary to set in motion all the forces of
antagonism and the strongest revolutionary energy in general,
and to represent the whole body of earlier heresy against
Catholic orthodoxy. In precisely similar fashion in 1847 the
Liberal middle classes styled themselves "Revolutionary"
and "Socialist," and enthusiastically championed the liberation of the peasant and workman.

Luther's strong nature broke out in the most unrestrained
fashion during this first period of his career. "If you (the
Roman priests) are to continue your mad ravings, in my
opinion there can be no better counsel and medicine to check
them than that Kings and Princes should interfere with force
and put an end to the business with arms, and not with words.
As we punish thieves with the sword, murderers with the
rope, and heretics with the fire, why should we not much rather
attack these dangerous teachers of destruction—Popes, Car-
dinals, Bishops, and the whole swarm of the Roman Sodom—
with every kind of weapon, and wash our hands in their
blood?"

This first fury, however, was of no long duration. When
the whole German people had been stirred to its depths,
when the peasants and poor citizens regarded Luther's outcry against the Popes in his preaching of Christian freedom
as the signal to rise against their oppressors, when the secular
authorities were only concerned to break the power of the
clergy, and to enrich themselves by appropriating Church
property, and when Luther was therefore forced to choose,
he did not hesitate for a single moment, protected as he was
by the Elector of Saxony, and surrounded by followers, who
constantly flattered the distinguished teacher. He allowed the

popular element to go its way, and joined the group of citizens, nobles, and Princes. The outcries for a war of extermination against Rome died away, and he proceeded to preach on behalf of a peaceful solution and of passive resistance, as did the German National Assembly in 1848, upon the occasion of the *coup d'état*.

When Hutten invited him and Sickingen to come to Ebern-burg, the centre of the conspiracy of nobles against the Pope and the Princes, Luther replied : " I have no wish that the cause of the Gospel should be advanced by force and blood-shed. By the Word the world has been overcome ; by the Word the Church has been maintained ; by the Word it will again be restored, and the Antichrist, as he came to his own without force, will fall without force." It will be seen that these are the words to which Lassalle represents Hutten as replying with his praise of the sword, in his drama, " Franz von Sickingen."

Luther's career now underwent a change, was occupied with bargaining and chaffering about the institutions and dogmas which needed reformation, and was filled with un-seemly negotiations, concessions, intrigues, and agreements, the result of which was the Augsburg Confession of Faith. To the undeceived Radicals of 1848, this result seemed typical of all the attempts at compromise and of all the haggling and chaffering which they had observed, as they watched the life of the German National Assembly. The very sublunary character of the official German Reformation seemed to them to show a similarity to the attempts of the citizen parties carefully wavering between a policy of abolition and a policy of maintenance.

In the history of the Reformation, however, a counterpart could also be found to the reversion of the citizen class to reactionary views. When the peasant war broke out, even in districts where the peasants were for the most part Catholics, Luther attempted to adopt an attitude of mediation. He made a decided attack upon the Government. Governmental oppression was to be blamed for the revolt ; the Government was rousing, not only the peasants, but God Himself. At the same time, the revolt was certainly sinful and contrary to the Gospel,

and for this reason he summoned both parties to concession
and agreement. The movement, however, rapidly spread, in
spite of these well-meant attempts at intervention, invaded
even Protestant districts, and rapidly outgrew the citizen
reform. When the most determined section of the rebels,
under Münzer, made Thüringen their headquarters, in Luther's
immediate neighbourhood, and when a few successful battles
would have sufficed to spread conflagration throughout
Germany, it was seen that intervention was hopeless. In the
face of the revolution, old quarrels were forgotten, and priests,
nobility, Princes, Luther, and the Pope, united in defence
against "the murderous and marauding bands of peasants.
They are to be cut down, strangled, and stabbed, secretly and
publicly, by anyone who is able, as if they were mad dogs,"
cried Luther ; "and therefore, my dear lords, liberate here,
bring safety there ; stab, strike, and slay them as you can ;
and should you die in the enterprise, well for you, for you
can find no more blessed death." Luther maintained that no
false sympathy with the peasants should be felt, as God
Himself had no sympathy with them. At a later time the
peasants themselves would be glad if they were forced to
surrender one cow, that they might eat the other in peace.
" Only let them hear the whistle of bullets, for otherwise they
will be a thousand times worse." Was there any great difference, people asked, between this language and that which
was used by the citizen classes of Germany and France,
notwithstanding their one-time inclination to Socialism and
Humanitarianism, when the proletariat demanded their share
of the fruits of victory, after the March revolution ? The days
of June, 1848, in Paris, when workmen were shot down by
thousands, seemed to be a commentary upon Luther's old text.

Luther had placed a powerful weapon in the hands of the
proletariat movement by his translation of the Bible. Over
against the haughty Christianity of the feudal period he had
placed a picture of the modest Christianity of early times,
and the peasants had availed themselves of this implement.
Luther now turned the Bible against them, and drew from
its contents a song of praise on behalf of the authority set up
by God. Princes by the grace of God, obedience unquestion-

ing, and even serfdom, were approved with the help of the Bible. Not only the peasant rising, but also Luther's own revolt against ecclesiastical and secular authority was thus disavowed. Had not rebels been shot down in 1848 in precisely similar manner, and thrown into prison in the name of Christianity ? Was not such action based upon a religion, the essence of which was a crude communism ?

Luther was confronted by the popular rebel, Thomas Münzer, whose father had died on the gallows, a victim to a noble's arbitrary will. His wide learning in the theology of the age had procured him a doctor's degree, but at the same time he treated the dogmas and the worship of the Church with the utmost contempt. He abolished the use of Church services in Latin long before Luther ventured to go so far. From the outset the object of his attacks was only the ecclesiastical power, and, like Luther, he urged the employment of force ; but his free-thinking doctrines were directed, not only against Catholicism, but against Christianity in general. Under mysterious formulæ, he taught a pantheism almost modern in character, and declined to regard the Bible either as the only means of revelation or as infallible. The only real source of revelation was reason, which had existed at all times and among all peoples. The Holy Ghost of which the Bible speaks was reason ; faith was nothing more than the life of reason in man, and therefore even the heathen could possess faith. By this faith man became divine and blessed. Heaven was not reserved for the life beyond the grave, for the Kingdom of God was to be set up here on earth. The only devil was the evil desires and lusts of men. Christ was a man like ourselves, and the Last Supper was merely a memorial feast. These religious views were accompanied by a corresponding Socialist programme, demanding a society without differences of class, without rights of inheritance, and without a Government from which the members of the State were excluded.

Münzer had broken with Luther and his party at an early period. Luther was necessarily forced to accept many ecclesiastical reforms which Münzer had introduced without consulting him. As early as the spring of 1524 Münzer had written to Melanchthon, saying that neither he nor Luther understood the movement, but were attempting to stifle it by their dogma of the verbal inspiration of the Bible.[1] Challenges issued by Luther to meet him in theological disputation were declined by Münzer, who replied that if Luther's intentions were honest he would use his influence to stop the persecution of Münzer's printers, and to remove the censure from his books, in order that the struggle might be fought out in the Press without hindrance. Luther then came forward to denounce him in public. In his letter to the Prince of Saxony, "against the rebel spirit," he declared Münzer to be a tool of Satan, and invited the Prince to interfere and drive him out of the country.[2]

Similarly, in the French National Assembly before and during the presidency of Louis Napoleon, the so-called Liberal majority had disavowed its past. It had constantly thundered one single word against the minority—"Socialism." Even middle-class Liberalism was declared to be Socialist, and the same accusation was levelled against civic enlightenment. To build a railway where there was already a canal was Socialism. It was Socialism to defend oneself with a stick if attacked with a dagger. "The middle class," says Marx,[3] "correctly saw that all the weapons which they had forged against feudalism were turning upon themselves, and that all the means of culture which they had brought forth were rebelling against their own civilization. . . . But what they failed to perceive was the consequence that their own Parliamentary government and their political supremacy was now to be universally condemned as Socialist. . . . If they saw 'peace' endangered whenever the social organism gave signs of life, how could they lead society to champion the rule of unrest, their own rule, Parliamentary rule—the rule that lives in battle and by battle, to use the expression of one of their orators? Parlia-

---

[1] Dear brothers, away with your hesitation and delay; it is time, for summer is at our doors. Make no peace with the godless, who prevent the Word from working with full power. Flatter not your Princes, otherwise you will perish with them. Ye tender scribes, be not unwilling; I can do nought else.

[2] *Cf.* Karl Marx, *Neue Rheinische Zeitung*, 5, 6, vol. for 1850; "The German Peasant War," by Friedrich Engels.

[3] Karl Marx, "The Eighteenth Brumaire of Louis Napoleon," 26.

mentary government lives on discussion ; how, then, could it forbid discussion ? The strife of oratory in Parliament calls forth the strife of the scribblers of the Press. The Parliamentary debating club finds its necessary complement in debates held in drawing-rooms and in public houses. If those in power at the summit of the State proceed to pipe, why should they expect that those beneath them will not dance ? The middle class, condemning as Socialist what they had formerly honoured as Liberal, thereby admit that their own interest demands the abolition of the dangers involved by self-government, for the purpose of restoring peace to the country." To apply the conditions then existing in France to Germany was obvious, and a comparison between Luther's attitude and the position of the German citizen class at that critical age was no less intelligible.

People were inclined to think that they were living in an age which had begun the work of the Reformation period anew. Upon the theological side the Reformation had been continued by Strauss and Feuerbach, while the Democratic party hoped in the political and social departments to resume the ideas and plans of the Reformation which had never come to fulfilment. But the party was not sufficiently instructed upon the nature of the Reformation. It forgot that the success of that movement was solely due to the fact that it had been confined and limited, both upon its negative and positive sides, and also to the fact that, though it proceeded from a strong and vital moral sense, it had been able to attract political powers and passions. The Reformation had emerged triumphant from its duel, because it had been seconded by the political advantages of those in power, but the Revolution of 1848 was purely idealistic and radical ; it was anxious to transform everything at one blow. For this reason, " the old Socialists," Marx and Engels, go back to the peasant wars, and glorify them. Lassalle, like them, was attracted by these wars, but regards them with greater intellectual power and with more historical insight. He observes that the peasants who were enchained by medieval ideas regarded landed property, the economic power of the Middle Ages, as the qualifying condition for participation in the government, whereas it never occurred to them that a man might have a right simply as a man to a share in the governmental power. In contrast to Marx and Engels, Lassalle now directs his studies by preference to the aristocratic revolts of that time and to the rising of the nobility under Sickingen. His researches in this direction gave him the idea for his drama, " Franz von Sickingen." We must return once more to this important source of evidence upon Lassalle's mental life. In his preface to this work he mentions the erroneous idea that the spirit of the Reformation had been more or less created by Luther. He shows that this spirit not merely existed before Luther's time, but was also inspired by pure human enthusiasm, arising from the renaissance of the sciences, which Luther turned into the narrow channel of one-sided dogmatic theology. He further demonstrates that this spirit of reform, which existed before the Reformation, was wider, freer, and more human in its scope than its own fruit, the Reformation. A letter from Hutten to Count Nuenar, referring to Luther's first appearance, runs as follows : " They are beginning to destroy one another. Perhaps you do not yet know that a party has risen in Wittenberg, in Saxony, against the dignity of the Popes, while another party is defending the Papal indulgences. Both sides are using every possible means and straining their utmost. The leaders of either party are monks, and are shouting, howling, and complaining as loud as they can ; recently they have even begun to write. Paragraphs, pamphlets, and articles, will be printed and disseminated. I hope that they will contrive to overthrow one another (' Sic spero fiet, ut mutui interitus causas sibi invicem præbeant '). When a mendicant friar recently told me the news, I replied : ' Devour one another, so that none of you remain ' (' Consumite, ut consumamini invicem '). So I trust that our enemies will destroy and devour one another in their mutual conflicts."

It is thus not the theological, but the moral and political reform that is represented by the two heroes of Lassalle's drama, Hutten and Sickingen ; and, in order that the piece might fully represent the later fate of its writer, Hutten finally joins the leaders of the peasant revolt, and persuades Franz to take the lead of the rebel peasants.

CHAPTER V

In the spring of 1862 the days passed by in hard work and fruitful thought, but as yet without feverish haste or restlessness, in the well-known house in the Bellevuestrasse. The little winter garden, which was full of beautiful and rare plants, peacefully exhaled its scents into the rooms about 't. The beautiful life-size marble and alabaster statues which were there placed, and stood out most effectively from the dark velvet curtains, seemed to be in perfect harmony with the life and habits of their owner. The mirrors, bronzes, Chinese vases, the modern pictures on the walls, the old papyrus rolls and folios in the library, bore no indication that their possessor would soon be reproached for his ownership of such luxuries, or be told that he should distribute them elsewhere ; nor did they give any premonition of the approaching time when they would all be scattered to the winds.

In the evening old friends and acquaintances continued to gather together. Franz Duncker, the supporter of the party of progress and owner of the *Volkszeitung*, who was soon to quarrel with Lassalle ; the botanist Prietzel, a friend of earlier years ; Ziegler, formerly chief burgomaster of Brandenburg ; the old, simple, and undaunted battle-poet Scherenberg ; Martiny, Lothar Bucher, Boeckh, Von Pfuel, and others, were there. Sometimes the lively and excitable Hans von Bülow would sit down at the splendid grand piano, and Liszt's compositions filled the lofty room.

Much laughter went on in the study when Lassalle had thrown aside his pen, so weary of writing his sparkling commentary upon the spiritless and halting prose of Julian

Schmidt, under the cloak of the " compositor," that Lothar
Bucher was obliged to write the last third of the book, under
the cloak of the " compositor's wife." They read aloud the
preposterous ideas which the golden words of poor Julian have
transmitted to posterity concerning the Seven Wise Men of
Greece. They enjoyed his penetrating observations upon the
Schwabenspiegel, the famous medieval code of Suabian laws,
which he regarded as a modern German collection of songs of
innocence. They laughed over his serious criticism of " Faust,"
" the virtuoso with no idealism," and over his foolish, misty
phrases concerning Fichte and Hegel. There 'was laughter,
too, in the drawing-room ; jokes and sarcastic puns were
made upon the Progressive party that had recently been
founded under the intellectual leadership of Schultze-Delitzsch.
These people had not even the courage to call themselves
Democrats, and what in all the world did they expect to signify
or to represent if they were not ?

The breach between Lassalle and the Liberals had not yet
occurred ; it was not far off, but had not yet become irreparable.
Hence might be explained the circumstance that just at that
time Lassalle received a complimentary invitation from one
of the most cultured and almost official circles in Berlin—
the only official recognition which was ever offered to him
during his lifetime by high society. Philosophical society
in Berlin had taken him to itself unanimously, for the author
of " Heraclitus " was regarded as an obviously qualified
member. He was now requested to deliver the memorial
oration in the course of the celebrations which this society
and the Society of Art and Science proposed to celebrate in
memory of Fichte on May 19, 1862.

It cannot be denied that in this lecture, " The Philosophy of
Fichte and the Significance of German Nationalism," Lassalle
brilliantly performed his difficult task. Strictly scientific as
the lecture is, and wide as is the information given in very
narrow limits of space, it is none the less light in style and
characterized by noble simplicity. How clever and true, for
instance, is the illustration which Lassalle gives of Kant's
" Critique of Pure Reason," which, by the superiority of self-consciousness, is able to overthrow the certainty of the outer world,

the fragments of which reflect only the critique itself. Lassalle exemplifies this by quoting a passage from Goethe's " Faust."

" The giant spirit of Kant," says Lassalle, " is in reality the Faust to whom the chorus of spirits call "—

> " Woe, woe !
> Thou hast destroyed
> This beauteous world
> With mighty hand ;
> It falls, it fades !
> A demigod hath stricken it ;
> We bear
> The ruins over to the shades of night
> And weep
> For beauty perished : but thou
> Mightier
> Than the sons of earth
> Build it
> Once more in greater splendour,
> Build it up within thy heart !

" and even so," adds Lassalle, " as the poet's cry of yearning calls to Faust, did he reconstruct the world in his heart. The German spirit, while he reconstructs the world from his own inner consciousness, is Fichte."

But Lassalle's lecture dealt with Fichte, not as a philosopher, but as a patriot ; he lauded him as the enthusiast who brought enlightenment to the spirit of Germany, and as the prophet who announced her unity. His love of this idea and his faith in it formed the ultimate bond between himself and his compatriots of his own rank. Upon that evening he clung to it as if it were the last sign of communion between himself and his fellow-citizens, with their Liberal ideas and their scientific culture.

His efforts were in vain ; his views were already known, and he was himself unpopular. During the lecture he was interrupted by outcries, the doors behind him were continually opened and banged. The audience did not hesitate openly to show their anxiety to go to dinner, and the conclusion of this masterly speech was heard only by a small number of the public. Thus in due form he was expelled from the midst of the Liberal middle class.

The lecture which Lassalle had delivered in Berlin upon Constitutional theory had attracted the attention of the workmen. They were yet more strongly aroused by his lecture upon the connection between the present age and the aims of the working class, which he delivered on April 12, 1862, before a union of Berlin workmen in the suburb of Oranienburg. At the outset of 1863 a committee met to call a general meeting of German workmen in Leipzig. The leaders had been greatly flattered by the Progressive party, but had been unable to decide their course of action. They now determined to invite Lassalle to tell them what, in his opinion, would be the most correct and advantageous method for them to pursue.

He sent an Open Letter of Reply to the committee, in which he declared with great precision and clearness his programme, which was precisely opposed to that of Schultze-Delitzsch. His words made an irresistible impression, and shortly afterwards the Universal German Workmen's Union was founded.

It would be waste of time to explain his economic principles in the order in which he proclaimed them in his agitatory speeches and lawsuits. I will therefore give here a general view of them in compressed form as they may be found scattered throughout his writings.

Lassalle, as a true Hegelian, divides the past history of the world into three epochs, the two first of which form contrasts, while the latter unites the permanent elements in the two former. He then shows that all historical development has proceeded from corporate life and action, without which no civilization at all could have been formed.

Throughout antiquity and medieval times human solidarity or corporate life was regarded as based upon subjugation and subjection. The French Revolution of 1789, and the period which it dominated, sought for freedom in the dissolution of all solidarity and corporate life, though freedom apart from corporate life is mere licence. Finally, the modern period, which Lassalle regards as beginning in 1848, attempts to find the bond of union in freedom. It is instructive to observe in passing, that a philosophic historian of Hegel's school feels no hesitation in dividing the history of the world into three epochs of equal importance for the purpose of producing two complementary conceptions, though one of these epochs embraces some five or six thousand years, and the other scarce sixty. It seems more natural to regard the development after 1849 as a continuation of the movement begun in 1789 than to exaggerate contrasts and to ascribe so short a period to the second epoch, in order to produce the Hegelian tripartite idea, with its revulsion of concept.

Lassalle is, none the less, correct in proceeding from human corporate life as an actual point of departure. He concludes that the fact of human solidarity may fail to be realized, but cannot be abolished, and that it exists, even though social institutions fail to recognize or to guide it. In such cases it appears as brute natural force, while the individual who is forced to rely upon himself is at its mercy. The interaction of social forces, their rise and fall, brings wealth to one, throws others into poverty, and sports with the labour and industry of the individual. Lassalle therefore maintains that attempts to limit and overcome this intermittent action are by no means intended to remove the freedom and responsibility of the individual, but, on the contrary, endeavour to give this freedom every opportunity of expressing itself in a reasonable way. The unfortunate fact, in his opinion, is that favourable circumstances at the present day usually have but a very slight and transitory influence upon the condition of the working classes, whereas unfavourable conditions recoil with destructive power upon those who own no property. Immediate reduction of wages, diminution of employment or an entire absence of work, are the blows delivered upon the backs of the workmen by bad times and by the fluctuations due to the greedy rivalry of speculators.

The school of political economy, represented in France by Bastiat, and in Germany by the leader of the Progressive party, Schultze-Delitzsch, had regarded the mutual exchange of commodities as the whole secret of political economy. Against this Lassalle vigorously emphasizes the fact that human society and human work in the present age does not merely consist in the association of men within definite localities, and the interchange of the products of their personal labour. He shows that production is a common result of co-operation, produced by the complex activities of a numerous body, while at the same time the profits of production are not divided as common property, but, as products or values, become the personal possession of the contractor or manufacturer. The manufacturer thus makes labour productive, inasmuch as his agreements with the whole of the working class, whose co-operation has brought about production, are subject to that law of wages which must inevitably be developed under these circumstances—the law which plays so important a part in the works of Marx and in the agitation of Lassalle ; the law which, never denied except by Lassalle's most ephemeral opponents, was formulated by Ricardo and has been recognized by all economists of any reputation ; the law that wages, upon the average, are limited to the sum which is unconditionally necessary for the maintenance of life and the propagation of the species, and will vary according to the habits of the people in question. The current rate of wages will oscillate about this point, never rising far above it or sinking far below it. Thus, according to Lassalle, the profound contradiction in modern society is due to the fact that the principle of co-operation is invariably employed for production, whereas the distribution of the profits is made solely upon the principle of individualism.

The antiquated economic school of exchange had depicted conditions as if every man worked immediately for his own purposes, and then, under some idyllic system, proceeded to exchange such products as he could not use himself for those of his neighbours. Lassalle scornfully asks whether undertakers' establishments exist primarily to provide for cases of death in the family of the owner, and only when such cases are rare, exchange for other commodities such trappings of woe as may be superfluous.

The same economic school spread the doctrine that saving and hoarding were the only means by which capital could be formed. Lassalle shows how irrational is the assumption that such a purely negative procedure as saving and not consuming could ever be the source by which the capital of a State is formed. " What products of labour," he asks, " can be consumed, and what cannot be saved ? Corn, meat, wine, and similar articles of food and drink—these things which can be consumed, must be consumed in general within a certain space of time, because as a rule they will not keep ; but if we glance at the other products which chiefly compose the capital wealth of modern society, such as steam-engines and farming implements, houses, raw materials of every kind, such as iron bars, pigs of copper, bricks and blocks of stone, need we ask whether these commodities can be consumed or will not be saved ? Is it reasonable so zealously to crown the capitalists for their services in not consuming all these steam-engines, all this guano, all these bars of iron and blocks of stone, or will the statement be brought forward that they have not sold them ? But if we are discussing the political economy of the State, and not that of the individual, it is obviously a matter of indifference whether a thing belongs to Peter or to Paul. It is only a misunderstanding of Adam Smith's century-old definition of capital as accumulated labour that has led to the doctrine of saving.

Instead of making unscientific attempts to represent capital as a natural necessity of eternal permanence, Lassalle enters upon an investigation to show how capital actually arose in the course of history.

In ancient times a man who had a hundred slaves could very well consume the product of sixty slaves' labour, and accumulate the product of forty slaves. This, however, was not saving. In the Middle Ages the overlord similarly accumulated the labour of his servants. This, again, was not saving. Then came the Revolution of 1789, when labour was declared free by law. But obviously work cannot be begun without tools and without the means of maintaining existence while the work is in progress—in other words, without previous work, which means capital. Hence the workman is under compulsion no less onerous than before to give his master the whole profits of his labour so far as that profit exceeds his own daily wants. Thus the labour previously performed, the dead labour or capital, outweighs the living labour in every society which, like our own, produces under the laws of open competition and individualism.[1]

[1] " We have been reproached with a desire to abolish property personally acquired by a man's own efforts, property which is the foundation of all personal freedom, energy, and independence. Are you speaking of the pro-

The workman is killed by the products of his own toil. His labour of yesterday rises up against him, strikes him down, and deprives him of the profits of his labour of to-day. The work of the wild Indian, his hunting, produces no super-fluity. Superfluity is only produced by labour carried on under the principle of the division of labour, and the division of labour is only possible when capital has been previously formed. Labour divided or united, producing the culture of which it is the condition, was originally and for a long time only possible in the form of slave-labour, brought together and kept in subjugation by force ; but it is the task of our period to abolish slavery and its various forms, and therefore, in Lassalle's view, our age must not merely put an end to these conditions—so much is unquestionably its task—but it must make this end a new beginning.

History thus shows that capital funds have not been formed by saving or by individual labour ; equally impossible is their formation by these methods at the present day. They are formed by the interconnection of society. Capital profit is very far removed from the nature of a wage paid in return for personal inconvenience. On the contrary, it constantly accrues, although the capitalist has not raised a finger or denied himself the smallest pleasure. Such increment may occur, for instance, by a rise in the value of land or of railway shares. It was simply in order to avoid the admission that labour alone creates value that Bastiat invented service as an economic idea. According to his theory, the standard of value does not consist in the necessary work expended upon the production of a commodity, but in the work that the consumer

---

perty of the small citizen and the small peasant which preceded citizen property ? We do not need to abolish this, for the progress of manufacture has abolished it and is daily abolishing it. But does paid work, the work of the proletariat, bring property to the labourer ? By no means ; it creates capital, in other words the property which exploits paid labour. . . . By freedom we understand free trade, free purchase and sale within the present conditions of civic production, but if haggling comes to an end, even free haggling will cease. You are horrified because we wish to abolish private property ; but in your existing society, property is beyond the acquisition of nine-tenths of its members. It exists simply because it does not exist for these nine-tenths. You are therefore reproaching us for our desire to abolish property, the existence of which necessarily presupposes the incapacity of the vast majority of society to possess anything."—KARL MARX, "Com-munist Manifesto," 1848.

is " saved " by the transference of the commodity to him, and this " saving " contains the idea of service. Lassalle asks whether a railway company could reasonably ask a price for the ticket which would correspond to the trouble, loss of time, and expense to which the traveller would have been put if he had been obliged to make his journey on foot or by carriage.

Against this Lassalle urges with Marx that labour is activity, and therefore movement. But all continuous movement implies time ; the solution of all values as consisting in the quantity of labour expended upon them, and this, again, in the time expended upon labour, is Ricardo's contribution to the subject. All value thus amounts to the time necessarily expended in labour for the production of a commodity. Is, then, this time the time expended by the individual ? When the workman is isolated it is so. With reference to the commodity produced, it is only so if I produce objects for my actual personal use ; but if I produce commodities for exchange —that is, for the use of others—my labour includes general or society labour. Thus, the commodity in question implies not only individual time, the time spent in labour by me personally, but also general or social time spent in labour, and this it is which forms the measure of unity for the amount of labour represented by the commodity produced. Now, the time of a society expended in labour has an independent existence of its own as money. Money is social labour-time in tangible form, abstracted from the special purposes of the particular labour, such as may be spent upon needles, wood, linen, etc. It is only by taking a *salto mortale*, or leap to destruction, into the sea of money that commodities can prove the truth of their existence as social labour-time externalized in tangible form. The statement of Say, that products can only be exchanged for products, that the capital of a land consists in wares, and not in money, and that money is not capital, is a truth which is only true when abstracted from the actual objects of economic intercourse. In actual practice products are never exchanged for products, but for money, and so long as products avoid this *salto mortale* into the form of money they are not capital. They are potential capital, but nothing more.

The pulsation of capital, which interpenetrates the civic

process of production, is interrupted, and during the time of its interruption capital is known as commodities. When the circulation recommences, commodities are removed and consumed for the purpose of further production. Production is, therefore, a stream, the motive-power of which is formed by capital, and is brought to a standstill in the produced commodity. This commodity can only return to the form of capital if it is turned out of its fixed form and thrown once more into the stream of production—if, in other words, it ceases to be a product, whether it is a means of life, or whether it is raw material for further work. There is but one product in the case of which this circulation is never interrupted, but is as constant as the circulation of the blood—and this is money. Money is, therefore, capital in the truest sense of the word. Money was certainly borrowed in antiquity and in the Middle Ages, but only with the object of consuming the amount of the loan. For this reason high rates of interest—in fact, interest at all—was often regarded as something dishonourable. The point of departure was that a loan made only for the purpose of use, and which made the borrower no richer, ought not, therefore, to enrich the lender—in other words, it was regarded as disgraceful to use the necessities and the embarrassments of another man in order to plunder him. Among us, on the other hand, it is not loans of this kind, but productive loans, that play the most important part. The lender's whole object in this case is to enrich himself—an object which the borrower readily shares with him—and a loan thus implies the same as an economic share in business profits. Gold and the riches of the ancients were capital in embryo form, but not capital itself. When the commerce of the Middle Ages began to rise to importance, the embryo attained development ; but only after the French Revolution were all the barriers removed which prevented free competition, and only then did capital become a fully developed organism. Henceforward all legal conditions of production are absorbed in one purely practical condition, preliminary possession of the necessary money enabling the producer to have his capital in his hands. In the Middle Ages the value of commodities depended partly upon the intentions of the producer. He might, for instance, insist upon a profit corresponding to his social position ; but the price of commodities is now determined by the cost of production. Under the equalizing predominance of free com petition, one producer underbids another in order to secure the market for himself. Hence an actual advantage for the consumer is cheapness, but this fact again necessitates production upon a large scale, and a large amount of money in hand, or a large capital. Consequently, under our present social arrangements, all capital necessarily tends to become large in size and to absorb smaller capital sums.

The standard of value for the commodity—in other words, the amount of labour-time necessary for its production—may be called the conscience of civic production. Now, this conscience is necessarily and continually outraged by the continual oscillation of prices between excess and deficiency. This, however, is a matter only of importance for the individual capitalist. With regard to capital as such, the several swings of the pendulum compensate for one another. Like the price of all other commodities, so also the price of labour or the rate of wages is determined by the relations of demand and supply. Meanwhile, the price of every commodity is determined by the necessary expense of its production. What, then, does it cost a workman to be productive ? The ordinary and necessary expenses of life for him and his family—in other words, the costs of producing labour—are equivalent to the cost at which a workman can produce. What, then, would happen to the sellers of other wares, supposing they were unable to hold out for several weeks in succession against a demand that did not correspond to their prices ? The seller of that commodity known as labour cannot hold out. He must sell, under compulsion of hunger. The special characteristic of the civic epoch is the cold and impersonal attitude of the manufacturer towards the workman, as though he were a commodity like other commodities on the market, produced according to the law of the cost of production. In this way it therefore appears that the average wage is necessarily limited to the amount usually regarded by the people as necessary to maintain daily life. Any surplus profit of labour comes to benefit capital in its different forms, and becomes a bonus upon capital.

The secret of the fruitfulness of capital is thus seen to consist in the unfruitfulness of labour. In the difference between the amount of labour expended, which is paid for in the price given for the commodity produced, and, on the other hand, the sums paid in wages, lies the profit that accrues to capital, or bonus, which appears as the capacity and power of capital to increase continually, a capacity that first gains full liberty of action by means of free competition. The bonus on capital is not, as has been said, merely a wage due to the intellectual powers which guide labour. This idea can be refuted merely by considering the difference between the wages of a company director and between bonus. Nor do wages rise with an increase of annual production, for, though a larger amount may then be paid in wages, it is merely distributed among a larger number of workmen—in other words, according to Lassalle's theory, there is not, under existing arrangements, a single shilling earned by a workman or a single drop of his sweat which does not on the morrow produce a new and unprofitable drop of sweat for the workman and a new shilling for capital. The implement of labour—namely, capital—has then become separated from the workmen, and attained independence. Its suckers absorb all fruitfulness to itself, and concede to the workman merely the compensation for the vital force necessarily expended in the course of the work. Capital thus makes labour unfruitful. What, then, is capital ? It is an implement of labour that has become independent, that has changed parts with the workman, has reduced him from a living being to a dead implement, and has raised itself, a dead implement, to the position of a living and productive force. If a stronger definition be wanted, capital is an advance made in virtue of labour previously expended, an advance which is necessary during the division of labour under a system of production which depends upon exchange ; necessary also during the unrestrained course of commercial rivalry for the daily maintenance of the producer, until his commodities have been delivered to their eventual consumers ; an advance producing the consequence that the profits of labour which exceed the amount necessary for daily maintenance accrue to the man who has made the advance. The statement of Lassalle's

opponents is thus entirely true when they assert that the
market price of a commodity is payment for nothing else than
for human labour ; but, be it observed, the payment is made,
not to the workman, but is absorbed by the sponge of capital :
" the workman's own has become another's."

The most obvious revelation of the uncertainty of modern
social conditions, and the impossibility of basing calculations
upon them, is found by Lassalle in the procedure of the Stock
Exchange, with its gambling upon the rise and fall of stocks
and the investment of property in shares, State bonds, and
loans in general. Every event in Turkey or Mexico, every
act of peace and war, every change of public opinion, a false
telegram, a loan in Paris or London, the wheat-harvest on the
Mississippi, gold-mines in Australia—in short, any outward
event occurring by purely outward movements of society as
such, whether in the sphere of the State, or the money market,
or trade, daily produces upon the Stock Exchange some
alteration for the weal or woe of the individual, and creates
new conditions under which he must live. Lassalle asks how
Socialism may be well defined. It may be certainly defined
as the distribution of property by social means, but it is precisely this condition which is nowadays in force. The state
of things as prevailing is nothing else than lawless Socialism
in the guise of personal production. What Socialism as a
regulating force would abolish is thus not property, but lawlessness ; in fact, it desires to introduce no property except
personal property founded upon labour.[1]

If now, says Lassalle, we turn our gaze from capital property

---

[1] Marx, who was an even more tenacious adherent of Hegel's principles of
rhythm and symmetry in the philosophy of history than Lassalle, laid down
three main periods of economic history. In the first, the workman owns his
means of production and conducts a small business upon his own account.
In the next period, the accumulation of capital, when it is not the direct
consequence of the transformation of slaves and serfs into wage-earners,
is based upon the exploitation of the immediate producer—*i.e.*, upon the
disappearance of private property as acquired by individual labour. But
this first transition from scattered private ownership to capitalist ownership
finds its counter part in the transition from capitalist to social ownership,
as a negation of a negation. The first point at issue is the exploitation of the
people at large by a few robbers. But whereas centuries were occupied in
the first transition, Marx with his abstract radicalism imagines that the latter
transition can proceed so rapidly and easily as the progress of his own specula-
tions and be accomplished by one stroke and by a sudden revolution, a most
unhistorical point of view.

as existing, which has certainly accrued in due correspondence with the prevailing state of affairs, we have the indisputable right to make the property of the future, as yet unproduced, the property of labour, by reforming the methods of production. There is to be no breach with the division of labour, the source of all civilization ; only capital is to be once more reduced to its position as a dead implement of work in the service of man. For this purpose it is only necessary that throughout the realm of production individual private capital for productive purposes should be abolished ; that the labour of society, which was previously common, should be maintained in employment by the common capital of society, while the profits of production should be divided among the fellow-labourers according to the value of their achievements. The means of transition to this purpose, the simplest and mildest of all, are, in Lassalle's opinion, productive unions supported by State credit.

CHAPTER VI

WE have taken a general view of the theoretical foundation upon which Lassalle's polemical writings are based. We must now see what specially advanced points in his theory were brought under the enemy's fire during the progress of the conflict, and which of these points proved to be indefensible. We have held a rapid review of his forces ; we must now observe their attitude in attack and defence during the battle.

We will therefore take the first disputed point—the law of wages. Lassalle placed the law of wages in the front of all his economic arguments, calling it by preference the " cruel iron law." He told the workmen, when anyone spoke of improving the conditions of their daily lives, to ask him first of all whether he recognized this law or not. If he did not recognize it, further negotiations with him were not worth the trouble, for the law was recognized by all leaders of economic science. If he did recognize the law, the second question arose—How did he think the law could be abolished ?

The Progressive party of that time, led by Schultze-Delitzsch as representing their economic theories, was, however, very far removed from recognizing the existence of that law. Open refusal to admit, ambiguous denial, attempts to explain the facts away, the imputation of low motives actuating the declaration of this " untruth " — all these methods were attempted. Such procedure can be only partially excused by the unwarrantable and exaggerated conclusions which Lassalle deduced from this law. He represented as something peculiar and especially formidable to the working class the fact that its income should at all times correspond with its most urgent necessities, while at the same time the necessities increased with an increase of income. As there are extremely few men whose income perceptibly surpasses their requirements, this law does not express anything peculiar to the working class alone, nor anything which, considered in and for itself, should arouse horror ; but instead of emphasizing this circumstance, Lassalle's opponents attacked his principle as a pure piece of invention. Lassalle rightly says that the anger of his enemies was " boundless " after he had revealed this law in the argument of his " open answer." Men turned upon him, as in antiquity they turned upon a priest who had betrayed the mysteries of Ceres. " Had my enemies been Romans," he says, " they would have struck me down in open market, as the patricians once struck down Gracchus ; but my enemies are not Romans, and for that reason they attempt to strike me down with calumnies, and not with swords."[1]

Just at that time Lassalle had been condemned to four months' imprisonment, as a punishment for the pacificatory and purely historical tone of his " Workmen's Programme." The newspapers professed to have discovered at one time that his opposition to the middle class was based upon hopes of ameliorating the rigours of his confinement, or that he was acting as a deserter, or as a tool of the reaction, or, again, as an ignorant amateur in the department of political economy. None the less, no one succeeded in explaining away the existence of the law. Thus the only issue was to regard it as an economic law of nature which, as such, could never be overthrown, and this last resource was also adopted.

Lassalle asserts that all attempts to improve the position of the working class by means of savings-banks, sick-clubs, accident insurances, and the like, are invalidated by this law, and must ever be naturally fruitless. If these institutions are intended to counteract the manifold misfortunes—insanity, illness, old age, etc.—which reduce individual workmen by chance or necessity below the general level of their class, they have a relative though a very subordinate value ; but for the welfare of the class as such they are purposeless. Lassalle

[1] " Labour Problem."

then considers the co-operative societies of consumers, founded by Schultze-Delitzsch for similar humanitarian purposes. He shows that the workmen require help, not as consumers, but as producers, for all men as consumers stand, comparatively speaking, upon the same level.   The point is to relieve pressure where the shoe pinches. He then examines the credit and raw material societies, and points out that the inevitable movement of industry is daily killing the labour of the individual handicraftsman by the system of manufacture on a large scale.   Hence these unions, which at most place the poor craftsman in a position to compete with the prosperous, do but unnecessarily prolong the deadly struggle of individual labour with the larger manufactories.

Finally, he draws attention to the illusory nature of the comparison constantly made between the position of the workman to-day and his position in earlier centuries, by which the true question is quietly obscured.   The point at issue is not the position of the workman in comparison with his position three hundred years ago, but his position in comparison with the necessities and customs of life at his time.   The cannibal savage cannot be said to regard the lack of a decent coat as a want.   Similarly, before the invention of printing, the workman felt no privation if he were unable to procure a useful book.   Privation is the point at issue.   Lassalle finally demonstrates that such retrospective views of the history of civilization are of very doubtful value, for the manufactured products, which tend to become cheaper, are consumed by the workman to a far less degree than the necessities of life, which show no similar steady tendency to cheapness.

Thus the usual considerations and compensating measures leave the law of wages untouched, and are therefore, in Lassalle's opinion, of no importance to the working class, considered as a class.   Hence he takes the view that the only remaining remedy is State interference.   To oppose this position, his adversaries changed their tactics, and asserted that the law of wages is a law of nature, against which, therefore, the State ought not to fight.   Lassalle's view was, as we have already seen, that economic laws are not natural, but historical.

A short explanation of this disputed point now becomes

necessary. Ricardo's theory of wages is the following :
Everything has a natural price and an actual price, and labour
is no exception. The natural price consists in the amount
of labour expended upon the production of the commodity.
If this object is labour itself, the natural price of labour consists in the expenditure necessary to produce a workman—that
is, in the sum absolutely necessary for the support of himself
and his family. The actual price of every article depends upon
supply and demand, but, as a rule, will only diverge from the
natural price for short intervals of time and to an insignificant
extent. As regards labour, a steadily increasing demand for
it will naturally produce a rise in wages, but at the same time
will produce a greater influx of workmen. If the demand is
reduced, the resulting distress will diminish the number of
workmen, and therefore again produce a rise in wages.

The point below which wages cannot fall is most intimately
connected with the mode of life under which the workman
finds he can live and rear his family in any particular land or
at any particular time. The reasons which prevent wages
from falling below this point are stated by Lassalle, in his
answer to the Workmen's Committee, to be emigration, the
fall in the marriage rate, artificial sterility of marriage, and
the diminution of the working population by distress.

Of these causes, the last alone is decisive. The connection
of the marriage and birth rates with the general prosperity,
and especially with the price of corn, is universally recognized,
but will not explain variations in the rate of wages ; for these
occur within spaces of time too short to admit the influence
of variations in the numbers of the rising generation. Emigration and migration within a country are merely forms under
which distress is outwardly expressed. This, therefore, remains the only material influence.

No one will deny that this law of wages is as hard as
" iron," as Lassalle called it, if he knows the difference between
the longevity of the rich and the poor, and realizes that want,
even if it claims victims only sporadically, none the less steadily
undermines vitality. Its influence is almost equally oppressive
whether the average prosperity of the population is high or
low ; for when the average is high, the workman will cling as

long as possible to the objects characteristic of his social status, which can be seen and are regarded by him as outward tokens of his position, and will do this even at the sacrifice of the greatest necessaries of life.

It was certainly a gross mistake on the part of Lassalle's opponents to dispute an assertion which he could so easily prove, as that all scientific authorities are agreed in regarding the law of wages as really existing. He was equally correct in pointing out the deceptive nature of comparisons between the present position of the workman and his position in earlier times ; but, none the less, one circumstance exists which, if it does not invalidate the existence of the law, invalidates Lassalle's conclusions—namely, that wages within recent years have, as a matter of fact, risen.

The law by no means excludes the workman from the possibility of improving his mode of life, in consequence of the progress of civilization, and even if the law cannot be abolished under existing social conditions, the conclusion does not follow that an improvement in the workman's position under present society is impossible. Such an improvement has been actually brought about in spite of the law, and to this Lassalle's action has largely contributed ; for such progress has been due, partly to the interference of the State in the most obvious abuses, partly to the fear of a threatening social revolution, and partly to the sympathy which a few leading men were able to arouse on behalf of the working class ; partly, also, to the co-operation of the workmen for the protection of their common interests—all of which influences were either furthered or in many cases created by Lassalle's agitation.[1]

The second point at issue is the alternative of self-help, or State-help. The destructive influence of a system of support and the strength inherent in the principle of self-help were generally acknowledged in Germany, which regarded England as the pattern State, after the abortive revolution of 1848. Hence we cannot be surprised at the outcry of disgust aroused by the word " State-help." Lassalle replies by urging that it is obvious foolishness to be continually calling upon the

---

[1] F. A. Lange, " The Labour Problem," 161-172 ; Lujo Brentano, " The Position of Labour in Modern Law," 179 et seq.

workman to help himself. The individual without capital is helpless, and one might as well call out to a man who had fallen into the water, with a weight of a thousand pounds in his pocket, advising him to swim to the shore. In the second place, Lassalle emphasizes the fact that State interference by no means excludes social self-help. No one, for instance, prevents a man from climbing a tower by his own strength, if he lends him a ladder for the purpose. Nor, then, does the State prevent youth from developing their own powers by providing teachers, schools, libraries, etc., for their benefit. Thirdly, he proves that the Manchester school itself was so unprincipled as to demand State-help, on finding itself unable to procure other resources, at a time when it was necessary to stop the emigration of workmen during the cotton famine, brought about by the great American War.

In these general statements Lassalle is correct, but he shows a tendency to hair-splitting in his fourth criticism, which is directed against an enterprise of his chief opponent, Schultze-Delitzsch, who attempted to find enough capital among the workmen to found a bank, which is still flourishing at the present day. This bank was to give credit to workmen's unions which really deserved it, and Lassalle criticizes the idea as if Schultze-Delitzsch had dropped his own principle and adopted Lassalle's. Schultze-Delitzsch always formulated his principle as follows : He stated that the weak forces of the smaller workmen and craftsmen would always be able to obtain credit if they would unite for purposes of self-help. After he had covered Germany with a vast net of unions, with a turnover of many millions, he crowned his system with the bank, that by this means he might be able to divert a large amount of capital into the smallest channels of his widely distributed unions. He conducted this plan upon such strict business principles that the shares of the bank even to-day enjoy the best of reputations upon the Berlin Stock Exchange ; while the industrial bank founded by his Conservative opponent, Privy Councillor Wagner, Bismarck's factotum, has disappeared from the Stock Exchange quotations. Lassalle is certainly correct in stigmatizing the attitude of Schultze-Delitzsch as shameless, when he made his appeal to the working class : " If you are to choose between Herr Lassalle and us, we need only say, ' There fine phrases, and here capital.' " When, however, Lassalle asks whether it would not be better to accept help from the State than receive it as alms from private individuals, we must point out that in this case there was no question of charity, but of an actual business enterprise.

The central point of his demonstration is to show that the vast majority of the population are without means, and that the State is, in reality, nothing more than an association of its population. " Why, therefore," Lassalle appeals to the working class, " cannot your great association, the State, exert a fructifying and stimulating influence upon your smaller associations ?" This the State not only can, but must do. Its task and its intention is to facilitate the progress of civilization among mankind. For this purpose the State exists, and has always existed. Without State interference neither canals, highroads, railways, nor telegraphs, would have been introduced. England paid twenty millions of pounds for the abolition of slavery in her colonies, and if the fact be established that free competition, as it exists among us, means for the poor that they must fight with teeth and nails against cannons and firearms, why should the State not interfere in this case also ?' [1]

If we examine these two catch-words, " Self-help " and " State-help," from the historical point of view, as they were understood in Germany in 1863 and 1864, both will be found to suffer from great lack of precision. As we have already observed, Schultze-Delitzsch a few years previously had succeeded, after making a small beginning in his own town, in creating a connected series of unions to advance cash and raw materials, founded upon the principle of " self-help." In connection with these, a number of workmen's educational unions, conducted in the same spirit, was gradually founded. This spirit was very different from that which prevailed in the English workmen's associations, which were based upon actual self-help. In the case before us the workman had or

---

[1] *Cf.* Lassalle, " The Labour Problem "; " Open Letter of Reply "; " The Workmen's Handbook " ; " Indirect Taxation."

took no initiative ; his position was determined upon a patriarchal system, his education was guided by those in better positions than himself, to whose interest it was to prevent the existing difference between the advantage of the manufacturer and that of the workman from ending in open struggle, for the manufacturer naturally regarded a settlement of contradiction by peaceful means as most important. In other respects the movement displayed all possible sympathy towards the working class : there were credit unions for those of them who already possessed a little capital, and wished to rise slowly above their class. Popular lectures were given upon astronomy, geography, natural science and history, whales and electrical machines, but politics were taboo. The workmen would then automatically join the Liberal party. This system was called self-help, for all were entirely agreed that there should be no State-help for the working classes. " No State-help granted from above, lest the Conservative party should be strengthened, and no State-help extorted from below, because the sense of democratic independence among the workmen necessary to secure such extortion was detested."[1]

In opposition to this system, Lassalle propounded his solution of State-help, which was intended to induce the workman to help himself with serious intent, but also to call in the State as a regulating power. We have already seen what he was able to say in general in favour of State interference, and how he emphasizes the duty of definitely forwarding objects of civilization as incumbent upon the State. Upon this point thinkers of the most different schools agree with him to-day, but it cannot be denied that even before Lassalle's time such agreement was also widely spread. Schultze-Delitzsch, for instance, had often emphasized this duty of the State, but with regard to the limits within which the State could justifiably interfere there was, and there still continues, much divergence of opinion. It is, however, certain that one of the most fruitful branches of Lassalle's activity is to be found in his vigorous emphasis of the rights and duties of the State, as against the one-sided views of the Manchester school.

[1] F. A. Lange, " The Labour Problem," 361.

We must now conclude with a glance at his practical
proposals.

Here we have the third point in dispute—productive unions
supported by State credit. Lassalle has nothing to say concerning any State organization of workmen, and makes no
proposals in the least resembling the national factories erected
in Paris in 1848 (by the enemies of the Socialists), which
inevitably ended in disaster. He demands the voluntary
co-operation of individuals. He only asks that these unions
may be enabled to begin their existence by an advance of the
necessary capital from the State. The State is thus to help
them by giving them credit, but is not to " organize " them,
and is not to carry on the work at its own expense or in the
position of a manufacturer. On the contrary, it is, by giving
credit, to enable the workmen to organize themselves and to
work for their own advantage.

But for the success of his plan not only must a credit
union include all existing workmen's unions, but an insurance
system must embrace the several unions within any one
branch of trade and thereby provide a balance to cover
practically all losses. Capital risk, therefore, does not exist
for individual unions, since competition is excluded. The
common organization of all the unions in the country would
at any rate go so far that they would keep one another informed of the conditions of production and the state of the
markets. The business books of the several unions would be
audited by a central committee appointed for the purpose,
and thus would become a real foundation for scientific statistics
of the conditions of production. By this means it would
be possible to avoid any likelihood of over-production, and
even so long as this object was not attained, over-production
would simply become production by anticipation, as the
colossal capital of the unions would abolish the necessity of
competitive sale. Thus society would be saved the crises
brought about by over-production, and this advantage, in
Lassalle's opinion, would be accompanied by a great and
positive addition to the wealth of the community.

To what an extent expenses are cut down by production
upon a large scale is universally recognized. It has been

proved, for instance, that by combining the bakeries of Saxony into large firms, with uninterrupted production, at least a million thalers a year would be saved in fuel alone. Lassalle maintains that such great co-operative enterprises would not only transform the problem of distribution, but would increase production to an unexampled extent by abolishing the haphazard methods at present in vogue. He further asserts that the markets of the world would consequently belong to the nation which first resolved to introduce this social transformation.

With regard to Lassalle's proposals for the future, it should be observed above all things that he never regarded them as containing any solution of the social question, nor did he ever profess to anybody that he could solve that problem. He has repeatedly asserted that this solution was a task demanding generations, and perhaps centuries, of time. In his pamphlet, " Open Letter of Reply," he never once used the phrase, " the social problem," and even less did he speak of its solution. Such a phrase was repugnant " to his conscience as a thinker," to use an expression he employs in a letter. His habitual term invariably was, " the improvement of the position of the working classes." Productive unions supported by State credit were to him merely the necessary first step upon the road which he was firmly convinced posterity would and must follow.

Many elements in Lassalle's fundamental views were derived from Hegel, and ascended the throne in company with Bismarck. One of these is his exaggeration of the State as the highest moral unity in which the individual can be merged. For Lassalle, with his love of power, it was a matter of indifference whether a decree from above forced society to modify its nature or whether such modifications were gradually introduced as the outcome of the widest possible political freedom. Though he was a lover of freedom, he was by nature a dominating, commanding and patronizing character, and regarded the independence of the masses as no more than a very remote object. I do not believe in the vitality of a union which is not independently developed, and does not conduct its own affairs. An official body in charge of the details of organization would be more likely to stifle than to stimulate any inclination to independence on the part of the workman, which is the great point at issue. The principal question is whether such unions would increase the scale of production above its present extent. It is not so much defective methods of distribution as the necessary limitations upon production which are the causes of the oppression under which the poorer classes labour. At the present time, with the stimulus of competition, with long hours of work and the subjection of the workmen, we are unable to produce more than we do, and is it likely that production could be increased under new regulations less severe in their operation ? Is it true that co-operation alone would produce so material a change in the conditions of production ? In the opposite case the productive union would be unable to guarantee the participants any profits much beyond the present rate of wages, simply because the capitalist, or, in other words, the bonus on capital, had been excluded from the enterprise. Let us suppose that a great manufacturer has four thousand workmen, and makes an annual profit amounting to the colossal sum of £10,000. If we regard this sum as a bonus on capital, and divide it, each workman would annually obtain an addition of only £2 10s. Lassalle has apparently over-looked the fact that private landed property is the first to profit by a rise in values produced by labour, and that such property, without any expenditure of labour, chiefly absorbs the fruits of labour.

While Lassalle continually repeats the fact that capital is in immediate enjoyment of all advantages, he lays no weight upon the fact that it is also immediately exposed to all risks and losses. Risk and loss do undoubtedly affect the workman indirectly, but he does not directly bear them. Obviously, the productive unions which could only be organized by slow degrees would never be able to bear a loss unless they were supported by State credit. The capitalist who has £100,000 can lose £50,000, and is not reduced to beggary ; but if we suppose that two thousand union workmen lost a similar amount—workmen living immediately upon their incomes—how could their difficulties be in any way relieved without drawing upon State credit to an almost unlimited extent ?

If the existence of Lassalle's productive unions is to be assured, the simultaneous erection of all unions in one branch of trade becomes necessary.

Even in such a case State-help in this form would scarcely be a permanent guarantee, unless we possessed the Universal State. A State can also suffer loss, and against such loss there is no insurance. It is surely superstitious to suppose that the connection between the price of commodities and prevailing circumstances can be severed. Surely, in opposition to Lassalle's view, the first State to introduce the new order of things would be in the worst possible position in the markets of the world, because it would be the least able to bear a loss.

Finally, the productive unions supported by the State, which are intended to abolish class differences, would inevitably introduce a new system of class differences by introducing new privileges. The object of Lassalle's historical efforts may be briefly stated as an attempt to replace the predominance of the third estate by that of the fourth, which he regards as synonymous with the human race. He readily admits that the third estate, when it rose against the classes favoured with privileges and protected by inequality in the sight of the law, during the great French Revolution, did regard its cause in its initial enthusiasm as the cause of the whole nation and of humanity at large (the declaration of the " Rights of Man ") ; but at the same time he maintains that this estate was speedily seen to be bringing with it a new privilege—the privilege of capital—and that it necessarily concealed among its numbers a new and unprotected estate, the fourth. Then this fourth estate, which can show no exclusive qualification for a share in the governmental power, neither nobility nor landed property nor capital, becomes for Lassalle equivalent with the human race, and its freedom is the freedom of the human race, " for we are all workmen." Here I will only point out that the fourth estate, as described by Lassalle, is not a reality, but an ideal of his own conception. Even if this estate were unwilling to offer any fresh privileges either to nobility, landed property, capital, or education, its ideas would follow the obvious course of argument and it would probably infer : because I am neither rich nor noble nor educated, I have a right to maintenance and to a share in the Government. But there is a far more obvious danger apparent. Would not the gradual formation of productive unions supported by State credit place the workmen who were not members in a critical position ? The gradual formation of such unions would reduce to a lower stage the working class who were forbidden by the nature of their occupation to make any use of such a union (such as porters, hodmen, and casual labourers of every kind). The foundations of a fifth estate would then be laid. The process would be repeated which occurred after the declaration of the " Rights of Man." It would be seen that the new programme was incapable of embracing more than one class, or of forming anything else than a new aristocracy.[1]

All these objections, whatever their justification or importance, are of no considerable interest here, for the simple reason that the question of productive unions supported by State credit was of very subordinate importance to Lassalle himself.

It is true, he thought, that the formation of such unions upon a large scale would be a means of accommodating supply to demand, as the enormous credit which these unions would enjoy would secure them against the necessity of selling commodities regardless of times and seasons ; but for him they were nothing more than a means to an end.

On April 22, 1863, he writes to Rodbertus, who did not believe in the value of the productive unions : " If you can show me another means equally effectual, I shall be equally ready to accept it and to subscribe to it. I have only proposed the association temporarily, because at the moment I really see no means which would be, relatively speaking, so easy and so effective. For the workman must have something quite definite and tangible proposed, not a mere law, to become interested in it." A month later he writes again : " Here we are only dealing with a practical means of transition, and not with a theoretical and final solution of fundamental importance. This you yourself will hardly expect for another five centuries. That this solution can be *gradually brought about* by the association, and *facilitated* by it to an astonishing extent,

---

[1] F. A. Lange, " The Labour Problem," 361.

seems to me indisputable, and I will do my best to prove it to you. Moreover, I do not see *any other* means of transition *equally* practicable. You have yourself admitted and most strongly emphasized the fact that a final solution, which you do not expect for five centuries, will only be brought about by a series of transitions, and cannot possibly be produced at one stroke. At the same time, it is quite possible that you may have devised an even better means of transition than mine. In this case, as I have said, I will most readily support it."

Rodbertus, who wished to retain and modify the principle of wages, does not seem to have been able to indicate any other means. In any case, the utmost interest attaches to the fact that in September, 1878, Bismarck expressed himself favourably upon Lassalle's proposal. He declared the foundation of productive unions to be an idea concerning the inexpediency of which he was by no means convinced. " I cannot say," he states, " whether I have been impressed by Lassalle's arguments or am still influenced by the convictions which I acquired in part during my stay in England in 1862 ; but it seems to me that the foundation of productive associations, such as are flourishing in England, would provide a possibility of improving the position of the workman, and giving him a material share in the business profits." He asserted that the attempts made in Germany proved nothing, as they had been carried out upon too small a scale. He referred the idea of these unions to the " sensible efforts " which at that time were the driving-wheel of the Social Democratic movement, and summed up his exposition in the following terms : " What Lassalle told me on this point was stimulating and instructive, for he knew and had learnt a great deal."

The statements quoted prove, in the first place, that the system of productive unions supported by State credit, proposed by Lassalle as the immediate object of the agitation, was in itself for him simply a means to attain a distant and final object—the abolition of landed and capital property. In a letter to Rodbertus he describes this as being the essence of his views, since he had begun to study political economy at all. He adds that this was an object which he certainly would not venture to put before the mob, and which he had therefore been careful to avoid mentioning ; but, on the other hand, his statement undoubtedly shows how entirely he was convinced of the correctness and practicability of his means. He firmly believes that unions supported by State credit would, in the course of some centuries, inevitably lead to his object. Rodbertus, in his " Posthumous Papers," says upon this point : " It must be said, without any desire to cast the smallest slur upon Lassalle's character, that there was an esoteric and an exoteric Lassalle, and in my opinion such practical questions as the social problem must always be discussed from these two points of view." These words were at once connected by Lassalle's opponents with those previously quoted (see, for instance, the impudent and valueless plagiarism from Becker : A. Kutschbach, " Lassalle's Death "), and were adduced as a proof that he did not himself believe in the means which he propounded to the workmen, whom in reality he regarded as the mob ; but such an assertion contains a double untruth. It is untrue to say that Lassalle had no confidence in this means, and it is untrue to say that he regarded the workmen as a mob, for he applies this term, on the contrary, to the vast and half-educated forces of Philistinism.

However, the fact is clear that the economic position of society cannot be permanently relieved by purely economic methods. Lassalle, with his excessive belief in the efficacy of outward methods, forgot that greater and richer production can only be attained under the influence of intellectual and moral education. He certainly manifests his anger against the large production of senseless objects of luxury. He reasonably attacks the middle classes for the foolishness with which they confuse the expensive with the beautiful. In other words, he clearly saw the desirability of removing the steadily increasing difference between the modes of life followed by the lowest and the highest groups of society. This change could be produced by substituting a larger production of indispensable commodities in place of our modern requirements. But, this sensible and justifiable praise of equality is not supported as its interests imperatively demand, by due emphasis of the fact of inequality. The master-workman should and must earn more than the apprentice ; the foreman deserves more than the labourer, and the overseer more than all. In other words, when Lassalle appears as a demagogue, we feel the want of any desire to inspire respect for intellectual work or to stimulate his hearers to rise to a higher stage of culture. They are to him an imposing force, as indeed they are, merely by numbers and weight. Thus, in his zeal to obtain another mode of distributing surplus products, he never says a word in any of his pamphlets on behalf of attempts to secure an increase in the value of products, such as a radical improvement in elementary education under the cheapest possible conditions. Only once in the long article which appeared in the *Kreuzzeitung* of July 19, 1864, does he ask for " the education of the working classes to a far wider extent under compulsion." Perhaps it is too much to ask that he who was obliged to create this movement from the outset should also have an eye to every consideration or reservation which was desirable.

In this point also he disagreed with Rodbertus, and their want of harmony upon this question was the reason that Rodbertus, though he approved Lassalle's principles and theories, declined to support his agitation with the great influence of his name. Lassalle wished to make the Socialist party a political force ; Rodbertus wished to confine its efforts to economic objects. Lassalle declined to join him unless he would take political action. This condition he based upon the view that under Schultze-Delitzsch the workmen had become a political force, but had been led astray into wrong economic paths, and that only by a stronger political agitation could they be led back from their economic aberrations. Hence he placed universal franchise as the first immediate object before himself and his opponents. The Liberals, who were fighting for free trade, were by no means favourably inclined to this demand. On this question he writes to Rodbertus in May, 1863 : " I have no intention of allowing the social question to be overpowered by the electoral question. You may rely upon me for that, but both myself and my party are injured by pseudo-democratic arguments (we neglect the development of political freedom, etc.), and so I must outbid my opponents upon either side, and defeat them both as a Democrat and as a Socialist."

To the best of my understanding, under existing circumstances no other path was open to Lassalle than that which he chose. His genius grasped the situation completely, and dominated it with tactics in which no fault can be found. It was his intention in the first place to raise the workman in the political world, and only then could he contemplate the task of improving and securing his social position.

CHAPTER VII

IF we are to form a correct estimate of the agitation created by Lassalle, we must consider the political conditions under which it began. These conditions seem very remote, because even greater political changes have taken place in Germany since that time than in the previous half-century. The Government was then supported by the *Kreuzzeitung* party. The Progressive party, generally corresponding to the National Liberals of to-day, had entered the political arena in 1861, and had thus waged for only one year their apparently hopeless war against those in power, which was continued until 1866. This conflict produced no result, until the Government, after all possibility of ending the strife by overthrowing their opponents was removed, cleared the way by war after war, and partially carried out the programme of the party whose views had hitherto been desperately opposed. The old German democracy of 1848 had left the scene, or had resigned itself to join the Progressive party. To Lassalle's restless spirit it seemed daily clearer that this party was lacking in political capacity and energy. At the outset of 1862 he seems to have entertained some weak hopes that the opposition would change their tactics, and would definitely insist upon their desires (the speech " What now ?"). When these hopes had vanished, he necessarily turned his gaze in another direction. His answer to the Workmen's Committee in Leipsic became, as we have mentioned, the occasion for the formation of the General Union of German Workmen, with the attainment of universal and direct suffrage as its object, and the presidency was offered to Lassalle. He was not particularly anxious to accept it, as the prospect of acquiring immediate power by which any serious achievement could be secured was very small. As he says in one of his letters : " Political action means immediate and instantaneous effectiveness. Everything else can be secured by scientific methods."[1] He yielded, however, to the persuasions of Countess Hatzfeldt, and undertook the difficult and harassing task of organizing and guiding a great workmen's union in face of the passionate opposition of the ruling classes, who were ready to use any means that came to hand.

The political object of his agitation can be described in a few words. Like Marx, he held the fundamental view that the whole course of social history, as known to us, has been a history of class warfare. In his book " The Italian War " he demonstrates the erroneous nature of the view that the French Revolution of 1789 was a purely political movement. It was a social revolution, and consisted in the overthrow of the old feudalism by modern civic society. With the object of destroying the new social order, feudal Europe joined in alliance against France. To defend and to secure its social significance, the Revolution abandoned its political form under Napoleon and became a military dictatorship. The French middle class, under Napoleon, fought for the confiscated property of the *émigrés*, which was estimated to be worth twelve milliards, for the abolition of monopolies and for freedom of competition. The object of the French middle class at that time was to overthrow feudal methods of production in manufacture and agriculture, and to secure freedom of capital. For these purposes the middle class displayed both energy and vigour. Purely political freedom, on the other hand, according to Lassalle's views, would never have been able to inspire the middle class with a readiness to self-sacrifice, for such freedom is never regarded by this class as of sufficient importance.[2]

[1] B. Becker, " Revelations Concerning the Tragic Death of Ferdinand Lassalle," 28. The genuineness of the letters printed in this low pamphlet is not disputed. Yet the possibility of falsification in points of detail is not excluded in the case of copies taken secretly, as these.

[2] Lassalle, " The Italian War," 54 ; " The Workmen's Handbook," 63-65.

Hence Lassalle's idea was to make class and social interest the moving force behind the cause of political freedom, and the only interest to be found was that of the poorer classes, whose numbers make them formidable indeed. He made the acquisition of universal franchise a question of daily food for the workman. In the working class he found the only adequately imposing force which could cope with the forces of political reaction prudently equipped with all the instruments of power. " Give me," he cries optimistically, " five hundred thousand German workmen as members of my union, and the reaction is no more."

If we can contrive to imagine ourselves in his position, we cannot refuse him our admiration. Schultze-Delitzsch was at that time the man of the hour. All the forces of independent thought flattered him, venerated him and followed him. Even Bebel was then walking in his footsteps. His doctrine of self-help was the only solution. From the moment when Lassalle rose against him he received as his portion scorn and mockery, and outbreaks daily renewed of hatred and overflowing contempt. The Liberal party believed, as one of the tenets of their faith, that Lassalle was in the service of the reaction—unconsciously, according to the calmer spirits ; with firm intent and purpose, said the hotheaded members of the party. The efforts of the Liberal leaders must have made him appear a secret reactionary to a large proportion of the working class. The sharp-sighted regarded him as a Socialist, as a man dangerous to society, and therefore to be treated as an outlaw. At the same time the philosophers of Socialism—Rodbertus, Marx, and Engels—wrapped themselves in profound silence which could only be interpreted as disapproval and necessarily aroused distrust.

In this apparently desperate situation Lassalle showed himself really great. It was impossible for him to follow Rodbertus, and, while agreeing to sacrifice the political element in his movement, to restrict himself to proposals aiming at social improvement, as purely theoretical disputes naturally would have been their only outcome. By such methods progress would have been impossible. Equally impossible was it for him to follow the example of Marx, and to preach revolution and the violent overthrow of every form of social order hitherto recognized, while declaring the abolition of private property as the object of his movement, unless he wished to end his time in penal servitude or in London, like Marx, who had fled the country. He came forward with perfect knowledge of men. He knew very well the strength of the Prussian monarchy, the slackness of the middle classes, and the thoughtlessness of the workmen. The middle-class cry for freedom produced no impression upon the working class. The working class had been aroused by the proclamation of equality, for which their first demand was expressed in their desire to exercise universal and direct suffrage. But it was not only necessary to arouse the working class, but to strengthen their sense of honour and of independence. Lassalle attained this end by disseminating his pamphlet, " Science and the Workmen." He showed the workmen that the highest culture and the greatest knowledge then existing were in alliance with them. It was further necessary to inspire them with the confidence of victory, and here Lassalle succeeded by explaining the numerical relations between the prosperous and the poor, and by showing the working classes in how diminishing a minority their favoured opponents were.

At the same time, in order to stir even the most indifferent among his hearers, he produced official statistics of the death-rate among the children of factory-workers, and appealed to paternal feeling and the love of mankind when his appeal to the love of freedom failed to strike home.[1]

Throughout the course of his agitation he used no single inflammatory or illegal phrase. No other object was proposed or admitted except the improvement of the condition of the working classes.

He was ready to dominate and to use threats, and did not shrink from the danger of stirring the powers of the uneducated against society ; but he was anxious to control and organize the masses, as indeed he did, by inspiring them with great ideas. " What is the origin," he asks in one of his speeches in his defence,[2] " of the political fear which the middle classes entertain of the people ? " He replies : " The recollections of

---

[1] C. A. Schramm, " Rodbertus, Marx, Lassalle," 70.
[2] " Science and the Workmen," 24 *et seq.*

the spring of 1848, when police discipline was broken down, when the people filled all the streets and public squares, and everyone was completely in the hands of men like Karbe, Lindenmüller, and other thoughtless agitators of the time—men without knowledge, culture, or insight, whirled to the surface by the storm which stirred political life to its very depths." At that time the middle classes shut themselves trembling in their houses. "Where," asks Lassalle, "were the intellects of Berlin, the men of science and of thought?" "They were not cowardly," he replies, "but they told themselves, 'the people does not understand our ideas or our language.' Now, gentlemen," he exclaims, "are you so certain that a political convulsion will never return? Do you wish that your lives and property were again in the hands of men like Karbe and Lindenmüller? If not, you may thank the men who have devoted themselves to the work of filling the abyss which divides scientific thought and scientific language from the people. You may thank those men who have undertaken at the expense of their own intellectual efforts a work, the results of which may benefit you all, every one of you. Maintain such men at the public cost in the Prytaneum, and do not subject them to prosecutions."

The movement which Lassalle's action accelerated was not directly marked by any characteristic repugnant to the constitutional system of monarchical Prussia. Even in his earliest youth, when he admitted in open court that he was "an adherent of the Social Democratic Republic," he possessed sufficient self-command and insight most decisively to restrain the workmen from any attempt to preach a State revolution. He says in his first speech before the Court of Assizes : "I turned to the workmen, I adjured them never to give way to the idea that they might use the opportunity to proclaim a Republic forthwith. Such action would be treachery to the common cause, for it would cast the apple of discord among the ranks of the citizens, who must now join like one man to avenge the insults offered to the law."

If such was his language as early as 1848, obviously in 1863 he was still further removed from any inclinations to come forward as a Republican. On the contrary, a mind so supremely

practical as his, far from entertaining desires for the overthrow
of the ruling powers, was prepared to make a compromise with
them, and to use them as a support where possible. In a
word, he had considered all the given circumstances, and had
resolved to make himself as few enemies as possible.

In this respect Lassalle is utterly different from Karl Marx.
Marx in character is as remote from Lassalle as a slowly moving
mind filled with profound and bitter resentment is remote from
a versatile and eloquent spirit, but in theory he is related to
Lassalle as the power of generalization to the power of dealing
with particular conditions.[1] Marx had the whole world before
his eyes ; Lassalle was concerned only with Germany, or, more
correctly, only with Prussia. The difference between their
doctrines is immaterial, but their methods were different.
Marx was international, Lassalle was national. Marx regards
social equivalence as only feasible in his Social Democratic
Republic, from which religion was banned, and his idea is a
federation of European Republics. Lassalle saw that the
European nationalities were still firmly established, that
national ideas were a factor of supreme importance, and that
religion would long retain an influence which no one could
afford to neglect, and he thought it possible, even under
existing political circumstances, to give the initial impulse to
a movement for transforming social conditions. As he so often
said, all he asked from the State was the " little finger."
Eventually he thought he had found in the Prime Minister of
that time, Herr von Bismarck, a man who was capable of
carrying out the work.

The complaint, which is justified up to a certain point, and
can be raised against Lassalle from the outset of his agitation,
is that his words at times ring with the true spirit of the demagogue. In his " Workmen's Programme," he flatters the
working class and heaps charges upon the upper classes to
an unjustifiable extent. However vigorously he may state
that the legal accusation against him was founded upon
stupidity and misunderstanding, the moral accusation remains.
A man is guilty who tells his workmen that the ruling classes

[1] Rudolph Meyer, " The Ominous Development of Socialism and the
Doctrine of Lassalle."

are forced in their own interests " daily to oppose all that is great and good, invariably to regret its success, and no less invariably to rejoice at its failure," etc.[1]

However far this may be true of individuals, a man does but rouse the hatred and passion of the blind mob when he enumerates such actions as demonstrable in the case of whole classes of fellow-citizens, many of whom have shown themselves capable of rising above their own class interests. It is little use for Lassalle, in attempting to defend his assertions concerning the necessary immorality of the upper classes, to appeal to the far stronger expressions of the Gospel. The Gospel was not an authority for him, and is equally little an authority for the rest of us, and such a wrong by no means makes Lassalle right.

It is also impossible to acquit Lassalle from the reproach of appealing indirectly to the brute force of the masses, for he never utters a word to explain the low and subordinate value of such brute force in every case where an intellectual point is at stake. His excuse is to be found in his principle that there is nothing more nearly related to pure intelligence than the sound common sense of large masses of men, and also in the principle which he had proved by practice that nothing is so amenable to organization as these great masses. In short, from the outset, the men of the French Convention were his real political ideals, and force gradually became all in all to him.

The place which he thus gave to force brought a change, at first imperceptible but by degrees quite obvious, upon the character of his agitation. It had begun as a purely Democratic movement, but the bitter and very personal feud which the several organs of the middle classes immediately opened against Lassalle were so many speedy intimations to the reactionary party that a new force had here appeared in the political arena, alliance with which might be well worth their trouble to obtain. By an old historical and political law, extreme parties are invariably drawn to one another; so it now happened that these several reactionary papers, henceforward designated Conservative by Lassalle, joined his side.

[1] " Workmen's Programme," 25.

The Liberals, as we have already mentioned, attempted to alienate the working class from Lassalle by the unanimous cry that he was the servant and tool of the reaction. About this time Lassalle made the personal acquaintance of Bismarck. His first visit to the Prime Minister is said to have been occasioned by the telegram to Bismarck, printed at the conclusion of Lassalle's Rhine speech (" The Festivals," etc.), demanding compensation for the violence of the police towards him. In my opinion, the form of the telegram indicates that the acquaintance had already been made. Lassalle found Bismarck's table covered with his pamphlets, and he found in the Prime Minister a kindred spirit who was entirely captivated by his personal influence, though this in no way prevented successive criminal prosecutions being brought against Lassalle.

About the time when he came in contact with Bismarck he received support of another kind, which he thought he could not venture, for reasons of prudence, to reject, but which injured his cause with good reason in the eyes of free and honourable thinkers, on account of the manner in which he used this help. He accepted the overtures of the clergy. This step was certainly not taken without some reluctance. Spielhagen is doubtless correct in reference to Lassalle when he depicts Leo as forced at the end of his career, with inward reluctance and many searchings of heart, to make common cause with the most reverend Privy Counsellor Urban. The Catholic clergy, which can never be accused of stupidity and invariably moves with the times, immediately saw that popularity and advantage might be gained by showing Lassalle the honour that was his due, and by supporting his efforts for the welfare of the lower classes. The Bishop of Mayence, afterwards the well-known Ketteler, was the first who openly declared for him. Lassalle was delighted at the acquisition of this new ally. In his speech at Ronsdorf, he declared with his usual emphasis that " the most brilliant representatives of German science, and the most distinguished names, before which even the State Counsel and the Judges must bow," had expressed by writing and word of mouth the highest approval and the most enthusiastic esteem for his book, " Bastiat Schulze." He then continued : " I will, however, give you a proof which is far more cogent than any that I have yet adduced. I will mention a name which will be heard by any court of justice on the Rhine, not only with the respect which those other names command, but with the highest reverence. A short time previously no less a person than a servant and Prince of the Church, the Bishop of Mayence, Freiherr von Ketteler, was impelled by his conscience to pronounce his views upon the workmen's question. He is a man who enjoys the reputation almost of a saint upon the Rhine, a man who for long years has devoted himself to scholarly research. He has published a book entitled ' Christianity and the Problem of the Working Classes,' and in this work he has declared for each several point in my economic principles and theories, in opposition to the so-called Progressives."

It is indisputably somewhat strange to hear from Lassalle this increasing emphasis of expression which advances from respect for great scholars to reverence for the clever priest in the princely cloak. It was also hardly worthy of Lassalle to appeal to the innocent confidence of the ignorant mob, who were thereby induced to regard as a saint the well-paid Bishop, who in after-years defended the syllabus and championed the Obscurantist party. Nor does he improve his case by introducing such qualifications as : " You know, my friends, that I do not belong to the pietists." He was obviously entering upon an undesirable alliance, but in his position Lassalle would none the less have been acting senselessly if he had rejected so powerful an ally who voluntarily offered his support. Moreover, at that time he had reached the highest pitch of irritation, in consequence of his lack of success and the opposition he encountered—irritation which history shows is experienced by those who attempt to make a disputed idea prevail against superior force. " The Messiah of the nineteenth century," as Heine, with poetical boldness, called Lassalle, was suffering the universal fate of Messiahs ; the tokens of his approaching downfall were manifest.

However, immediately before his downfall he was to experience yet one more triumph, such a triumph as had ever been his dream, amid thunders of applause, the enthusiasm of thousands, and a short enjoyment of the sweets of power.

As an agitator he had constantly shown his possession of the most remarkable gifts for winning the support of the masses ; devotion, admiration, blind obedience, and even absolute reverence were the feelings which the workmen displayed for him. The fact is the more remarkable, as Lassalle had hitherto never maintained a permanent connection with members of the working class. A talented workman, however, by name Kichniawy, had possessed his full confidence in Düsseldorf, and during his lifetime Lassalle was always in closest intimacy with this man ; but at the present moment enthusiasm for him spread like wildfire. I have already mentioned how, like a second Napoleon, he won over to his side in Frankfort the troops which his opponents brought against him. His journey through the Rhine Provinces in September, 1863, was not so much a tour to raise agitation as a magnificent review of troops.

From town to town Lassalle reviewed his adherents. In Elberfeld he spoke before an audience of three thousand and in Solingen before five thousand under one roof ; when the meeting was broken up by the police upon a pretext, and Lassalle was arrested, he was accompanied by ten thousand workmen, amid a continual storm of cheers, from the place of meeting to the telegraph-office, where he telegraphed to Bismarck, as we have stated.

This arrest, which became a triumphal procession, was unwisely described by part of the Liberal Press as if the police had been forced to accompany Lassalle to secure his personal safety, and had been obliged to protect him against the curses of the population with fixed bayonets. Naturally, such a falsehood produced no effect upon the eye-witnesses of the occurrence, and only served to evoke the angry devotion which is the reward and the satisfaction of men who are attacked with such weapons.

But all the ovations of this first campaign were as nothing to the triumphs which Lassalle gained when he made another tour through the Rhine Provinces in the spring of 1864, and for the first and last time took a personal part in the festivities celebrating the foundation of the Universal Union of German Workmen. Little harm was done by the fact that the hired quarters of the Union were found closed almost everywhere, for the reason that the police, with threats which were anything but ambiguous in character, had induced the landlords to break their word.   Other meeting-places were soon found.   In every case the same scenes occurred.   Hundreds of workmen met him at every station, offered him their greetings at the various stopping-places, accompanied him in procession to his lodging, which was decorated with wreaths and flowers, and presented him with testimonials.   In all the towns and upon all the roads were serenades, gateways of honour, garlands, inscriptions, endless cheering, and the delighted uproar of a thousand voices. Workmen, young and old, wherever he appeared, pressed forward about his carriage, which was decked on every occasion with flowers, wreaths, and flags, to shake his hand or to gain a word from him.   Sometimes as many as twenty-five decorated carriages followed him as a procession of honour.   This feeling was the more remarkable, as Ronsdorf and the neighbouring town of Solingen are among the few districts in the Rhine Provinces which both before and afterwards sent members of the Pro-gressive party of the time to the German Reichstag.   To give a correct idea of it, I will quote an extract from a newspaper report of the time, dated Ronsdorf, May 23 :

" As the carriage approached the limits of Ronsdorf it could be seen even from a distance that old and young were abroad, for the heights were thick with people.   At the boundary of the town was an archway with a wreath which bore the inscription :

'Welcome to Dr. Ferdinand!
A thousand welcomes to this our land !'

With wreaths and garlands and inscriptions of this kind the road was decorated throughout its length.   At the boundary the President's carriage, which could be recognized by its decoration and the transparency, ' Be at One !' was con-stantly overwhelmed with a rain of flowers, thrown with sure and laughing aim by the factory girls.   At this point the workmen of Solingen and Wermelskirch were drawn up in thick array to receive the President and to join the procession.   The enthusiasm was indescribable.   Till Rons-dorf was reached there was a continual round of greetings and cheers. Where the road turns and goes downhill a very interesting sight was afforded, as the masses of the people who had come out to the welcome attempted to keep pace with the carriage downhill, and ran either upon the side-walks or upon the road itself in pursuit of the procession ; so great was their zeal and enthusiasm that most of them reached Ronsdorf together with the carriages."

Such reports of tours made by royal personages or high officials are common enough. In these cases public feeling is easily aroused to enthusiasm by various motives—the loyalty of subservience, the hope of promotion and rank, the fear of reprimands or the anxiety to be noticed ; but such spontaneous expressions of gratitude and enthusiasm as are above described are unusual among the unemotional peoples of the North. Indeed, as Social Democracy was never able to gain a firm footing in this district for a long time afterwards, the enthusiasm seems to have been as short-lived as its blaze was fierce for the moment.

The speech which Lassalle now delivered, amid tumultuous cheers, to celebrate the foundation-day of the Workmen's Union, entirely corresponded with the prevailing enthusiasm. It was a long and proud retrospect of the results attained, of the rapidity with which the Union had spread and the ready reception it had received from the working classes in all German towns and districts from the greatest to the smallest. Lassalle, as we have mentioned, referred to the testimony of great scholars and of the venerable Bishop on behalf of his cause, and proceeded to emphasize the fact that King Frederick William IV., who had sent bayonets against the Silesian weavers in 1844, had shortly before graciously received a deputation from Silesia, and had directly promised to consider the miserable position of the workmen in the cloth factories. All these facts Lassalle summed up in the cry : " We have now forced workmen, people, scholars, Bishops, and the King, to testify to the truth of our principles."

At the moment when Lassalle uttered these words he reached the zenith of his life and his influence. His words were truth, and their truth was power. " Wherever I have been," he said, " I have heard observations from the workmen which may be

summed up as follows : We must weld our wills unanimously
into one single hammer, and put that hammer in the hands of
a man whose intelligence, character, and good-will we can
trust, that he may raise the implement and strike." And in
virtue of the dictatorship of insight he now held this heavy
hammer in his hand, and was as happy to feel its weight as
the god Thor when he again grasped his long-lost Mjölnir.
Like the god, Lassalle had now gained the desired weapon,
without which he was not entirely himself. For a moment he
brandished it rejoicing, as if he had reached his goal, though
in his thoughts he must have reviewed the strange vicissitudes
of his life, of which two whole years had been spent in prison,
while five fresh criminal actions were now threatening him—a
life which had passed through fire and storm, but had been
filled by an invisible harmony, the twanging of the bow-string
and the sounds of the lyre. His heart swelled beneath the
enthusiastic applause of the grateful crowds, but at the same
moment the picture changed, and he saw in giant outline before
his eyes the many anxieties which he had kept from the knowledge of his hearers—the dangers which threatened him, the
attempts which had failed, the weakness, the indifference, the
hatred, the envy, the brutality and the power against which
he had to fight. Such was the darker side of the picture.
News had reached him the previous day that he had been again
condemned to four months' imprisonment *in contumaciam* (as
he had failed to appear within the limits of time appointed by
the court), and he knew that the judges in the Rhine Provinces
were almost exclusively composed of members of the Progressive party. He also knew that the position of the Workmen's
Union was by no means so brilliant as he thought prudent to
represent it, to describe it to his warmest friends and to see
it in his optimistic moments. The Union exhausted his powers,
absorbed his property, which had been considerably increased
by his father's death, and was far from making the progress he
had expected. Lassalle's letters at this time complain bitterly
that everything might have been very different " if the working
classes had done their duty." And he was well aware that his
enemies were infinitely more energetic than his friends. No
wonder that thoughts of death and downfall arose within him

during this moment of brilliant enthusiasm. He concluded this last speech which he delivered to his adherents with these words :

" Well, I hope to refute these two charges, as I have refuted so many others. Strong, however, as a man may be, he is lost when confronted by a certain bitter antagonism. But this troubles me little. As you may think, I did not raise this standard without full knowledge beforehand of the possibility that my own downfall might be the consequence. (General sensation throughout the meeting.) The feeling that overcomes me upon the thought that I personally may be set aside cannot be better expressed than in the words of the Roman poet, ' Exoriare aliquis nostris ex ossibus ultor '; or, in German, ' If I am overthrown, may some successor and avenger arise from my bones.' May this great and national movement towards civilization not come to an end with myself. On the contrary, may the fire that I have kindled spread and devour as long as one of you draws breath. Such is the promise that I ask from you, and in token of it I will ask you to raise your right hands."

It might be thought that when Lassalle uttered these words he had a clear premonition that three months later he would be a corpse. A week previously, in a meeting of the Union at Düsseldorf, he had said to the members : " Next year you will be obliged to drape this room with mourning." Possibly he even foresaw that this national movement, if it did not die with him, would lose its national and monarchical character, and that the organization which he had founded would be absorbed in a few years by International and Republican Socialism.

Upon several subsequent occasions, though his health was shaken, he was obliged to speak in public. In the course of the prosecution directed against him at Düsseldorf, he who had shattered I know not how many criminal charges vainly made a last effort to win his freedom. The court condemned him in the first instance to six months' imprisonment. He felt deeply despondent. When Paul Lindau, the young editor of the *Düsseldorfer Zeitung*, who had done Lassalle the courtesy of reproducing verbally his speech in his defence, called out to him, as they took leave of one another, "We shall meet again, Herr Lassalle!" he replied, "Who knows?" And when Lindau looked at him in surprised interrogation, he added : "I cannot endure imprisonment for a year or even six months. I simply cannot stand it, and should prefer to go into exile. My nerves are completely broken down." Weary in body and soul, he went to his usual watering-place in July, at Rigi-Kaltbad. Here he was again overwhelmed with work, but attempted to restore his shattered health by feasting his eyes upon the beauties of Nature, and then it was that the fate overtook him which became his death.

CHAPTER VIII

WE have seen that Lassalle understood that his efforts for the moment were fruitless. Countess Hatzfeldt had written to him : " Can you not content yourself for a time with science, friendship, and the beauties of Nature ?" He replied from Rigi on July 28 : " You think that politics are a necessity to me. How little you know my nature ! I desire nothing more earnestly than to be rid of politics once for all, and to be able to retire to science, friendship, and the beauties of Nature. I am tired and weary of politics. Doubtless my political ardour would flame as fiercely as ever if any serious incidents called it forth, or if I had power or saw a means of gaining it —a means that I could suitably adopt, for without supreme power nothing can be done. I am too old and too great a man for mere child's play. For that reason I was very unwilling to accept the presidency. It was only at your request that I gave way, and it is at the present moment a heavy burden. If I could only lay it down, I could decide at once to travel with you to Naples, but how can I be rid of it ?"[1]

This is not the kind of thing that one would have expected to hear two months after the speech at Ronsdorf, but it is the language of weariness and overstrain. A few days before this was written, on July 25, a young woman had called upon Lassalle at Rigi. This incident was to lead to the conclusion of his life. It is an incident of which the low tongues of scandalmongers have made great use, but it will only be described here as far as it illustrates Lassalle's character or is explicable by it.

Fräulein Helene von Dönniges was the daughter of a dis-

[1] B. Becker, " Revelations," 28.

tinguished Bavarian diplomatist.   Her father was an influential
Privy Counsellor of King Max, and since the early sixties had
gathered round him at Munich a circle of cultured scientific
men, legal authorities, historians, and poets, including such
men as Liebig, Bluntschli, Sybel, Geibel, Heyse and Dingelstedt.
He was known throughout Bavaria for his hostility to the
power of the Catholic Church.   Her mother was a beautiful
Jewess, who had been converted to Protestantism in order to
marry her father.   The parents lived a luxurious, worldly and
pleasure-seeking life.   Their daughter, Helene, was left greatly
to herself and to a devoted maid in her youth, and became a
spoilt and neglected girl of lively spirit, impressionable and
thoughtful at an early age—in short, a premature woman of
the world.   When she was twelve years old she was as fully
developed as an ordinary girl of nineteen.   She was unusually pretty, of sensual and challenging beauty, with a
magnificent head of fiery red hair—one of the beauties who
invariably gather men round them in any company, because
they show without ambiguity that men are the chief object of
their interest.   Her ambition was to be the most daring of
horsewomen and the most desirable partner at balls.   At the
same time a tendency to enthusiasm for art and artists and for
men of greatness and daring slumbered in her heart.   When
she visited Berlin in the winter of 1861 she had a pleasant
South German or rather Southern manner, showed a readiness
to please and a somewhat imperious spirit.   She had been
already involved in several love affairs, and her reputation was
widespread.

She frequented those circles of Berlin society with which
Lassalle was connected, heard accounts of him here and there,
and heard even the most fastidious men speak of him in terms
of admiration.   One day a clever man whom she met for the
first time said to her after a short conversation : " You are
the first woman whom I have ever been able to think of as
Lassalle's wife."[1]

[1] Dr. Oldenberg has assured me that he actually did speak these surprising
words, which were repeated almost literally by Helene von Dönniges, or
as she afterwards called herself, using the name of her first husband, von
Rackowitza (afterwards Friedmann, and now Schewitz), in her book, which
in all material respects is reliable and truthful, " My Relations with Ferdinand
Lassalle," 1879.

They met one another at the houses of common friends, and
fell in love immediately.   Each of them had then become the
subject of conversation on account of their respective minor
love affairs—Lassalle for an intimacy with a lady of Berlin,
and Fräulein von Dönniges for the ardour with which she was
pursued by a young Wallachian Bojar named Yanko, Prince
of Rackowitza, to whom she had hitherto regarded herself as
half engaged.   But these new feelings dispelled any that they
had hitherto entertained.   As Lassalle immediately said of
them, " each was the other's fate."

Helene's passion was of the overpowering kind which may
bring a spoilt and unusually brilliant woman to worship the
man in whose neighbourhood she first feels that her will is
subordinate to another far stronger will ; that her pulses stand
still in fear and delight ; that her mind sinks beneath the
domination of a superior nature, and rises in yearning towards
it.   Lassalle's feeling for the young lady was calmer, but by
no means cool, and she made no concealment whatever of her
lively interest in him.   His period of youth was at its close.
He was seriously thinking of marriage, and something in
Helene's character attracted him so strongly that the idea of
a marriage rose in his mind at their first meeting.

The couple, however, had but few opportunities of seeing
one another.   Helene lived with her grandmother, who knew
nothing of Lassalle except that he was a " horrible demagogue,
who had once been involved in a prosecution for theft."   Her
house was therefore closed to him, and invitations from Lassalle's acquaintances were declined.   At the same time there
is no doubt that the lovers met oftener than Helene von Rackowitza declares.   I have certain information of the fact, but her
silence upon the point is natural, and in any case no definite
plans for the future had yet been made.

On that July evening at Rigi Lassalle saw her on horseback with a whole company of strange ladies and gentlemen.
In his delight at meeting her again, so fair and radiant, Lassalle
immediately resolved upon the serious step of a definite engagement.   Half jestingly and half seriously he proposed, in order
to avoid all difficulties with respect to parental objections, that
they should elope to France, and there be married.   She replied,

as was quite natural, that in case of necessity she was prepared to agree, but she asked him first to make a serious attempt to gain her parents' consent. Lassalle promised to offer his proposals for the hand of the young lady, and immediately communicated his intentions to the Countess. She wrote a letter attempting to dissuade him, to which he replied : " You say in your letter that I should feel some doubts, as I was recently head over ears in love with another girl, and I reply that the expression, being head over ears in love, can never apply to me. But in any case, it is no small piece of fortune for a man already thirty-nine and a half years of age to find a woman so beautiful, so free, and so entirely suitable to me, who loves me so much, and who finally will give up her will entirely to mine, which is an absolute necessity for me."

We see that Lassalle, in this letter of August 2, discusses the subject with a certain calmness and coldness, though such a tone is less surprising, as he is writing to the Countess. As a matter of fact, he was neither calm nor cold. He had spent the week after July 25 in a whirl of love and happiness. Politics, the agitation, and his many vexations were all forgotten. He had become young again. His relations with Helene were innocent and youthful. She could do with him as she would. She played with him as with a great dog, and if she said " Lie down !" he was prostrate at her feet. When she had gone away, he used to do his work in the telegraph-office of Rigi in order that he might be able to send her a message whenever he felt inclined. The tapping of the instrument calmed his nerves. Moreover, within three days he sent her six stormy love-letters—effusions of wild adoration. He followed her to Bern, read poetry to her, gave her books to read, told her of his life and his struggles, and allowed this adoring woman, twenty years of age, to learn full details of his plans, while she before her idol, her Cæsar, her royal eagle, again became a child and rejoiced at her happiness. His love was that of a student or a poet. He has " window dreams " while sitting on her window-sill during a beautiful moonlight night, lost in imaginings of the future and the wildest aspirations of youth. She may still see the day when he will be able to place the crown of victory upon her brow. Would she like a triumphal entry into Berlin in a carriage drawn by six white horses ? Our enemies are as numerous as the sand, but we shall drive over their bodies with people rejoicing and cheering about us, " Ferdinand the defender of the people !" a (proud title, isn't it ? " Long live the Republic and its golden-haired lady President !" But they return to earth. From one who was supposed to be Bismarck's right-hand man she had heard that Lassalle had visited him, and that he was " awfully impressed." Is that true ? Has Lassalle been to him, and on what account ?

He is silent, and plays with her hand. "What a child you are! It is absurd with such small fingers—for, you know, it *is* absurd to have such small fingers—I say it is absurd with these fairy fingers to try and pry into my deepest secrets, which I preserve as precious stones in the strong-box of my heart. Yes ; I did visit Bismarck. The great man of iron tried to captivate me, and iron is a precious metal, so strong and hard, so reliant for cutting and thrusting. What is there that iron has not secured in this world ? Almost everything has been wrought and founded by means of iron. I tell you, almost everything. But there is another metal more pliable and more seductive, useless for heroic exploits and deeds of arms, and yet more powerful than this omnipotent iron ; it is gold. What iron has destroyed gold rebuilds. It is very questionable which of the two metals is the stronger and more effective, but effect, after all, is the one important point. And, finally, iron grows rusty in course of time, and the place for rusty iron is the lumber-room. Away with it to history, the lumber-room of centuries. I prefer gold—such gold as my darling wears upon her head, and has been given to me, in my mysterious power to attract men and to make them mine. You shall see, my beloved, that our gold can attain everything."

" But you yourself speak a great deal about weapons and blood, and battles and revolutions cannot be brought about without weapons and without iron."

" Child, why talk of all this upon so beautiful a moonlight night ? To talk of battles and the call to arms is by no means the same thing as to hew down one's brothers and one's fellow-men with cold, hard, and blood-stained hands. Don't you understand what weapons I mean ? Don't you know that I mean my golden weapons of intellect, the art of speech, the love of humanity, the task of improving and raising the poor, the miserable, the toilers and moilers, and, finally, and above all things, the will ? Don't you know that I desire to use these noble and really golden weapons for more noble and beneficent purposes than the murderous implements of the Middle Ages ? Blood and iron are but the last necessity, when men will listen to nothing else ; but I think they will learn to fear us without any drawing of swords." Then followed a long embrace, kisses, whispering, and farewell.

This week, with its bright hopes and its long whispered conversations in the moonlight at the low window, was the poetry of their love, its true life, disturbed by no hostile elements and no violent passions. Indeed, this week, with its forgetfulness of the world and its surrender to love, marked the height of peaceful joy that was granted to both of them. A few days later the card-castle of happiness was overthrown.

Lassalle generally and in theory was aware of the fact that he was hated and abhorred by the upper classes of German society, but he had never yet attained any keen or true realization of the height which this hatred and this bitter abhorrence had reached. He saw himself as he was, with his great gifts and capacities, with his defects, which as a whole were not repellent, and he forgot how distorted a caricature of himself was in circulation among society, and how much dirt his detractors had cast upon his name. He was a simple nature, and he thought in his simple pride that he could easily bring two reluctant parents to reason. The only point was to discover " what they had against him." He relied upon his gift of attraction and upon his rights. He had the girl's consent, and he was no ordinary man. Moreover, Helene was of age, and a statesman like her father would hardly be likely to cause unnecessary scandal by a refusal.

On the morning of August 3 Helene von Dönniges came to meet her parents at Geneva. On the afternoon of that day Lassalle was to arrive at an hotel in the town. Helene found her relatives in a state of cheerful excitement. One of her sisters had become engaged to a man after her parents' hearts, a Count of high rank. She determined to take advantage of the prevailing good-humour, and to tell her mother everything, and she informed her that she was engaged to Lassalle.

Had she informed her mother that she had brought a formidable and deadly poison, and was proposing to administer it to the whole family, she could hardly have aroused greater horror and dismay. In spite of Helene's requests, her mother hurried away in tears to inform her father. He rushed in, thundering : " What is the meaning of this horrible affair with that scoundrel Lassalle ?" The friends of the family intervened, each with some dreadful story of Lassalle and his life with women, his relationship to the Countess, and his pernicious energy as an agitator. What was Lassalle ? The braggart chieftain of a marauding robber-band, with a prosecution for theft in his past history. Of all those present, the most poisonously disposed was a man whom Lassalle had once ordered to be thrown out of a public assembly, and who had sworn to repay the insult.

The girl remained unshaken in her declaration that, sorry as she was to vex her relations, she was none the less determined to marry Lassalle. Her father with curses informed her that if she persisted in her resolution he would permit no further intercourse between her, her mother, and her brothers and sisters. She ran out of the house unobserved, and hastened to Lassalle's hotel, where she had sent her maid a few hours previously with a letter of warning. Lassalle's train, however, was late. He had only just reached Geneva, had not received the letter, and Helene met him at the door of the hotel as he was getting out of the carriage. He was surprised by her desperate and distracted appearance. He opened the door of a room in the hotel. She fell down before him, calling herself his wife and his property. Now was the moment to flee to France by the next train.

She was right. The moment had arrived, and would never return. It was the only possibility of saving their future. Lassalle laughed at her. He could not understand or realize the state of affairs, and was simple enough to believe that Helene was exaggerating. Why in all the world could he not openly obtain his bride like other men ? What reasons called for a romantic elopement ? At that moment of his life Lassalle was not himself, and he never forgot it. For the first time in his life he acted irresolutely and according to social convention, and instead of escaping with Fräulein von Dönniges, he gave her his arm and took her to a lady friend. There her mother found her, and treated Lassalle, who maintained his calm demeanour, as an outcast whose observations demanded no reply. Stricken with stupidity and blindness, he gave Helene back to her mother in order to show her his power over her daughter, in the foolish belief that he could easily persuade a sensible and educated man like her father, and in the desire of paying his addresses in legal and conventional form. Her father now proceeded to pour the vials of his wrath upon the girl. Seizing her by the hair, he dragged her across the road to his house, locked her up, and began to subject her weak and broken will to a system of compulsion and persuasion which would have deprived a stronger woman of all power of action.

When Lassalle discovered that his access to Helene was cut off, he broke into despair at what he himself called his " drivelling," and made a firm resolve to recover Helene at any cost. The difficulties with which he was confronted raised and were to raise his passion to the highest degree, which was further inflamed by his scorn of himself for casting away by his weak and conventional action the happiness which had readily been offered to him. When, however, Lassalle's passion reached boiling-point under the influence of these events, the bold and enthusiastic pride of the girl was broken by the interpretation which she placed upon his action, and which we can easily understand. She loved Lassalle as tenderly as ever, and doubtless believed in his power to secure their union, but the fiery and dauntless character of her feelings had expired. She had staked everything upon one throw. Weak as she was, she had completely surrendered to him, and had acted with a desperate determination unusual in her sex and her youth, and her overflowing passion had been greeted with prudential considerations. Her violent adoration for him whom she called her beautiful and noble eagle began to fade from the moment when the eagle appeared to act like a common domestic fowl, and then her doubts began to rise. Was he really hotly in love with her ? Had he been entirely serious, and, if so, why did he thus voluntarily give her up and hand her over to her parents ?

By August 4 her father extorted from her a declaration, which was handed to Lassalle, in which she broke off their engagement. Lassalle was prepared to believe anything, except that the girl's passion for him had faded, as his feeling for her had now reached the point of madness. He correctly interpreted the declaration as extorted by force, suspected that his beloved was kept in confinement and ill-treated, bribed the servants to open communications with her, began legal proceedings to remove her from the guardianship of her father, and, in short, stirred heaven and earth. With his preference for forcible measures, even when milder means would have afforded more prospect of success, he travelled to Munich, interviewed the Minister who was the superior of Herr von Dönniges, in the hope of working upon his anxiety by threats. He telegraphed east and west to his friends, induced them to negotiate with Herr von Dönniges, with his daughter and with the people of the house, and inquired of Bishop Ketteler, through the Countess of Hatzfeldt, whether he would be prepared to marry himself and Helene if he became a convert to the Catholic religion. At the same time, he did not conceal that the reason for this inquiry lay less in his own convictions of the truth of Catholicism than in the fact that Helene professed this religion. As a matter of fact, she was a Protestant ; but Lassalle proceeded in such frantic haste that he never gave himself time to verify the fact, and the inconsiderable influence exerted by questions of creed at the present day is well evidenced by the fact that this loving pair had never yet exchanged a word concerning the religious communion of the bride.

A thousand plans shot through Lassalle's brain, while his proud heart rapidly sank at the idea that his efforts might possibly be shipwrecked by an actual change in the girl's feelings. But about this time a successful issue appeared possible. It is extremely difficult to prevent two lovers for any length of time from exchanging letters or from meeting, and a single conversation between Lassalle and Helene would have been enough to clear up the misunderstanding and to secure the future. Unfortunately for him, he chose, as if he had been stricken with insanity, the most disastrous method of opening negotiations with Helene.

As long as he felt no doubts of her love he had fully understood that his continued friendly relations with Countess Hatzfeldt might lead Helene's parents to regard him with disfavour. He had promised Helene that, when they were married, they should not be troubled with the continual presence of the Countess, and he also saw that his proposed marriage would find in the Countess herself an adversary who could not very easily be appeased. In his letters, therefore, he was careful to keep her away from Switzerland, and eventually he ordered her in somewhat unceremonious words to "obey his command" and to stand aloof. Hardly, however, had his doubts of Helene's loyalty arisen, hardly had he begun to fear that he had been mistaken in the woman whom, with considerable lack of prudence, he had belauded in a letter to the Countess as the one woman in the world for him, than he became anxious to find someone upon whose devotion he could unconditionally rely, and, following the habits of the last twenty years, he applied to the Countess, asking her to use her "eloquence" to strengthen Helene in her determination. He probably thought that a woman would more easily find access to the house than himself, and he was at the same time detained in Munich by his attempts to influence Herr von Dönniges through the Minister of Foreign Affairs. He did not consider that the Countess had already regarded Helene with the mistrustful eyes of jealousy, had begun to despise the girl from the bottom of her heart since the failure of her courage, and was therefore much more likely to do her best to dissolve an engagement which she could only regard as disastrous to her friend. But before Lassalle had applied to the Countess he had summoned by telegraph his friend, the well-known historian, Colonel Rüstow, and had commissioned him, while he was otherwise occupied, to discover Helene's real feelings, to find out her place of residence after her removal from Geneva, and to bring about her liberation. He forgot, or did not consider, that Rüstow and Countess Hatzfeldt were at that time

14

quite unanimous and more than intimate. As a matter of fact, the Countess inflicted a deadly insult upon the girl by demanding a meeting with her " to settle the question of her relations to Lassalle," in terms to which only a refusal or no answer at all was possible. Rüstow at the same time appeared as Lassalle's ambassador, and frightened Helene by his cold and hostile bearing. Were these Lassalle's best friends ? Were these the people in whom she was to confide ? People who could not see or understand, or would not realize, that she was acting under threats and compulsion, and that her every word was dictated by her selfish and imperious father.

Meanwhile Lassalle was daily writing long urgent letters of ardent and beseeching explanation, in which he told her that both in Swiss and Bavarian law she was of age, and could marry anyone she liked, that there was no material objection to their marriage, etc. But by a really tragical fate, and by a sinister consequence of her father's plans which Lassalle did not expect and never learnt until his death, not one of these letters was read by Helene. One alone reached her hands, but only after she had given her father her word of honour to return it unread.

Why did she not break her word, and abandon all other considerations ? It is perfectly obvious that some fibre in her being had been broken when Lassalle handed her over to her parents. Her feelings for her lover changed at the moment when he deserted her. She was bewildered at never hearing from him ; she was insulted and wounded by the hostile attitude of his ambassadors. The compulsion to which she was subjected in her parents' house broke her spirit, and accustomed her to the idea of abandoning Lassalle. She was incapable of taking any step whatever on her own responsibility. Help must come from without, directly from Lassalle, and she had seen him for the last time upon the day when he gave her back to her mother.

Half intimidated by her father's threats, and partly led by her repulsion to Rüstow, bewildered, disheartened, exhausted, and vacillating, she declared before her father and Lassalle's friends, Rüstow and Dr. Hänle, that she regarded her relations with Lassalle as at an end and desired no further communication with him. At that moment the family sent for her former fiancé, Yanko von Rackowitza, with whom she had broken since her acquaintance with Lassalle, and hurried on preparations for his marriage with Helene.

As long as Lassalle was in doubt concerning a change in Helene's feelings he was utterly harassed and despairing. Such phrases as the following from a letter to the Countess are not of rare, but of constant occurrence : " I am so unhappy that I am weeping—the first time for fifteen years. You are the only one who knows what it means when a man of iron like myself writhes in tears, like a woman." And he writes to Helene : " I am suffering a thousand deaths hourly." The word death is of frequent occurrence in all these letters.

Lassalle definitely felt that if he were humiliated and beaten in this affair he was overthrown for ever. He realized that the pride and self-consciousness which had carried him through so many hard struggles would be shattered, and that his belief in his " star " would be gone for all time. To regard the cause of his overthrow as wounded pride is too severe a judgment. His belief in other men and his confidence in himself were suddenly destroyed at the moment when he was forced to regard the passionately desired object of his adoration as faithless.

In one of his letters he says : " If I am now overthrown, it will not be by brute force, which I have so often defeated, but by the most unparalleled vacillation and flightiness on the part of a woman whom I love beyond all permissible bounds." Elsewhere he says : " So I fall with and through her will—a dreadful example of the fact that a man should never tie himself to a woman. I am overthrown by the most horrible treachery and the most repulsive felony which the all-seeing sun has ever beheld."

His bitterness at the " boundless ridicule " to which he would be exposed for stirring up a whole Ministry for the sake of a girl who would have nothing to do with him, as he imagined, is also to some extent responsible for those exaggerated outbursts which were dictated by the extremity of despair ; but he would never have spoken of downfall and death if the vital power within him had not received some flaw, and if he had not thought that he had lost all control of his fate. Moreover, his despair now brought to the surface all the coarser elements of his disposition—elements the existence of which he had hardly suspected in his better moments. His letters to Rüstow contain passages which cannot be printed, so hideous is the feeling by which they are inspired.

As soon as apparent certainty had replaced the period of painful doubt, Lassalle sent a challenge to Herr von Dönniges, and a letter full of the coarsest insults against Helene to Herr von Rackowitza, which was bound to evoke a challenge from the bridegroom. Herr von Dönniges speedily left Geneva, and the challenge which Lassalle received from the insulted bridegroom decided the matter. The seconds agreed upon a duel with pistols, the conditions of which were as follows :[1]

" CONDITIONS.

" The combatants to stand firm at fifteen paces, to fire within twenty seconds marked by counting one, two, three, at the beginning, middle, and end of the time. Pistols to be smooth-bore, with fore and back sights. The combatants to adopt any attitude they please, each to have three shots. Refusal to fire to count as a shot. The same second to load both pistols on each occasion. Seconds to draw lots for their turn in loading. Count Kayserlingk and Dr. Arndt to procure the surgeon. Meeting-place, the omnibus terminus in Carouge, at half-past seven in the morning, August 28. R. I., A. II., B. III. Each combatant leaves in the hands of his second a statement that he has committed suicide in case of eventualities."

Lassalle's second and intimate friend, Colonel Rüstow (who committed suicide in 1879), says that at midday on the 27th he informed Lassalle in the Victoria Hotel of these conditions, earnestly begged him to get some practice in shooting and told him of a place where he could find opportunities. Lassalle, however, spoke of this advice as "nonsense." His opponent was of another opinion. The same afternoon he

---

[1] Carl Schilling, "The Expulsion of President Bernhard Becker from the General Union of German Workmen," 31.

fired 150 shots in a shooting-gallery. I now quote a few passages from Colonel Rüstow's description of the next morning :

" At midnight I went to bed in Lassalle's rooms. At three o'clock the next morning I got up, and, after dressing, hurried to my lodging, where I had several small things to fetch. Then I went to the gunsmith and found him at work at four o'clock repairing a pistol-spring. I took the pistol from him, and went back to the Victoria Hotel. At five o'clock I woke Lassalle, who was sleeping quietly. He happened to catch sight of the pistol. He seized it, fell upon my neck and said : ' It is just what I want.' We started for Carouge. On the way Lassalle repeatedly asked me to see that the duel was carried out upon French soil, that he might be able to stay in Geneva and to settle affairs with the old ' runaway.' Glad as I was to see him so confident, I thought this was a little too much. I pointed out to him that he was not the only combatant, and that every bullet might find a mark—that one should never despise one's opponents. My words, however, made no impression. We reached Carouge before seven o'clock, and as the other parties had not yet arrived, we waited. Lassalle, who betrayed not the smallest excitement, drank a cup of tea. At half-past seven the others arrived. They had Dr. Seiler with them, who knew a suitable place. They were in front and we followed. Near the place which Dr. Seiler wished to reach, we got out of our carriage, and went through the bushes until we had reached the spot. When we drew lots it fell upon me to load for the first shot, and to give the word of command.

" The parties were led into position while I loaded. I was several times urged to give the word of command loud and distinctly—naturally an unnecessary request. Twenty seconds were allowed for each shot, and were to be marked by the second who loaded by calling one at the beginning, two at ten seconds, and three at twenty seconds. I was careful to call, ' Are you ready ?' beforehand. I gave the first word of command. Hardly five seconds afterwards the first shot exploded, fired · by Herr von Rackowitza. Scarce a second afterwards Lassalle replied. He missed, for he had already met his death. It is surprising that he was able to fire at all.

After he had fired he made two involuntary steps to the left. Only then did I hear, for I had been obliged to look at my watch, that someone—I did not know whether it was General Bethlen or Dr. Seiler—asked : ' Are you wounded ?' Lassalle replied : ' Yes.' We immediately placed him on a rug, and temporarily dressed his wound. While the opposite party went away, Dr. Seiler and I took Lassalle to a carriage, and helped him in. We both went with him, and supported him on the way as well as we could. I made the coachman choose a way where there were no paving-stones, which we were only obliged to cross for 200 yards. Lassalle was very quiet during the drive. Only when we came upon the rough paving-stones did he speak of the pain caused by the wound, and asked whether we should soon be home. The bullet had entered the lower part of his body in the left side, had injured all the chief organs, and issued at the right side. In spite of his pain, he went firmly up the hotel stairs in order not to frighten Countess Hatzfeldt, who was waiting to know the result of the duel. He then lay in pain for three days under continual infusions of opium. We knew from the outset that his wound was mortal, and he died on August 31."

CHAPTER IX

So poor and melancholy—indeed, so unworthy—was the death that ended a life of great promise and full performance ; but this death was no mere accident. It was a fate necessarily resulting from the nature of his character. Whatever Lassalle had accomplished in life he owed to himself, and to no outside help. He was also the destroyer of his own fortunes, and went to his doom as though of set purpose.

The words found upon the breast of the wounded man were :

" I hereby declare that it is I myself who have put an end to my life.

" F. LASSALLE.

"*August* 28, 1864."

These were the last words that he ever wrote, and were intended to disseminate an innocent untruth for the purpose of shielding an opponent, but they contain a higher truth and express the full nature of Lassalle's fault. No one but he could have ended his life in so unworthy a manner—a life to which he himself had given so great an importance and on which he had laid so great a responsibility. The strain of pride and of despotism in his nature, which prevented him from devoting himself entirely to his own business, moulded as he was for one purpose, brought him to his downfall.

As soon as the news of his death spread abroad, a committee was formed in Geneva of Republicans from every country for the purpose of arranging a magnificent funeral. The members of this committee included Colonel Johann Philipp Becker for Germany, Generals Georg Klapka and

Bethlen for Hungary, Bakunin and Alexander Herzen for
Russia, Thaddeuz Strynski and Fr. Bosak for Poland, Elie
Ducomme and James Fazy for Switzerland, Francesco Garrida
for Spain, Giuseppe Pino and Giuseppe Zamperini for Italy.
The funeral, which was attended by more than four thousand
persons, took place on September 2 in the Temple Unique at
Geneva.

The Countess had Lassalle's body embalmed, and took it
with her to Germany, with the intention of laying it in state
wherever he had worked and gained adherents, but this project
was forbidden both by his family and the Prussian Government. None the less, his funeral was celebrated with fanatical
grief and sorrow in the towns by the " communities," then
comparatively few, which Lassalle had founded. Men lamented
as if a national liberator had died, and even to-day the Socialist
workmen of Germany remember the anniversary of his death
as the death of the Redeemer is remembered by the Christian
Church.

Lassalle's body reached Breslau on September 14, and was
laid in the family vault in the Jewish churchyard. A simple
monument raised above him bears the following inscription,
composed by Boeckh, then eighty years of age :

" HERE REST THE MORTAL REMAINS OF
FERDINAND LASSALLE,
THINKER AND WARRIOR."

He never lived to see any of the ideas for which he had
struggled brought to realization. His grave lies at the en-
trance of that bloodstained road upon which a new Germany
strains vigorously forward towards a goal which he and many
others had before their eyes—the power and unity of the
Empire—but which was attained by means which his enthusiasm and intelligence alone could indicate. Probably
Lassalle, like his friend Lothar Bucher, though in another
way, would have been a political support to Prince Bismarck
during his struggle for the formation of the German Empire,
had his life been prolonged ; on the other hand, he would have
laid great demands upon the Government for social measures
—demands which the Government never thought of satisfying

after his death. But it is certain that the coldness of the Government towards burning social questions has contributed more than anything else to abolish Lassalle's national Socialism, which disappeared with the condition which secured its supremacy—its easy practicability. Within a few years after Lassalle's death, if his adherents were unable to secure the election of their own candidates, they preferred to vote for a Conservative rather than for a member of the Marx-Bebel party. In no long time the Social Democratic groups were divided upon trivial personal questions, and Lassalle's Workmen's Unions invariably voted for the most radical candidates when elections by vote took place. The unions have now been amalgamated. As long as Prussia remained a kingdom in black and white in the old style, the working-class population was either without influence upon politics, or followed Liberal leaders. It was not until the North German Federation was founded that Social Democrat principles began to spread through Germany, and it was not until the conclusion of peace with France that their astonishingly rapid growth began. The movement seems to increase in proportion to the disappearance of the spirit of provincialism.

The fact is still remembered that the attempted assassination of the German Emperor gave Bismarck the opportunity of passing a law which temporarily outlawed the German Socialists, and it is a well-known fact that after he had proclaimed and begun to carry out a complete revolution of the economic policy of the Empire, he attempted to complete his Socialist legislation by his State Socialism, and put into practice several of the main principles contained in the programme of the exponents of Socialist theory.

During the first discussions upon the Socialist legislation in September, 1878, when Bebel and Bismarck were the chief speakers, the latter discoursed at considerable length upon his relations with Lassalle.

Bebel's most important arguments were that the Government had always attempted to use the Social Democratic party for its own advantage, and as he devoted much of his speech to the meetings and the close relations between Bismarck and Lassalle, the Chancellor was obliged to go into this burning question in some detail. But no one believed that he would have confined himself exclusively to these personal recollections, to the complete neglect of the real nature and the practicability of the law. After delivering a· blow at the previous speaker, Professor Hänel, and declaring his inability to follow him " upon the main battle-field of rhetoric," he immediately attacked the personal question and delivered himself of a fragment of biography, together with a eulogy, of Lassalle, surprising in its warmth. Obviously, if Bismarck was not prepared with the curt denial (which a politician in necessity might have used) of Bebel's statements concerning his close intimacy with Lassalle, his only alternative was to represent Lassalle as by no means dangerous to the State ; but the warmth of his words was not necessary for political purposes, and was apparently the outcome of genuine admiration, nor do I remember ever having heard Bismarck speak with such full recognition of a political personality. He first emphasized the fact that it was Lassalle who had approached him, and not *vice versa*, as against Bebel's statements, and then continued :

" I saw him, and since the first few hours conversation with him, I have never regretted my action. I did not see him three or four times in that week, but have seen him perhaps three or four times altogether. Our relations could not possibly take the form of political negotiations. What was there that Lassalle could have offered or have given me ? He had nothing behind him. In political negotiations, the principle of *do ut des* (I give that you may give) is an implied principle, though dignity may forbid the expression of it—(laughter)—but if a man is forced to ask himself, What can a poor wretch like you give ? the principle does not hold good. He had nothing which he could have given me as a Minister. What he had was something which attracted me extraordinarily as an individual. He was one of the most intellectual and amiable men with whom I have ever had to deal—a man who was ambitious upon a large scale, and by no means Republican. His ideas were very definitely national and monarchical, and the ideal before him was the German Empire. Here, then, we found a point of contact. Lassalle,

I say, was ambitious upon a large scale, and whether the German Empire was to end in the Hohenzollern or the Lassalle dynasty was to him perhaps a matter of doubt—(great laughter) —but his ideas were thoroughly monarchical. Had he been confronted with the miserable epigoni who are now boasting of him, he would have launched upon them a *quos ego*, would have hurled them scornfully back to their nonentity, and have made them powerless to misuse his name. Lassalle was an energetic and very clever man. A conversation with him was most instructive. Our talks lasted for hours, and I was always sorry when they came to an end. At the same time it is wrong to suppose that I came to any rupture with Lassalle concerning our personal relations and personal goodwill, as he apparently entertained the pleasant impression that I regarded him as a man of genius whose society was agreeable to me, while he also had the no less pleasant impression that I was an intelligent and interested listener. Thus, there can be no question of negotiations, for the simple reason that I had but little chance to speak in our conversations. (Laughter.) He took the burden of conversation on his own shoulders, but in a pleasant and attractive manner, and everyone who knew him will agree with my description. He was not a man with whom definite agreements upon the basis of *do ut des* could be concluded. I am only sorry that his political position and mine did not allow a more extended intercourse between us, and I should have been glad to have a man of such talents and intellectual capacity as a next-door neighbour. (Laughter.)"

If these assertions be regarded with the eye of criticism, one point appears of very subordinate importance—the question whether Bismarck saw Lassalle some twenty or thirty times, as the Countess Hatzfeldt asserts, or whether they had three or four interviews, as he himself states. A man's memory may easily deceive him upon such points after the lapse of fifteen years. Probably the Countess is exaggerating and Bismarck is underestimating, but an error upon such a matter is immaterial. This, however, is not the case with reference to the nature of their intercourse. We can easily understand that Bismarck would attempt to represent this as innocent and unimportant from the political point of view, but is such a statement in any way probable or credible ? The Chancellor, who was well able to make the best of his capacities, did not disdain to declare with humour half good-tempered and half malicious that Lassalle was rather too fond of hearing himself talk, and thus prevented the conclusion of any arrangement between them. He forgets that a moment previously he had spoken of Lassalle as free from all petty pride, and had described him as ambitious in a great style. Then he proceeds to dispute the possibility of a *do ut des* between himself and Lassalle, between the Revolution as engendered from above and from below. He says that Lassalle had nothing behind him. Nothing ? Bismarck in 1863 was not so simple as to regard the great German Labour party, which had just been founded, as nothing. What Lassalle had behind him and could offer was a very valuable alliance for the Government in times of struggle, and if this alliance was not then accepted, it certainly was not rejected. Finally, if, as Bismarck asserts, the principle of *do ut des* forms the political rule of negotiations, why did Bismarck give something to Lassalle, who could offer him nothing in return ? Universal direct suffrage was Lassalle's requirement and only his programme, and this Bismarck conceded. Productive unions supported by State credit were only Lassalle's idea and his immediately practical object, and Bismarck induced the King of Prussia to give a large sum of money from his private chest to support the first attempts in this direction. Bismarck's expressions upon this point are somewhat ambiguous. " Our conversation certainly turned upon the question of universal suffrage. . . . I am readily convinced, and I see no harm in discussing the question with a clever man. . . . I am quite sure that we have spoken about it."

So it was not in virtue of conviction that Bismarck introduced universal franchise. He adopted it " with a certain reluctance, as a Frankfort tradition." It was during the political struggles of those days " a card which had previously been played, and was left lying on the table." The undoubted result was that this card was played against the ruling middle classes, and that the advantage of it was bound to fall to the lot of the pure Democracy.

In this connection the point of chief interest to myself in these assertions is not the political question, but the picture which they give of Lassalle in private life, as he appeared to the gaze of the greatest statesman of the age. We have here a sketch of Lassalle immediately before his fall, which forms an historical counterpart to the portrait of him drawn by Heine at the outset of his career.

The consideration, what future would have been reserved for Lassalle if he had not been taken away in the prime of life, may be attractive, but is futile. Everyone appears in history characterized by what he has been and what he has done, and no figure is more clearly stamped than that of Lassalle.

In the German literature of the nineteenth century we become acquainted with three successive generations of minds. First comes the romantic school, who avoid the present and practical realities of life, and forget the poverty of daily life in a world of their own imagining. Then, about the time of the July Revolution, appear the first political authors, such as Börne and Heine, who desire to liberate the whole race from all the bonds of law and tradition, and cry aloud to humanity as a whole in the course of their attempts to shake off the oppression of State religion and despotism. Young Germany is the continuation of this Radicalism, which is rather universally humanitarian than political. Among the Hegelians of the Left, such as the talented Ruge ; among such writers as Gutzkow, Herwegh, Prutz, Freiligrath, Moritz Hartmann ; and among orators like Kinkel, the revolt against the existing system—a movement also supported by high capacities for poetry, thought, or oratory—retains the vagueness of outline which marks the liberationist group before the month of March, 1848. Then comes the third and present generation, in love with power. In them the vague and lyrical element has passed away. They are marked by their close and often harsh grip of reality, while they rest upon a broad basis of knowledge. This is the generation which Bismarck has impressed with the mark of his genius, and which has gradually subjected itself to him, as the French Republicans of 1793 subjected themselves to the bold despotism of Napoleon.

But though he had no experience of Bismarck's performances

and though he was uninfluenced by Bismarck's spirit, Lassalle, in spite of the fact that he descends from 1848, bears the strong intellectual impressions of New Germany—complete freedom from doctrinaire traditions, the keenest practical insight, the gift of energy based upon scientific training. With regard to social questions, he has seen into the future to a point beyond any that we have yet reached, and so far he belongs, not only to the present, but to the future. Beneath the political and social surface of Europe is fermenting a great and comprehensive idea which many years ago Lassalle announced to a few thousand men, and which is now supported by four millions of German voters—the idea that our present economic system cannot be maintained, that it must be remodelled, and that in place of the domination now supported by brutality and injustice, conditions must supervene under which our accumulated and as yet untried economic science can be used in the service of liberation and order ; and the fact that this idea has become a universal sentiment is due to Lassalle more than to anyone else.

Nature had endowed Lassalle with great and fine capacities ; she had given him a will of Spartan strength, intellectual and oratorical talent ; like a youth from Athens of old he had the bow and the lyre. But from the harmony of these great gifts rose a character unequally developed. There was an impure deposit of pride and haughtiness—a " Hybris," to use the Greek term—and this pride became his ruin. Circumstances granted the opportunity which his capacities demanded in theory only, and not in practice. Throughout his life, in freedom or in prison, he was a caged eagle, and under stimulus his force of will rose and became overstrained until it overpowered his other abilities, and destroyed the equilibrium of his nature. Other men might die of undue greatness of heart. Lassalle died of undue greatness of will, but this will or self-confidence, excess of which caused his death, had at the same time maintained him throughout his life. He stands in history as a monument to will-power. The romantic school had found employment for their self-confidence in the caprices and tricks of humour. The revolutionary political school satisfied their self-confidence in a struggle for freedom conducted with genius, but necessarily without political purpose. Lassalle's self-consciousness obliged him to provide within this period a great and memorable example of personal energy, dispersed and concentrated in a manner wholly characteristic of him.

For these reasons all that he has done will ever arouse an interest which is purely human and partially independent of scientific considerations.

INDEX

BILLING AND SONS, LIMITED, PRINTERS, GUILDFORD